Random Harvest

MODERN HEBREW CLASSICS

David Patterson, Series Editor

This series presents formative works of lasting significance that have appeared in Hebrew, as well as more recent critical work. The series is designed to acquaint the English reader with the quality of modern Hebrew writing in its period of revival and renaissance and to reflect the cultural, religious, and social conditions and conflicts in Jewish life in the nineteenth and early twentieth centuries.

Random Harvest: The Novellas of Bialik,
translated by David Patterson and Ezra Spicehandler

The Experienced Soul: Studies in Amichai,
edited by Glenda Abramson

Joseph Perl's *Revealer of Secrets:* The First Hebrew Novel,
translated with an introduction and notes by Dov Taylor

Tradition and Trauma: Studies in the Fiction of S. J. Agnon,
edited by David Patterson and Glenda Abramson

Random Harvest

THE NOVELLAS OF BIALIK

translated by

David Patterson
Ezra Spicehandler

Westview Press
A Member of the Perseus Books Group

Modern Hebrew Classics

The publication of this collection was made possible by the generous assistance of the Institute for the Translation of Hebrew Literature.

Published in 1999 in the United States of America by Westview Pres., 5500 Central Avenue, Boulder, Colorado 80301-2877, and in the United Kingdom by Westview Press, 12 Hid's Copse Road, Cumnor Hill, Oxford OX2 9JJ

Library of Congress Cataloging-in-Publication Data
Bialik, Hayyim Nahman, 1873–1934.
    [Novellas. English. Selections]
    Random harvest : the novellas of Bialik/translated by David
Patterson, Ezra Spicehandler.
        p.   cm.—(Modern Hebrew classics)
    Contents: Random harvest—Behind the fence—The shamed trumpet—
Big Harry—Short Friday—The legend of the three and four.
    Includes index.
    ISBN 0-8133-6711-5
    1. Bialik, Hayyim Nahman, 1873–1934—Translations into English.
I. Patterson, David, 1922–   . II. Spicehandler, Ezra.   III. Title.
IV. Series.
PJ5053.B5A6   1999
892.4'35—dc21   99-10677

                                                                                                          CIP

The paper used in this publication meets the requirements of the American National Standard for Permanence of Paper for Printed Library Materials Z39.48-1984.

10   9   8   7   6   5   4   3   2

Contents

Preface

Although Ḥayyim Naḥman Bialik is known primarily as a poet—perhaps the greatest Hebrew poet in the past six hundred years—his novellas and other fictional prose writings are also of the highest quality and deserve the attention of a wide reading public.

Four of his stories, translated into English by I. M. Lask, came out in New York in 1939 under the title *Aftergrowth and Other Stories,* and the same translator had a fifth story appear under the title "Aryeh the Brawny" in *Israel Argosy 7* in 1960. Similarly, Herbert Danby's translation of "The Legend of the Three and Four" was included in *And It Came to Pass,* published in New York in 1938. These translations have great merit, but they have been out of print and virtually unobtainable for many decades. Moreover, over the past half century English itself has undergone considerable changes and acquired a greatly expanded vocabulary.

In the light of these factors, a new translation of Bialik's five novellas, together with *The Legend of the Three and Four* (Second Version), seems both appropriate and timely. These works are presented to the English-language reader in the hope that they may help to illustrate the quality of modern Hebrew literature in its period of revival.

David Patterson
Ezra Spicehandler

Acknowledgments

At every stage in the preparation of this volume we translators have benefited from the tireless and good-humored efforts of Jackie Finlay. We would also like to thank the Oxford Centre for Hebrew and Jewish Studies and particularly the able library staff for their unfailing and courteous aid.

This book has been published with the assistance of the Institute for the Translation of Hebrew Literature in Ramat Gan, Israel. Permission to publish the English translations granted by Zmorah Bitan Publishers, Tel Aviv, is gratefully acknowledged.

D. P. and E. S.
Oxford and Cincinnati

Introduction

Ḥayyim Naḥman Bialik (1873–1934) is considered to be the greatest modern Hebrew poet. His career spans a crucial period in Jewish history, and he belongs to the golden age of Eastern European Hebrew and Yiddish literature.

Biography

Born in the village of Radi in the Ukrainian province of Volhynia to a middle-class family that had become impoverished, Bialik was raised in the nearby town of Zhitomir, whose Jewish community had still preserved an almost medieval religious culture. He received a strictly traditional education (Bible, Talmud, and Midrash) and at the age of seventeen (1891) was sent to study at the great Yeshivah (Talmudic academy) of Volozhin. By the time he arrived there, he had already fallen under the influence of the *Haskalah,* the Jewish enlightenment movement, which had aspired to integrate Jews into the predominant European culture of the countries in which they resided. The naive *Haskalah* hopes, however, were shattered by the Russian government's adoption of reactionary policies following the assassination of Czar Alexander II in 1881. Most Russian Jews despaired of ever gaining emancipation under the oppressive czarist regime. Millions, driven by poverty and discrimination, began a mass emigration to Western Europe or to the United States, where economic and political conditions were more amenable.

A large segment of the Jewish intelligentsia who remained in Russia was attracted either to its rising revolutionary movements or to the *Hovevei Tsion* (Lovers of Zion), the pre-Zionist movement, and its call for Jewish auto-emancipation in a reestablished Jewish homeland in Ottoman Palestine. Bialik and many of his fellow students became supporters of the *Hovevei Tsion*, and many became followers of Aḥad Ha-am, who advocated a cultural Zionism, which would primarily attempt to preserve the ethical values of Judaism by redefining them in secular terms. Although not fully rejecting the political objectives of Zionism, Aḥad Ha-am argued that the post-*Haskalah* generation had to solve what he called the problem of Judaism—that is, how to maintain Jewish cohesion in an age in which religion was losing its sustaining power. He urged that the primary goal of Zionism be to establish a Jewish center in the ancient homeland, which would serve as a focal point for a Jewish cultural renaissance.

Bialik began writing Hebrew poetry even before he left Zhitomir. Anxious to publish his early poems, he went to Odessa, then the center of the Lovers of Zion and a capital of Hebrew letters. During his first short stay in Odessa, he met I. H. Ravnitsky, the editor of *Ha-Pardes,* an influential Aḥad Ha-amist journal. Ravnitsky recognized Bialik's literary talent and agreed to publish one of his earliest poems. Unable to establish himself in Odessa, however, Bialik returned to Zhitomir. By the time he married in 1892, he was recognized as one of the most innovative and talented young Hebrew poets of his generation. In the 1890s, he engaged unsuccessfully in the lumber business, a trade that both his own family and his father-in-law had pursued. Like many Hebrew writers of his generation, he was compelled to turn to the teaching of Hebrew for his livelihood. Nevertheless, Bialik, encouraged by Ravnitsky, first his mentor, then his close friend and collaborator, continued writing poetry.

Bialik's poems during his early period often reflect his despondency at his "failure" in Odessa and his reluctant return to provincial Zhitomir. Personal anguish is aggravated by his concern for the sociopolitical state of Russian Jewry:

> *Who knows how many tears are yet to fall—*
> *What storms will yet descend upon our heads.*
> *Before a good and powerful wind [spirit]*
> * bursts forth*
> *And drives the clouds into the desert*
> *Wiping away the veil obscuring our skies*
> *And blocking our cries from reaching heaven.*
> **"Wandering Afar"**

His verse is suffused with a deeply passive resignation to the poet's tragic fate:

> *God has not summoned me to blow the trum-*
> *pet blasts of battle*
> *The very smell of war fills me with terror*
> *I cringe whenever the bugle sounds on high—*
> *Between violin and sword I choose the violin.*
> **"The Song of Israel"**

Yet his Aḥad Ha-amist hopes at times reinforce his faith in ultimate salvation:

> *You shall not totter, O tent of Shem*
> *From your piles of dust I shall rebuild your*
> *walls . . .*
> *And when I restore God's ruined sanctuary*
> *I'll widen its curtains, cut windows in it.*
> *Then the light will drive away the dark shad-*
> *ows.*
> *And when the covering cloud shall rise, God's*
> *glory shall descend.*
> **"At the Threshold of the Beit Midrash"**

In the great poem of those sad years, "Ha-Matmid" (The Diligent Talmud Student), while lamenting the seemingly meaningless fixation of the pious student on archaic texts at the cost of his health and the suppression of his natural adolescent instincts, he is able to declare:

> *And I recall how strong the seed, how healthy*
> *The grain buried in your stunted field . . .*
> *And how great the blessing might be wrought*
> *Were a single ray of sunlight to heat it with its*
> *passion.*

This faith that the remnant spark of a dying fire, the surviving seed of an abandoned and desiccated field, might still be rekindled into a luminous flame, is the other side of the despair that had darkened the young poet's world.

In a sense, the hero of his first story, *Aryeh Baal Guf (Big Harry)*, serves as an antipode (to use a phrase coined by Jacob Fichman) to the pale, aesthetic Talmud student. Harry's vitality, despite his vulgarity, almost unwittingly attracted Bialik's imagination.

In 1900, Bialik finally settled in Odessa and, except for a short stay in Warsaw, lived in that city until he left Russia in 1921. He soon became an intimate younger colleague of Ahad Ha-am and the important Hebrew and Yiddish writer Mendele Mocher Sefarim. Within a decade Bialik emerged as a leading figure in the Jewish cultural life of Odessa and in its coterie of Hebrew and Yiddish writers and intellectuals. With Ravnitsky, he established Moriah, an important publisher of Hebrew and Yiddish books. Moriah specialized in Hebrew readers and children's books—many of which were written or scrupulously edited by Bialik himself. Two of its "best-sellers" were Bialik's poetical works and *Sefer ha-Aggadah,* the masterful anthology of Talmudic and Midrashic legends and anecdotes that to this day enjoys an enthusiastic readership.[1]

After the Communist revolution in 1917, Bialik realized that Jewish culture had no future under an antireligious and anti-Zionist Bolshevik regime. In 1921, through the intervention of the Russian writer Maxim Gorky, who admired his poetry (in Russian translation), Bialik succeeded in obtaining exit visas for his family and several Jewish writers and their families. He moved to Germany, where he reopened and expanded his publishing house, Moriah, and also established Dvir, originally devoted to more scholarly works. In 1924, he was able to realize his youthful dream of settling in Palestine, by then under British Mandate. He moved to Tel Aviv, transferring his publishing houses to that city. There he became the leading writer and literary mentor of an entire generation of Hebrew writers and a major figure in the growing Jewish community in Palestine. In 1933, the entire Jewish world celebrated his sixtieth birthday. He died the following year and was mourned by thousands of his ardent admirers.

Bialik was primarily a great Hebrew poet. He began writing as a *Hibbat Tsion* (Love of Zion) poet, although even then, he tried to tone down the prevailing sentimentalism and the fine phrasing that

---

[1]An English translation of this work, entitled *The Book of Legends,* was published by the Jewish Publication Society, Philadelphia, 1992.

characterized most of the works of his older contemporaries. As an Aḥad Ha-amist, he believed that the battle against the old religious culture had ended and that the central problem was how to enter the modern world and at the same time preserve and advance the rich heritage of the Jewish past. In this stage of his career, he believed, as did Aḥad Ha-am, that Hebrew writers should confine their writings to Jewish themes, although he did write several personal poems whose contents were more universal.

During his Odessa period, he increasingly turned to lyrical themes, writing poems about the inner struggles of the self, the creative artist, and nature and love. The sunny, quasi-Mediterranean Odessa led to somewhat "sunnier" works. Bialik had reached the peak years of his creative enterprise.

In 1902, his collected poems finally appeared. The reception was enthusiastic. Josef Klausner's laudatory review was typical: "Bialik must be considered to be the Jewish national poet ... not only a Hebrew poet, but one who fully (expresses) the Jewish national spirit." The volume closed the first phase of his career, largely dominated by poems on Jewish themes. He was, however, moving to a more subjective, universal period, although he never completely abandoned "national" subjects. Victor Ehrlich reminds us that nineteenth-century Russian poets often saw themselves as prophets and were viewed as such by their audience.[2] The overwhelming impact of the Hebrew prophets upon Hebrew readers led them even more to endow their "national poet" with the mantle of prophecy— a role that Bialik frequently declined and yet often assumed. He described his Yiddish poem "The Last Word"—as "prophetic." Its first line is "I have been sent to you by God."

As the *Haskalah* came to a close, some Hebrew poets began replacing the syllabic meter used by their predecessors with the accented meter prevalent in romantic German and Russian poetry. Bialik was among the earliest Hebrew poets to adopt this new metrical system. However, his stresses followed the Ashkenazic pronunciation of Hebrew, which ignored the biblical accentuation, a system scrupulously observed by the Sephardic pronunciation and employed by speakers of modern Hebrew. Although Bialik pre-

---

[2]Ehrlich, Victor. *The Double Image*. Baltimore: Johns Hopkins Press, 1960. Pp. 18–20.

dicted that a later generation of Hebrew readers might not "hear" his superb rhythms or be familiar with many of his rhymes, he used the Ashkenazic pronunciation current in his day in most of his verse.

Poetry

In Odessa, he composed four long poems (*Poemas,* as the Russians called them): "The Dead of the Wilderness," "The City of Slaughter," "The Scroll of Fire," and "The Pond." Of the four, only the last was purely lyrical, whereas "The City of Slaughter" was clearly "national." "The Dead of the Wilderness" and "The Scroll of Fire" fall somewhere in between. Although they involve national themes, they do so subtly and symbolically. They can, therefore, also be read as "universal" poems. "The Dead of the Wilderness" has the plasticity characteristic of an epic poem. "The Scroll of Fire" is written in a strongly lyrical vein, with allusions to the poet's personal struggle with his identity as both a Jew and an artist endowed with a unique mission.

"The City of Slaughter" (1904) is the longer of two powerful poems composed in the wake of the Kishinev pogrom of 1903, an event that, although dwarfed by the Holocaust of the 1940s, in its day shocked the entire Western world. It is written in a "prophetic style"—God addressing the prophet—but is revolutionary because it turns the traditional Jewish *kinah* (lament) on its head. The accused are not the perpetrators of the massacre or the unforgiving God who inflicted a deserved punishment upon his wayward people, but the bloodless Jews who passively endured bloody outrages without the courage to resist their savage attackers.

The God of Israel who addresses the poet is reduced to a helpless bankrupt whose once-great values are ignored by humanity. He is no longer capable of stemming the gross tide of murder inflicted upon His chosen people. The poem was immediately translated into Yiddish and Russian and became the rallying cry that evoked a more aggressive response to later attacks upon Jews.

"The Dead of the Wilderness" (1902) is based upon a Talmudic legend according to which the members of the generation of the Exodus, condemned for their insolence against God to perish in the wilderness and not to enter the promised land, never really died.

Instead they lay eternally asleep in the desert, ready to rise at redemption's call.

The poem opens with a powerful description of the army of dead warriors stretched rank upon rank in the scorched desert sands. Periodically they are attacked by predators: an eagle, a lion, and a snake, but each retreats before striking the valiant army, repelled by the power and majesty it exudes. According to Numbers 14–15, the warriors, upon hearing God's cruel decree, attempt to advance up the hill country toward Canaan in revolt but God cruelly crushes their mutiny. Bialik expands the story and has the Israelites rise in revolt against God several times in different historical epochs, only to be repulsed each time and return subdued to their slumber. At times the desert, too, rises in stormy rebellion against its Creator: "[It] wakens to avenge the desolation imposed by Him. Dares to pour out the basin on His face . . . and wreak havoc upon His world, restore chaos upon His throne."

One may read the poem "straight" as a magnificent epic poem. F. Lachover, in consonance with his generation, gives it a national interpretation.[3] The dead, he suggests, symbolize the dormant Jewish people confined to exile, yet possessing a latent power that from time to time impels them to revolt against their fate, attempt to force God's hand and regain their freedom. The predators, he contends, are symbols representing Israel's oppressors: Egypt—the snake; Babylon—the lion; Rome—the eagle (these symbols are found in the Bible and Midrashic literature).

Others have suggested that the poem is a hymn celebrating man's Promethean struggle against the restrictions imposed by God, the Creator—humanity's eternal struggle to alter the natural order with the power of science and intellect.

Like Yehuda Halevi, his great medieval predecessor, Bialik expressed his dissatisfaction with the alien metrics and rhyme patterns adopted by Hebrew poetry throughout the ages. Despite his mastery of these forms, Bialik felt that they often jarred the natural cadences of the Hebrew language. On various occasions he composed poems in free verse but usually reverted to the accepted European models. "The Scroll of Fire" (1905) was his boldest experiment to free his poetry from these conventions.

---

[3]Lachover, Fischel. *Bialik Ḥayyav Vitsirotav* (Vol. 2). Tel Aviv: Dvir, 1950. Pp. 400–406.

During his relatively short stay in 1904 in Warsaw where, for a time, he served as the literary editor of *Ha-Shiloah,* he may have read some of the great Polish national poets—Adam Mickiewicz, Juliusz Slowacki, Jan Kasimierz, and Krasiński—and been impressed by their recourse to ancient Polish myths and folklore. He probably also came across the prose poems of the Russian and European symbolists and neoromantics. Yet the form he chose for "The Scroll of Fire" was essentially his own. He described it as "a mosaic of legends reworked by his imagination." The basic plot had its archetype "in the quest for the Holy Grail." He drew upon two older Jewish myths: the first was the rescue of the holy fire from the destroyed Temple of Jerusalem, as related in Maccabees 1:18–2:13 and retold in the medieval *Chronicle of Josipon.* The prophet Jeremiah rescued the sacred fire that had descended from heaven and carried it to Babylonia, where he hid it in a cave. There it remained until Ezra and Nehemiah rebuilt the Temple and restored it to its new altar. The second was the Talmudic and Midrashic legend about two hundred youths and two hundred maidens who were taken captive by the Romans at the fall of Jerusalem to be enslaved as prostitutes in Roman brothels. Apprised of this scheme, the chaste maidens leaped to their death into the sea and the youths followed suit (Babylonian Talmud 75b and Midrash to Lamentations 1:45).

In Bialik's version, the act of rescuing and concealing the fire recurs following the destruction of the Second Temple (70 C.E.). This time the holy fire is salvaged by an angel, who is also charged to guard "the cup of tears" shed by God whenever Jews suffered. When filled to the brim, the cup signals redemption. The angel flies with the flame to a desert island and places it atop a craggy hill. God orders him to guard the fire as well as the "Hind of Dawn," the symbol of the Jewish people and its messianic hopes. Shortly thereafter the two hundred youths and the two hundred maidens taken by the Romans are cast away on an arid desert island. The groups are placed on either side of a deep ravine through which a perilous river flowed. Among the youths, two tall males of equal height stand out above the others. One is a gentle youth whose clear eyes are fixed upon the sky as if he is seeking for the star of his life; the other is a wrathful young man with sullen eyes cast down upon the earth, searching for what his soul has lost.

The bright-eyed youth appears to represent the optimistic aspect of Jewish history, and the dark-eyed youth, Jewish despair and loss of hope. In various works, Bialik referred to the negative reaction that persecution and anti-Semitism provokes among despairing Jews—the other side of Jewish messianism. If God or man denies them salvation, its frustrated victims should turn to terrorism, an attempt to undermine Western civilization from within. The bright-eyed young man rejects this spirit of despair and calls instead for a song of consolation and reconciliation, for ultimate salvation.

Before the bright-eyed young man sets out on his quest, he suddenly sees the maidens across the chasm, marching in single file, hands outspread to the sky, eyes moonstruck, heads crowned with thorns. Oblivious of the danger threatening them, they reach the edge of the ravine and tumble like a flight of white ostriches into the abyss below. The youths leap after them in a vain attempt at rescue. All drown. Suddenly a heavy, black object floats after the drowned bodies. Is it a ship or a coffin?

Only the chosen, clear-eyed youth survives.

After much agony and many trials, tribulations, and temptations, he finally reaches the craggy cliff on top of which glows the holy fire. Of all the obstacles he meets on the way, temptation is the most onerous. He constantly encounters two maidens—one a pure-eyed, innocent maiden over whose head the Hind of Dawn hovers; the other, a luscious, earthy, seductive maiden, whose image is reflected in the dark waters of the abyss. Both struggle for his soul. During his journey, he also encounters an elderly holy man who teaches him how to overcome his passion for the earthy maiden by devotion to religious asceticism. The youth seems to evade temptation and ultimately reaches the holy fire. However, just as he seizes it, he again succumbs to the allure of the lusty maiden and leaps after her into the abyss. He has failed.

Unlike the other youths, however, he survives. The dark waters carry him to the shores of a distant land. He becomes a wandering exile among his brothers, suffering with them and, at times, showing them great compassion.

And when his heart oppressed him very much and his great dreams and true torments found him . . . he would go out of the city and sit under a desert bush raising his eyes toward the Hind of Dawn, searching for her image in the waters of the river . . . and looking at the void within his heart, facing the world in silence with his great grief, the grief of the individual.

And the young angel . . . charged to guard the Hind of Dawn,
would quietly tip the cup of silent grief, dropping from it one drop after the other, in the quiet dawn.

The two youths seem to symbolize the two possibilities of salvation—a hopeful, optimistic, and creative course or a pessimistic,
vengeful, and destructive course. Bialik himself hinted that the
camps represented the gap between two different manifestations of
Judaism. This has been taken by some to mean the difference between Western European Jewry—in Bialik's time—optimistic and
enlightened, and Eastern European Jewry—pious, mystical, and of
isolationist mentality.

Baruch Kurzweil has argued that the poem should be read on two
levels.[4] It depicts the inner conflict that Bialik had experienced
throughout his life—between his profound sense of mission as a
poet called to give voice to his people's tragedy and its struggle toward its national renaissance, and his personal predilection as an
artist seeking to express his selfhood. The maidens symbolize the
eros—passion, beauty, nature; the youths and the old sage represent
the puritanism of the Jewish tradition—ascetic, ethical, and devout.
The subject of the poem is the age-old conflict between the Hellenic
view of life and the Jewish view. The two maidens also represent the
conflicting attractions of the eros itself—the innocent, angelic female as against her seductive, sensual counterimage. For Kurzweil,
the destruction of the Temple alludes to the destruction of traditional Judaism by the forces of modernity (European civilization).
The flame salvaged by the angel symbolizes the core of Judaism that
Aḥad Ha-amists had hoped to salvage by giving Judaism a moral,
positivist, and historical interpretation. The failure of the youth to
hold on to the flame expresses Bialik's fear that Aḥad Ha-amism
might fail to salvage the holy fire.

In "The Pond" (1904–1905) Bialik is at his lyrical best. He began the poem while in Warsaw. Members of Warsaw's corps of
Hebrew and Yiddish authors were more "European" than the
staid Odessans and subject to the influences of the neoromantic
and symbolist literary trends that had begun to dominate conti-
nental writing:

---

[4]Kurzweil, Baruch. *Bialik ve Chernikhowsky* (Bialik and Chernikhowsky). Tel
Aviv: Schocken, 1967. Pp. 47–51.

> *In the thick foliage, isolated from the world,*
> *In the shadow of a tall oak, blessed by light*
>   *and taught by storms,*
> *It [the pond] dreams alone of an upside down*
>   *world spawning its golden fish,*
> *Yet who knows what is in its heart?*

Are these echoes of Dante's forest, symbols for the turbulent visible world—and does the pond, the mirror reflecting the forest and contemplating its true essence, signify the mind and heart of the artist?

The poem's theme is the dilemma of the artist who in childhood experienced the world as a unified whole but, with maturity, has lost this sense of wholeness. In Bialik's generation this dysfunction is linked to the loss of faith in God. The artist (the pool) is (or holds up) a magic mirror to the universe, restoring its shattered unity.

Yet Bialik at times doubted whether this quasi-Platonic idea could indeed fill the void left by this severance.

> *But who knows perhaps it [the pond] dreams*
>   *secretly*
> *And that only in vain does the prince wander*
> *Searching in the primeval forest, in desert*
>   *sands, and sea beds*
> *For a lost princess*

"The Pond" is structured in patterns of contrasts: morning, then moonlit night, a stormy day, and a serene dawn. It closes with a lyrical intrusion of the speaker's self, shifting the discourse from the third person to the first.

> *In my youth . . .*
> *When the wings of the* Shekinah *first fluttered*
>   *over my head*
> *And my heart knew how to yearn unto death*
>   *. . .*
> *Seeking a refuge for its prayers,*
> *I would sail forth in the heat of a summer's day*
> *To the glorious kingdom of serenity—*
> *To the forest's thicket.*

Among God's trees that never heard the sound
of an ax . . . ,
I would wander for endless hours
Alone with my heart and my God until
I came upon
The forest's holy of holies . . .
Inside the curtain of leaves
Is a small green island, soft with grass
. . . Secluded, as if it were a world by itself,
A sacred shrine . . .
Of venerable forest trees . . .
Its ceiling—a small blue dome . . .
Its floor—glass: a pond of lucid water,
A silver mirror framed in wet grass
Containing . . . a second universe.

The poem closes with a hymn, which translates the array of images into the secret language of the gods. It is a secret, wondrous,
soundless language in which God reveals Himself to His elect. It is a
language in which the Ruler of the World contemplates His profoundest thoughts and in which the creative artist gives concrete
form to the meditations of his heart, finding in it the solution to an
ineffable dream. It is indeed language of imagery.

And here follows a rich catalog of contrasting visual images: the
broad strip of blue sky and its expanse, the white and black little
clouds; the tremor of a golden stand of wheat, the stature of a cedar;
the flutter of a dove's white wing, the soaring pinions of an eagle;
the beauty of a man's body, the brilliance of the eye's glance; the
wrath of a sea, the gay mischief of its waves; the silence of falling
stars, and so on.

In this language, the language of all languages,
The pond spells its never-ending riddle to me.
And secreted in the shade, bright, serene, and
silent
Seeing everything and seen by everything
within it,
It seemed to me to be the open eyelid of the
prince of the forest, great in mystery
And steeped in thought.

Stories

At the urging of his colleagues Bialik again returned to writing prose fiction. This was in keeping with Russian literary traditions. Great poets like Pushkin and Lermentov wrote not only poetry but works of fiction as well.

Mendele Mocher Sefarim (1835–1917) was the most important writer of Hebrew and Yiddish fiction at the time. He was influenced by the social realism that pervaded contemporary Russian letters—a realism with a satirical bent that lashed out at the social problems afflicting Russian society. He realized that writing in the lofty classical Hebrew style then used by his contemporaries to describe the impoverished and folksy masses of Russian Jewry was awkward and inappropriate. Thus Mendele, who began as a Hebrew writer, shifted to writing his works in Yiddish, the spoken language of his characters. In the 1880s, however, in response to the prompting of many of his Hebrew writing colleagues (including Bialik), he began adapting, not merely translating, his Yiddish works into Hebrew. To do so, he felt he had to fashion a new modern Hebrew idiom that blended the "high" Hebrew style of the Bible with the "lower," more mundane, Hebrew of Rabbinic literature. This newly forged medium was seized upon by the fiction writers of Bialik's generation and became "the style" in which many of them wrote their stories and novels.

Bialik never completely confined his prose writing to "the style." Although a number of his fictional works were influenced by Mendele's astute combination of realism and satire bordering on the grotesque, even in Bialik's earliest stories (*Big Harry,* for example), his writing is more objective and his satire modulated by a certain empathy for the butts of his humor. His cast of characters also included men and women who were less "lumpen proletariat" than those who inhabited Mendele's world. Raised as he was in a family of lumber dealers, he often depicted the milieu of middle-class merchants and dealers, who were more representative of his generation. Moreover, whereas Mendele does include gentiles in his cast of characters, they are, on the whole, alien "types" rather than real individuals. Bialik, too, maintained a certain "distance" in his treatment of gentile figures, but he had a more intimate knowledge of them (see *Big Harry, The Shamed Trumpet,* and *Behind the Fence*).

He was also attracted by the growing symbolist movement. His extraordinary command of all facets of traditional Hebrew literature was skillfully mined. As he reached the zenith of his career, both his poetry and prose writing were enriched by the use of inter-textuality. His subtle employment of these subtexts appealed to his many Hebrew readers who, like him, were well acquainted with the various levels of Jewish literature. Bialik's symbolic catalog includes references to the animal world—snakes (original sin), eagles or hawks (ideals, optimism), lions (righteous anger), deer, does, and fawns (positive signs), sun, sunsets, white clouds (vision, natural beauty), the pool or pond (the inner world of the artist). These mo-tifs repeat themselves throughout his works.

In reading the novellas, the reader will become aware of the devel-opment of Bialik's narrative skill. In *Big Harry* Bialik's style is slightly marred by digressions and lengthy descriptive passages. Works like *The Shamed Trumpet* and particularly *Behind the Fence* are more tautly constructed. *Short Friday* is a charming, humorous portrayal of the naive world of a country Rabbi and is free of any digressions.

Elements of social realism abound in Bialik's stories. Referring to *Big Harry* in a letter to Aḥad Ha-am, Bialik asserted that Harry was a "new type," not yet described in modern Hebrew litera-ture—a brawny, self-confident, and ignorant entrepreneur. Harry's son, Moshe "the Candidate" (the sobriquet given to him by his fa-ther), is portrayed as a social-climbing young man who imitates in manner and mien the elegant and cultured members of the Polish gentry.

A whole galaxy of non-Jewish types populate Bialik's prose works: the peasant friends of Harry and Noah *(Behind the Fence)*; the faithful, quasi-"Judaized" servant Yavdoha, totally familiar with Jewish customs and traditions, Styupe, the loyal jack-of-all-trades, both employed by Yose the village Jew, and the peasant boy who is sent to ḥeder to learn how to read and write at least in Hebrew *(The Shamed Trumpet)*; the lovely Marinka and her witchlike anti-Semitic "Auntie" *(Behind the Fence)*; Ivan, Reb Getzel's street-smart servant *(Short Friday)*; and Makarka, Noah's bosom friend *(Behind the Fence)*. This cast of gentile characters also includes the various officials, high and low, ranging from sympathetic, apathetic, to hos-tile, whom Yose "the villager" must court, cajole, and bribe in his vain effort to remain in the countryside *(The Shamed Trumpet)*.

Of course, greater attention is given to Jewish characters: Harry, his sons, and his social-climbing wife; Alter—Harry's angry and virulent competitor; and the "fine Jews" *(Big Harry)*; Noah, the Jewish child and adolescent, with his gentilelike love of nature and sport, his conventional parents, his classmates, his cynical and lusty tutor *(Behind the Fence)*; the world of the Jewish children *(The Shamed Trumpet* and *Random Harvest)*; the stern and abusive fathers, the caring *Yiddishe mame (Random Harvest* and *Behind the Fence)*; the naively religious Pesach-Itzi, the dairyman *(The Shamed Trumpet)*; and Reb Getzel, the tax collector.

Bialik's fiction concentrated upon those elements of the Volhynian Jewish milieu most familiar to him: the Jewish lumber dealers, the village Jews in charge of tree cutting or the smelting of tar, the religious functionaries: Rabbi Lippa *(Short Friday)*, the pious but naive Rabbi; Reb Gadi, the *shohet (The Shamed Trumpet)*; the innkeeper, the poverty-stricken, incompetent, and often cruel *melamdim*. We may note Bialik's penchant for the simple, unlearned Jewish classes, despite the fact that he himself was raised in the home of his erudite and moderately prosperous grandfather, had studied at a prestigious Yeshivah, and in his youth associated with Zhitomir's intellectual elite. Like his contemporary, Shalom Aleichem, his attitude to the "common folk" was on the whole sympathetic rather than critical, his humor more ironic than satirical.

His later prose writings were no longer constrained by traditional literary techniques. In *Random Harvest* he records his pseudoauto-biographical memoirs, giving free rein to his brilliant poetic imagination, with seemingly little concern for the structural demands of what may have been a novel he had planned to write. The unstable conditions in Russia during World War I and especially during the Bolshevik revolution, his subsequent immigration to Germany and finally to British Palestine, his multifarious activities as publisher, scholar, and active participant in communal affairs also did not allow him the leisure required for the writing of so long a work. Indeed his literary output during that whole period was quite scant. Such works as he managed to write were shorter literary pieces, including several remarkable children's stories.

As the coeditor of *Sefer ha-Aggadah (The Book of Legends)*, Bialik had a profound knowledge of the vast repository of Talmudic and Midrashic materials. In his many children's stories he had drawn upon these legends, revised and expanded them. He was particularly attracted to the legends about King Solomon, whose reign marked the golden period of the ancient Davidic monarchy.

The Legend of the Three and Four, written several years before his death, is an exciting experimental-symbolist work. Its semiarchaic Hebrew style is disarming. Bialik resorted to ostensibly older forms of Hebrew literature to write this quasi-allegorical story, open to a rich variety of interpretations. It is a veritable masterpiece.

Modern Hebrew literature has canonized Bialik as its greatest writer. His writings express the yearnings of the modern Jew for a synthesis of the hallowed traditions and ideals of a dynamic Jewish culture that evolved over three millennia and the Helleno-European culture that has permeated the modern world. His poetry deals with the crisis engendered by the loss of faith and the endeavor to salvage those elements of a religious tradition and a rich literary heritage that remain relevant in a modern age. It expresses the despair of those who, shattered by the decline of religious belief, lose the sense of wholeness, and the quest not only for a new reading of ancient texts, but also for a renaissance of Jewish culture in the new-old national home. It both personalizes and universalizes the tragedy and the quest. Although the world he described has long ago sadly disappeared and been replaced by the new, dynamic, but often brash, Israeli society, Bialik has retained much of his relevance because of his compelling literary achievement.

1

Random Harvest

❖   ❖   ❖

Random Harvest is an incomplete work of fiction. Seven chapters (2–8) appeared in 1908 in *Ha-Shiloaḥ*, the literary journal on which Bialik once served as literary editor. Seven additional chapters (9–15) were published in 1919, and the opening chapter appeared in 1923.

Some scattered prose fragments found among Bialik's literary remains deal with a young man called Shmulik, the very name of the hero of *Random Harvest*. It would seem that Bialik had intended to write "the novel of his generation" but never finished it.

Although *Random Harvest* contains some autobiographical elements, it is a fictionalized autobiography. Bialik had occasion to criticize those readers who naively took everything he wrote in the first person to be autobiographical. Zeva Shamir, a noted Bialik scholar, goes as far as to claim that Bialik "invented" a mythological autobiography that actually was a portrayal of the life of a typical product of the shtetl rather than a real account of his own life. This mythologizing, she claims, extended to Bialik's so-called autobiographical notes, such as his letter to Joseph Klausner. Even these alleged memoirs deal with stereotypical experiences that any one of his contemporaries may have had. She makes much of Bialik's description of his cruel schoolmaster and particularly of his stern father and of the putative poverty his family had suffered after his father's early death. Bialik actually came from a middle-class family; his widowed mother was never reduced to peddling in the town's marketplace (as he depicts her in one of his poems). He himself denied this last point. However, many of the incidents he described, particularly those reflecting the inner world of the imaginative child who was destined to become an important poet, have the ring of truth.

The Hebrew title Bialik gave to this work is *Safiaḥ,* a biblical term designating the aftergrowth of random fruits and vegetables following the Sabbatical year (when the fields in ancient Israel were left fallow [Leviticus 23:5])—hence our title *Random Harvest.* Bialik gave this term an additional connotation. He may have borrowed it from the Hebrew poet Judah Leib Gordon, who described the Hebrew writers and readers of his generation as *sefiḥim,* "the orphans of humankind, abandoned by their fathers and mothers . . . men incapable of any (productive) trade or who occupy themselves with outlandish matters." Bialik, too, extended this term not only to refer to the random chapters of this work but also to label his protagonist: "And before I begin to recount a little bit from here and there, a few chapters from the meanderings of the inner life, and the true dreams of a random son of Israel, may I be permitted to relate, without apparently any obvious connection to what has gone before or what will come later . . . "

Actually, most of the first segment (Chapters 1–6) forms a well-structured, lyrical, and fictionalized account of the narrator's earlier years in the village of his birth. Of these the first chapter is artistically the most moving, depicting the discovery of the future poet's "self":

> How true the saying is that a man sees and perceives only once: in childhood! The first visions, in that same innocence as on the day when they left the Creator's hand, they are the real essence and the very stuff of life; and those impressions that follow are secondary and deficient, seemingly like the first, but weak reflections of them, and not genuine. And from my flesh I saw this.

These primary visions are lost once the narrator leaves the village (his childhood Eden) and moves to the pitch-makers' quarter of the city (Exile). "[M]y world darkened a little and its radiance faded. In our new place of residence on the outskirts of the town, gray and noisy days confronted me, the life of a Jewish townlet with its vexation, anger, and unpleasantness." . . .

He recalls the rural landscape he was forced to leave: the green hillock with its two tiny white houses, the splendor of its sunset, the glory of its forests, the village pond that "sparkles at the side of the hill like a bright mirror," and above all his wondrous dream of walking in a tumultuous band of people, wagons, and beasts of burden trudging along a sandy road. Everyone is returning from an unsuccessful fair, and they are disgruntled, bickering with and shouting at one another. He is dragged along with the throng. Suddenly he finds himself alongside a stream, separated from the mob by a curtain of reeds. Through a break, he sees the image of a "mysterious creature" sitting alone beyond the barrier on the grassy bank of a stream, undisturbed by the passing caravan. He ponders the mystery as he finds himself separated from both the crowd and the enigmatic stranger. Suddenly it dawns upon him: "Surely I know him, surely I have been with him. Surely he is very, very close to me and to my soul. Surely he and I are one." The dream is about the self-image of the artist in society, and the conflict between his yearning to express his unique "self" while bound to the social milieu in which he dwells and to its demands upon his heart and his mind.

The remaining chapters of *Random Harvest* do not quite reach the lyrical quality of the first. With ironic humor they describe the awakening curiosity of the gifted child, his wonder at the riddle of the mirror, his inability to read the symbols of the alphabet. He is taught them in a conventional way but gives each letter his private and richly imaginative reading. He struggles against the obtuseness and conventionalism of his Hebrew teachers and the incessant taunting of his classmates. His teachers and his father are epitomic representations of the severe discipline and the rigorous proscriptions of the religious law. He tells of his fascination with sunsets, his fear of fire, his dream of encountering a band of dwarfs.

In the second group, the sketches lose their temporal and logical order. They continue with descriptions of an inspiring and imaginative schoolteacher; they depict fascination with the biblical narratives, which, in the mind of the child, become part of his immediate experience. He describes his life as a schoolboy, his encounter with peasant boys, the awakening of his libido—involving both his attraction to the lusty peasant girls and his memories of an idealized puppy love affair.

Bialik refers briefly to the village pond that became a recurrent motif in his poetry and to which he devoted his long poem "The Pond." Scholars have disagreed as to the symbolic meaning of the pond. For some, relying on Bialik's autobiographical letter to Klausner, it represents the mind or soul of the artist, which converts the illusory reality of the world into a truly metaphysical or aesthetic reality. Others argue that Bialik's realism precludes such a reading and suggest that the pond serves as the repository of the visions and images that are absorbed by the artist. They base their interpretation on a passage that appears in our text (Chapter 1):

Hardly had I bared to the heavens the little windows of my soul, my two eyes, when the visions of God came streaming unsummoned from the four winds. Sometimes they would well up to me from the depths of silence, in shapes such as appear in dreams or in the waters of a clear pool. There was no speech and no words—only a vision.

Random Harvest is a brilliant unfinished poem in prose written at the height of Bialik's career. The translators have tried to convey something of the magic of the original Hebrew.

❖   ❖   ❖

1

My Native Village and My Dream

I cannot remember how many summers and winters passed from the earliest moments I can recall in my native village until the time when my family took me to live in a suburb of the nearby town. As a little child, apparently not yet five years old, I was left to play on the garbage heap. But what sense of time does an infant have? In my native village the laws of nature never changed. The seasons came round at their proper time, and everything went on as usual. But that first early world I brought with me from the village, which is still concealed in its own special place in the recesses of my heart—that strange world, wonderful and unique—seems to contain no trace of autumn or winter. The whole village of those days, as far as my eye could reach, composed one single tract—and all of it pure summer. The sky was a summer sky, the earth a summer earth. Plants and animals were all summer; and Feigele, too, Feigele, a girl of my own age, my one companion in the whole village—she too was all summer. I can recall only one iron, wintry day of ice and frost, standing apart, cruel and angry, like a robber armed with an ax; and near it, cast aside in the mud like a trampled corpse, another solitary rain-swept day, melting with distress and dripping sorrow. But these are mere exceptions, blemishes. The world in all its purity, the one that stretches from the grass in the wall of our little house to the green grove that screens the eye at the end of the village—that world is all summer.

Here before me on this backdrop of blue skies and green grass are embroidered the pictures of my world in those first days; wonderful pictures, light and serene as pure mists, half secrets and half dreams—and nevertheless no scenes as bright and clear as they are, nor any reality as real. They are my soul's basic, elemental scenes, bestowed upon me freely from the skies, a gift of God and His goodness, because of my tender years and helplessness, my dumbness, and my heart's pining. I was little and tender and left to myself. I knew not how to ask or even call things by their names; nor was there anyone at hand to open my mouth and rouse my spirit, to take me by the hand or come to my corner. Like a forsaken fledgling I wandered alone about my nest; my father and mother left me to myself and there was no one else to look after me. Then God in His mercy took me under the shelter of His wings and allowed me to sit quietly at His footstool and play gently with the fringes of His garment and the edges of His mantle. By day He sent His hidden angels to amuse me with fancies and bring a smile to my lips, which no one saw; and by night He sent His little dwarfs to play before me by the light of the moon and banish fear from me, but no one heard. He set them all about me, seeing but unseen, placing them in every dark corner and in every lowly hollow, to fill my soul with the sweet dread and awe of God.

His hidden hand sowed all my paths with wonders and placed riddles in everything upon which my eye alighted. Every stone and pebble, every splinter of wood, was an inexplicable text, and in every ditch and hollow eternal secrets lurked. How can a spark be contained in a mute stone, and who puts the dumb shadows on the house walls? Who heaps up the fiery mountains in the skirts of heaven, and who holds the moon in the thickets of the forest? Whither stream the caravans of clouds, and whom does the wind in the field pursue? Why does my flesh sing in the morning, and what is the yearning in my heart at evening time? What is wrong with the waters of the spring that they weep quietly, and why does my heart leap at the sound? These wonders were all about me, caught me up, passed over my poor little head—and refuge or escape there was none. They widened my eyes and deepened my heart, until I could sense mysteries even in commonplace things and secrets everywhere.

Hardly had I bared to the heavens the little windows of my soul, my two eyes, when the visions of God came streaming unsummoned from the four winds. Sometimes they would well up to me from the depths of silence, in shapes such as appear in dreams or in the waters of a clear pool. There was no speech and no words—only a vision. Such utterance as there was came without words or even sounds. It was a mystic utterance, especially created, from which all sound had evaporated, yet which still remained. Nor did I hear it with my ears, but it entered my soul through another medium. In the same way a mother's tenderness and loving gaze penetrate the soul of her baby, asleep in the cradle, when she stands over him anxious and excited—and he knows nothing. And sometimes the visions came interwoven with fragments and combinations of sounds. The noises of the cosmos are legion, differing one from another in countless aspects. Who can fathom their meaning or understand their nature? The sounds of day and the sounds of night, whether impudent or modest, whether bold or faint, long drawn out, and suddenly cut short. The cry of a drowning man at the end of the earth, or the groan of murder hovering in the forest. To me they seem like disembodied spirits, the messengers of God, bearing His word, wandering to and fro on the wings of the wind, speeding arrowlike from one hiding place to the next, peeking out for a moment and disappearing suddenly; one cannot perceive them come and go, and the eye cannot discern them. And there were times when I heard the silence and saw the voices, for as yet my senses had neither bounds nor limits, but each encroached upon the other. Sound drew sight after it and sight, sound and scent—both of them. As yet I knew neither rhythm nor measure. The little mound in the field was a mountain; the pond, an ocean; the end of the village, the horizon of the earth.

How true the saying is that a man sees and perceives only once: in childhood! The first visions, in that same innocence as on the day when they left the Creator's hand, they are the real essence and the very stuff of life; and those impressions that follow are secondary and deficient, seemingly like the first, but weak reflections of them, and not genuine. And from my flesh I saw this. All the sights of heaven and earth, which I have blessed throughout my life, have received no nourishment except from the power of that first vision. In later life I have seen the skies of Italy in all their azure sweetness. My feet have trod the heights of the Swiss mountains. The sight of them enchanted me. But when have I known a sweeter blue than this? Where have I seen mountains loftier and more magnificent than these? Whenever I see the sun rise or set in all its brilliance, I stand amazed. But surely I have seen the sun rise and set even more splendidly, with even greater wonder! And when I pass across a green field, I know not why the sight of grass flashes for a moment before my eyes, the sight of that same grass, which first I saw in the village, when I was still attached to my old nurse—God grant she rest in peace! It was fresh and lush, alive and new, half-submerged in the limpid water, sown with little flowers delightful to the eyes, pushing their yellow, dew-flecked heads out of the grass, with a single pearl-like tear quivering in the eye of every one of them.

After we left the village to live elsewhere—I was about five years old at the time—my world darkened a little and its radiance faded. In our new place of residence on the outskirts of the town, gray and noisy days confronted me, the life of a Jewish townlet with its vexation, anger, and unpleasantness; and the greater the human tumult about me, the more I shrank into myself and the more the festive exaltation of my heart ebbed away. The ignorant *melamdim* into whose hands I fell, with their scowling faces and their straps, drove away my childhood visions. Those first heavenly reflections no longer appeared to me except when they encountered me alone, away from the daily tumult and the teachers' realm. They hid behind some curtain, and from time to time they would dart glances at me to revive my fancies and renew their power. Peeking out for a moment and disappearing, peeking out—and disappearing. Drop by drop, like some precious elixir of life, the splendor of those wonderful days dripped into my heart, and from my childhood world there appeared to me only bits and pieces as time passed by. Suddenly out of the air, fragments of pictures would blossom forth, severed pieces from the past: a distant patch of sky in pristine purity, a strip of earth at the beginning of spring, a rich, black fragrant strip—primeval earth, suddenly protruding from beneath a blanket of cold snow with its body still trembling. A lonely, deserted hut in an abandoned cucumber field. A glowing sunset at the edge of the firmament. The sound of howling from the forest. The eerie shriek of a bird at night. The moon suspended over a chimney on some roof. A festival minyan in my father's house, and a band of frightened youngsters bursting into the house and crying, "Wolves in the village!" And nearby—Jews dressed in their prayer shawls standing on the topmost roofs looking toward the forest in search of wolves, stretching their hands into the air and making threatening bearlike sounds, *"Ahoo-oo! Ahoo-oo!"* Suddenly Feigele, too, is here. She herself! Hiding behind the old oak tree, thrusting out her head at me for a moment and crying, "Cuckoo!"

Indeed in the sweet moments of divine inspiration, when the heart is as full and juicy as a ripe grape and the channels of mercy suddenly open of their own accord, it is enough for me to close my eyes for a moment, and there appear before me, like lightning flashes, all the paths of my life from its beginning, shimmering in the pure white glow that illumines them from end to end. At such a moment the vision of my native village will suddenly appear and stand before me just as it was, in all its kindly grace and all its pristine splendor. Like a fiery palm, a swift hidden hand, it suddenly appears and presents me with the essence of my childhood, the sum of days and years, all folded and enclosed in a little sheath of one split second. I see again precisely the houses from the morning of my life, the site of my first childhood, in all their fullness and with the universe surrounding them, all at once both great and small, with nothing missing—and once again I savor the taste of that first vision. Wherever it is, in some forgotten corner of Volhynia, from a haunt of reeds and swamps, from a place of endless forests, my native village suddenly appears, together with its days and nights, its festivals and Sabbaths, and all the fixed ceremonies of its year, looking just as God created it: small, peaceful, and humble. It stands there still, just as it has stood in its confined space from the six days of creation, half on the plain and half on the slope, hidden in the shade of bushes and trees and surrounded by its gardens and cucumber fields, bearing with quiet grief the burden of its chaste existence, quietly—as it always has done. Nothing in it has changed, not a pebble is missing, the very same clay houses and low wooden shacks strewn about the valley and the hill like startled flocks of sheep; the same silent grove plotting against me in the distance behind the village, with its cold darkness; and that very same green hill lies in front of me right opposite my father's house like some ravening, terrifying beast or some wild ox on the path, swallowing everyday at twilight a whole golden orb—the setting sun—a whole golden orb every single evening; the very pond that sparkles at the side of the hill like a bright mirror, where ducks purify and sanctify themselves, upending every few moments, ducking their heads in the water with tails toward the sky; those very paths, wriggling like serpents through fields and pastures, losing themselves with endless yearning in the hidden distance.

All the festivals of the year stand quietly before me as in a dream. Sabbath and weekday, summer and winter, days of contentment and times of anger, daytime joys and terrors of the night, they and their fragments and the fragments of their fragments, all things and their opposites beside them, join together—without canceling each other out. Every season has its own particular light, every day its own appearance. And all of them mingled together for all that—again as in a dream—into one complete entity whose name is: my native village.

Young days of spring, white with blossom and swathed in soft and tender greenery, sprout joyful and trembling alongside burning summer days weary with heat and laden with gold; and in their midst the sad evenings of the vintage season and the angry purple winter skies die away with quiet sadness over hissing, glowing coals. For a moment the first snow, too, flickers at me from their midst, the soft, sweet snow falling quietly and gently as though from a light sleep in the void of the world, touching my eyelids and bringing its fresh white coldness into my heart. It is a fugitive heritage in the treasure trove of my memories and a tiny remnant of a complete winter that has been stolen from my heart; I have no knowledge where it has gone. That winter has passed and no longer exists, just as there are blotted out from my mind the beginning and end of a great whirlwind that overtook me suddenly on a scorching day when I was returning home on a hillside path between the tall grasses. The storm rushed in from the ends of the earth and fell upon the village—and for a moment the ground trembled mightily. The heavens grew dark, blackness descended. The forest roared in the distance, trees were uprooted, and the grasses on the hill clung to the earth in terror. Columns of dust soared on high and straw roofs flew into the air; and before I could pull myself together—there I was flying! I tell you I was flying! A mighty gust of air suddenly engulfed me, lifted me up like a feather, and carried me to the bottom of the hill and to the top of the hedge surrounding our house. How I arrived or how I was afterwards carried into our house—I do not recall. But the experience of that flight—what fool would attempt to explain it to others? Only in dreams at night are there times when a person might savor a tiny fragment of it. . . .

Sometimes, in saner moments, I say to myself, it never happened at all! The village, that village which I see in my imagination, never really existed. Not it, nor the forest, nor the dwarfs, nor Feigele, nothing. They are only folktales and dreams that arise of their own accord like wild plants, based on a few true facts to make them appeal to children. In any event—I rationalize still further—the sequence of times must be confused and the incidents in disorder. Earlier episodes may have come later and vice versa. Imagination is fickle, and one cannot rely upon it.

Would it were so! My complete faith in the absolute reality of these legends is not affected one whit by all that. What difference if they actually occurred or not? They exist in my very soul, and their reality is in my flesh and bones. The finger of God engraved them on the tablets of my life, and who can erase them? If they are of the stuff of dreams—no truth and no reality is their equal. Like wine preserved in the grape, so they remain in a man's heart as long as there is breath in his nostrils. Their scent will never fade nor will their taste diminish. On the contrary, as the years pass, their sharpness and splendor increase, and the older they become, so their power grows and their sweetness abounds. No wine is as strong and as sweet as the story of our childhood! A single drop of it is sufficient at times to intoxicate the heart to the point of madness, to sate the soul! May the name of our good angel be blessed, for not allowing us to taste from the cup of its delights more than one drop at a time, and at long intervals. A single drop too much or larger than a measure—and a man's heart could perish at that moment from sheer ecstasy.

I am quite sure that when my own time comes, and the gates of this world open for my exit—at that last hour all the scenes of my childhood will peek forth once again from behind the curtain and raise themselves before me in one array. Every single one of them will come in all its sweetness and grace and in all its pristine splendor, just as I was shown them in the morning of my life. They will stand before me bright and clear and watch me silently. Suddenly the light of the seven days of creation will shine upon them—and fade forever with the light of my soul. . . .

Dreams tell lies—but not all of them. And before I begin to recount a little bit from here and there, a few chapters from the meanderings of the inner life and the true dreams of a random son of Israel, may I be permitted to relate, without apparently any obvious connection to what has gone before or what will come later, but only by way of a small interlude between them, one of my own dreams, a dream that was engraved in my heart in the past and has remained in all its clarity and all its detail to this day. I do not know whether I will be able to convey to anyone the feeling of a dream as it was, and in particular to taste the flavor of its special light and atmosphere—how difficult it is to do that with a dream!—nevertheless, come what may I will tell it. The dream is a true one, almost real. Therefore it contains no strangeness, confusion, or surprise. And it seems to me, this is the proper place for it.

I dream—before me lies a long road, heavy with sand and loaded with long, long convoys of wagons returning from the fair—and I among them. I do not know how or whence I was carried into their midst, but I walk on, swallowed up in a dense, noisy throng, and drag along with it almost unconsciously. All about there is noise, tumult, and shouting, carts and wagons, some empty, some loaded with goods, together with their passengers, drivers, and hands, men on horseback and on foot, man and beast in one great mixture, dragging on, and plodding forward heavily and fatigued, amid clouds of dust and deep sand. Walking is well nigh impossible. Wagons and men half sink into the deep sand. Dust, heat, and exhaustion. Everyone is weary and broken; everyone is dirty and soaked with sweat. Everyone looks irritable and sullen, and everyone shouts and beats the animals cruelly and in anger. The fair—it would appear—was unsuccessful. Not one realized even half his expectations. And so they vent their anger on the miserable beasts. And the worse the road becomes, the shorter their tempers, and the greater the noise and the confusion. No one listens to his fellow. They urge each other on and get in each other's way. "Hey there! Move along, man! Stop, stop, stay where you are, you son of a bitch!" But no one has the power to move or stop. One moves because the crowd moves, and stops when it stops, just like a flock of sheep. I, too, am one of the flock. I struggle among them, but do not know what I am doing there. I am tired; oh, my head, my head! I am on the verge of fainting, but I carry on. Involuntarily I carry on, as though dazed. And I am still walking when suddenly there seem to be green rushes in front of me. I open my eyes—upon my word, they really are green rushes, alive and fresh, tall and thick, stretching along the road on the right and forming a sort of green wall at its edge, separating the road and the wanderers from some other world, a mysterious world, behind it. As I behold the rushes, my spirits revive. How strange that I had not perceived them before. Here they are and here they have been all the time. But even now it appears that I am the only one that senses them. My heart goes out to the green rushes, and without taking my thoughts off them I continue to be dragged along with the stream. Over there, on the other side of the green partition, lies another world, a bright, serene world. I know it, but apart from me no one else knows. But I am still dragged along with the stream, on and on. Yet my eyes never leave the rushes. And—most wonderful of all—whenever I pass sections of the green partition that are less dense, or where there are little openings, there appears what seems the image of a mysterious creature sitting on the other side, alone in the grass on the bank of a limpid brook, his back to the rushes, and facing the clear, tranquil waters. The clamor of the convoys passing by on our side apparently does not penetrate to him, as though he is engrossed in another far-away world. He sits as though transfixed, facing the mirrorlike waters, quite motionless. Nevertheless, no matter how far I move on—he is still there. Again and again his dark image flickers at me from afar between the rushes, through every fresh lattice and opening that I pass, as though he himself, together with the limpid brook and all creation round about, accompany me silently, without my knowledge, moving along with me of their own accord, step by step, and imperceptibly—like the reflection of the moon in a stream. Who is that mysterious creature? Surely I know him, surely I have been with him. Surely he is very, very close to me and to my soul. Surely he and I are one. Surely I ought, come what may, to steal away and escape for a moment to that pure, tranquil world behind the green curtain. The bank of the clear, limpid brook is surely my place, and I am the one who sat there of old. But I am still dragged along with the current and walk and walk, on and on. Clouds of dust cover me, and a great tumult settles over me, and I walk on and on, farther and farther away. Where are the green rushes? Come and gone! I have left them all behind me, they and their pure world and the brook with its limpid waters, and the mysterious creature sitting forever on the brook's bank. Suddenly I remember and my heart leaps. This lone mysterious creature that I have left behind on the bank of the brook—it is me, me myself, me, and no one else!

That is the story of the dream—and the meaning may be left to God! Let us leave the mysterious creature for a while. Let him sit alone where he is, just as before. Let us not disturb his peace. Who knows, perhaps someday his image may appear again for a brief moment through the latticework. From now on, I will wend my weary way in the deep sand at the rear of the convoys.

2

MY THUMB AND THE SECRETS OF THE WORLD

There was never any real harmony between my father and myself. It would appear that he was set against me from the moment of my birth, like someone who has made a bad purchase and doesn't know what to do with it: with no conceivable use or possibility of sale. As luck would have it, I descended upon my father and mother by an oversight, after they had already married off most of their children and given up hope of additional offspring. I was eighth in line and a child of old age; and when the midwife congratulated my father about me with a Mazel Tov, he wrinkled his nose a little . . . so my mother told her neighbors. She also told them that thirty days after my birth I was sent into exile: I was shunted off to the bosom of a gentile wet nurse in a neighboring townlet. The wet nurse, begging your pardon, had dried-up breasts, and when I used to cry for milk, she would put my thumb in my mouth to suck. . . . When I was brought back from there, my legs were bowed, my belly was swollen, and my eyes protruded like two glass marbles. Apart from that, I had taken to eating plaster off the wall, munching on coal, and sucking my thumb. . . .

This habit of thumb sucking had become second nature, and I did not give it up for a long time. Whenever I lapsed into reverie, I would suck my thumb. My father, who was a martinet by nature, used to smack me for it and call me "thumb sucker" or "pipe man"—for the thumb between my teeth reminded him of a pipe in the mouth of an old man contemplating—but I remained indifferent to his slaps and nicknames. He went his way and I went mine; and whenever he left the house, I would take myself off into a corner, sit all alone, fall into a reverie, and suck. . . . What my reveries were about—I do not know. I would curl up like a lizard in some hole and daydream. Whatever I saw or heard around me seemed a sort of dream, and my heart was full with mute astonishment at reveries that had no name or form. Everything astonished me . . . the ticking of the clock, the shadow and the stains on the wall, the silence of an empty room, the darkness under the bed, the sandals lying there, the fine sunbeams glistening through the window, floating dust—all of these were deep secrets and mysteries requiring study, and I wandered about among them like an ant in the grass . . . they too had their own secret life like me and only my heart had any commerce with them. If anyone spoke to me, I only half heard what was said, and if someone asked me anything, I would narrow my eyes and remain silent. My heart was always fixed on some other place: on a spot on the wall or a fly in flight. My soul would enter the essence of everything, as though possessed, and dwell among the trees and the inanimate stones, soaking up everything from them and giving nothing in return. . . .

No one in the household paid me any attention. Father was a stern man, ground down, and worried. I do not know what worried him. My mother would remember me, but always after the event. "Oh my goodness, the infant hasn't eaten yet . . . the baby hasn't been washed yet. . . . Where's the infant?" And the infant, that is to say, me, Shmulik, would be sitting at that moment in some hidden place, under the bed or in the niche under the stove or in the yard behind one of the fences, sitting and playing by myself. The neighbors, when I came across them, used to peer at me suspiciously, putting a finger on their temple, to indicate that my mind was not quite right, the Lord preserve us, whispering and spitting.[1] And if my mother came upon them meanwhile, they would suddenly fall silent. . . .

Of all the household furniture, the old mirror hanging above the couch drew my attention most. In my eyes, it was the greatest of the secrets of my world. Every time I stood upright in front of it, I could see another room and furniture and myself and the cupboard facing it with its brass objects on top. The very same images, except that in the mirror all of them were perched on a slope, ready to fall at any moment; it was a knotty problem: in the first place, how did they all get into the mirror? And second, why didn't the cupboard with its brass objects topple over? . . .

I made up my mind to look into the matter properly at the first opportunity, and a favorable occasion soon presented itself. The other members of the household went out somewhere and I was left alone. It was twelve noon. In the middle of the floor the reflection of the window lay spread out like a pool checkered with light—with flies coming to bathe in it. A speckled hen was slowly walking about, step by little step, clucking softly and secretively, as though about to fall asleep. Each time she was swallowed in the pillar of light, her feathers turned to gold and she became transparent and radiant. I got up and climbed on the sofa and stretched myself in front of the mirror—there he is! a second Shmulik standing just in front of me with his nose touching my nose. I backed away a little— and he also backed away. I came closer—and he came closer. In that case, I grimaced and stuck out my tongue—and he did the same. "Ha, ha, ha," I laughed—and he too laughed, but without the "Ha, ha, ha," since his voice was not heard. All very strange. I am a little nervous—nevertheless I look . . . the floor in the mirror is sloping

---

[1]To ward off the evil eye.

and the pool of light in the middle is about to spill . . . and the other objects are also slanting or hanging there miraculously . . . oh, supposing, God forbid, the mortar, for example, might fall from the top of the cupboard—bang! It could break my skull. . . . My heart stands still with hidden fear, but at once I regain my courage and peek again. I have to get to the bottom of the matter—come what may! Behind the mirror, some hidden imp or sprite must surely be sitting, and it must be he who is performing the magic with his spells. To peek or not to peek? . . . Who knows whether some hidden hand might smack my face. Would that be too much for an imp? . . . I screw up my courage and grasp the frame of the mirror, peeking to see what is behind it—and back away at once . . . another peek—and once again a retreat . . . suddenly the mirror swung, and with it the floor, the room, the objects, I myself—bang! My heart jumped, my eyes grew dark, and I stumbled and fell under the debris. . . .

When I came to myself, I saw that the room, thank heaven, had not collapsed, but the mirror had slipped off its two lower supports and remained dangling by the upper hook. Between the side of the couch and the wall, Father's notebook stuck out a little. Clearly, it had fallen from behind the mirror and was caught between the two. The damage was slight; in alarm the hen had jumped on the table and knocked over a mug. A single splinter of glass had fallen into the pool of light, where it sparkled brightly, as though a miracle had suddenly happened to it. . . .

The end of the affair was the same as the end of all my activities in Father's house—smacks across the face.

And that very day I was sentenced to the ḥeder.

About this time my father moved his household from the village and set up house in a suburb of the nearby town, and I found myself in the domain of a first-grade *melamed*, a resident of that suburb.

3

THE ALPHABET AND
WHAT LIES BETWEEN THE LINES

In the ḥeder my luck did not improve. I remained aloof from my companions and they from me. I shrank inside myself, creating my own world, without anyone being aware of it. Even the *melamed* and his aide knew nothing of it. They knew only how to hit, each in his own particular manner: the teacher laid in with strap, fist, elbow, and rolling pin and whatever else that could cause pain, and as for the aide—he had an ugly habit of his own. If I didn't answer properly, he would at once spread and twist in front of my face five murderous fingers and begin jiggling my Adam's apple. At such a time he seemed to me a sort of panther or some other noxious beast— and the fear of death descended upon me. I was frightened he might scratch out my eyes with his filthy fingernails, and because of fright, my mind became so dazed that I would forget everything I had learned the previous day. He would show me with his finger the form of a letter and ask, "What's this?" and I would blink my eyes, quiver all over, and remain silent. The power of speech deserted me.

Really and truly their teaching entered my mind only through half an ear, by way of my left side-lock. My right ear was absorbing another teaching of its own accord, which came up out of the prayer book from between the lines and mingled with what was already in my mind. The lines themselves and the actual letters were only faint echoes of it. On the very first day that the aide showed me the alphabet chart set out in rows—there immediately sprang up before me rank after rank of soldiers, of the kind that sometimes passed in front of our house, with their drummer in the front: *trram—trram!* The rows of alephs and gimmels with the slanting dots below were very like them. They were real soldiers, armed from head to foot: the former, the alephs with knapsacks folded on their backs walked along, stooping slightly under their packs, as though setting out on "maneuvers"; the gimmels standing upright with one foot stretched out in front of them were ready to "quick march." My eyes began searching at the sides and edges of the chart. "Who are you looking for?" the aide asked me. "The drummer," I say with searching eyes.

The aide dropped the pointer from his hand, took hold of my chin, raised my head a little, and fixed his bovine eyes upon me . . . suddenly he aroused himself and said, "Go!"

One syllable and that was all. And another child at once ascended the bench in my place, while I got down in disappointment and withdrew to a corner, not knowing what the aide wanted. All that day I pondered on soldiers and the army. Next morning, when I was called again, the aide showed me the form of an aleph and said, "Do you see that yoke and a pair of buckets?" . . . Indeed, upon my life, a yoke and a pair of buckets. . . . "That's an aleph," the aide affirms. "That's an aleph," I repeat after him. "What's that?" the aide asks again. "A yoke and a pair of buckets," I say, delighted that the Holy One, Blessed be He, has furnished me with such lovely toys. "No, say 'Aleph'!" the aide says again, "Remember: aleph, aleph." "Aleph, aleph . . . "

As soon as I left him, the aleph flew straight out of my mind, and in its place there was Marusya, the gentile water girl. All day she never left my sight. I saw her just as she was: with her bare calves, her thick plaits, and the yoke and buckets on her shoulder. And there was the well with the trough beside it and the ducklings in the nearby pool and the garden of Mr. Alter Cuckoo. . . .

"What's this?" the aide asked me the next day, pointing to the aleph. "Oh, Marusya!" . . . I was delighted with the discovery. The aide flung the pointer from his hand and spread his fingers; but thinking better of it, he took my chin and said: "Goy, aleph, aleph! . . . " "Aleph, aleph, aleph! . . . "

The shape of other letters also appeared to me in various guises: in the form of beasts, wild animals, birds, fish, and crockery, or simply strange creatures whose like I had not yet discovered in this world for the time being. The letter shin—a kind of adder with three heads; the letter lamed—a stork stretching its neck and standing on one leg like the one that lived in a treetop behind our house; the gimmel—a riding boot, like the one pictured on the jars of shoe polish being vigorously rubbed by a little devil with a tail. . . . The dalet—looking like an ax, and so with them all . . . and sometimes one of the letters would appear to me in one shape today and in some other shape tomorrow. This happened of its own accord, without any intention or effort on my part. A form that I had grown tired of withdrew, and another one took its place.

When I came to combining the letters, I found a mixed multitude of the strangest creatures. They came striding along in great bands, side by side or following each other, neck in front of face and face opposite neck, with the simple nun and the squashed-nosed *pay* always striding on one foot at the head. The lamed walked erect with neck outstretched and head upright, as if to say, "Look at me; I am head and shoulders taller than them all." Meanwhile the yods pressed forward, such little creatures that seemed to me to have no shape or support, and nevertheless I liked them more than the others. They always seemed to be floating in the air or drawn along by chance—and I was very sorry for them. I was always afraid that with their diminutive size they might get lost among their companions and be crushed or trodden underfoot, God forbid, among them all. . . .

Such confusion prevented my ear from hearing the aide's teaching, and my windpipe seemed fixed between his fingers. With my mouth I repeated after him apparently every syllable, but my heart was minding its own business: forming one shape after another, combining forms, and daydreaming. Sometimes the sound of the syllables was woven into the fabric of my dreams and endowed them with fresh coloring or new features, whether pertinent or not. During my reading, if I chanced upon a grotesque combination of forms, I would suddenly start laughing; and my mirth would send the aide into a towering rage, drawing his whole fury upon me. I had no idea why my laughter affected him so.

My classmates paid no attention to me at all, and I took no heed of them. When they were playing inside the ḥeder—I would sit to one side and watch them or withdraw to a corner, suck my thumb, and fall into a reverie. I was drawn after the shapes in the prayer book, in all their combinations and patterns, as far as my power of imagination could stretch. My mind extracted from them whatever it could, eating the kernel and throwing away the husk; and when the children came out to play in the yard—I would seek out some hiding place, sitting alone and playing by myself. Whenever my turn to read came round, they searched for me until I was finally found sitting and sucking my thumb behind some fence or lying in a dark corner of the corridor.

4

I Am Weaned!

When I had spent two years in the ḥeder without much success with the Hebrew of the prayer book, my teacher introduced me to Bible— with considerable improvement: the prayer book was already "old hat," and its letters I considered lifeless. To what might it be compared? To someone gnawing and chewing empty husks. But Bible was different; it opened new windows to the world of imagination. First of all the petite aleph.[2] I found the little fellow at once, sitting opposite the tent of meeting at the beginning of Leviticus, awaiting my arrival. I was long acquainted with his companions, dwarfs like himself, from the "Prayer for Rain" in the prayer book, and I was able to convey greetings in their name. Second, the sheep and cattle and birds: ox, ram, goat, dove, and turtle dove . . . they were all well known to me and I was familiar with them. You might almost say that I had a share in them. The goat and the calf pasture in the meadow behind our house at the end of the suburb—I spend my free time with them; and the doves—they come from the dovecote of our neighbor Truchim, and they also have right of entry into our yard. . . . In the morning, when I leave for school, they come toward me strutting importantly, puffing out their crops and cooing, *"Tur, tur, tur."* . . . For some time I have had my eye on a pair of them and at Hanukah, may it come in peace, when I am in the money, God willing, I will buy, without commitment, that pair for ready cash. . . .

And when I reached the passages[3] in which are mentioned head and fat, innards, and shanks washed in water, "And he shall set them on the wood that is on the fire," nipping off the head and breaking the bird's wings, "its crop with its feathers," wringing out the blood, the offering in a pan, a frying pan, et cetera, et cetera—there arose at once in my imagination my mother's entire kitchen on the eve of a festival. My mother and the maid—aprons on their waists and sleeves rolled up to their elbows—stand armed with rolling pins, rolling the dough on the board, beating eggs in a dish, and pouring glistening oil into hollows in the mounds of white flour . . . the cat too is here: he lies in wait round the salting board casting glances at the "caul which is above the liver," the loins and kidneys, and the crops and shanks lying about in their salt and oozing a reddish juice . . . and the maid from time to time throws him a piece of intestine or white gut of fish roe or "the crop with the feathers" and the like, to keep him busy for the time being, and to distract his attention from the meat. The pestle and mortar sing out, "Pound it well, pound it well!" and my nostrils caught the sweet, refreshing savor of oven baking, and an offering of flour mixed with oil and

[2]The first word of Leviticus ends with a miniature aleph. It was customary to begin the study of the Bible with Leviticus.
[3]See Leviticus 1ff describing the sacrifices and offerings in ancient times.

egg yolks, and my ears picked up the sound of crackling and sizzling pancakes floating in fat in the skillet and the frying pan and the crackling sound of "the gift offering" and other pastries with the dough cut into strips like noodles or molded into pies and puddings coated with raisins, saffron, and cinnamon . . . the word "crackling" stimulated my appetite most, until my temples hurt and my cheek twitched: Cr-a-ck-li-ng! . . . I was overcome with hunger. My mouth filled with spittle and my thumb found its way unconsciously between my teeth. . . .

"Where are you reading?" . . . my teacher suddenly asked, strap in hand. All the pupils fall silent and fix their gaze upon me. My little finger wanders between the lines, a blind terrified wandering. . . . Brimming with tears, my eyes glance alternately at the Bible and my teacher's strap. The blurred letters dance in front of me. The teacher raises his hand and my right shoulder hunches in fear. In my fright I forget to take my thumb out of my mouth.

"Berele!" my teacher suddenly addresses a lively child. "Run along to Nahum the cobbler and bring me back a little pitch. Right away. Tell him, 'The teacher wants it.'" Berele hurried away. The children round the table whisper to one another, stealing glances at me and laughing, stealing more glances and laughing again. Why are they looking at me? Why are they laughing? Berele brings a little pitch on a splinter of wood and puts it on the teacher's table. "Come down!" the teacher orders me. I come down. "Come here . . ." I take one small step forward. "More . . ." Again a little step. "And again . . ." and I am standing held between the teacher's knees. God in heaven, what is he planning to do to me? . . .

The teacher bends his thumb backwards until a kind of little hollow appears next to the bottom joint. He fills the hollow with snuff and after inhaling a noseful, he stands up and suddenly sneezes right in my face: *"Attishoo!"* . . .

That done, his mind is cleared, and he addresses himself to the matter in hand: He pulls my thumb from my mouth and waves it in front of all the children, at the same time asking in schoolmasterly fashion according to the direct method, "Children, what is this?" "A thumb, a thumb . . . " "And what is this?" he inquires again regarding the pitch. "Pitch, pitch . . . " "And what is this?" "Snuff, snuff . . . " "And what should be done to a child who sucks his thumb?" This stumps the children and they fall silent. The teacher demands an answer with his eyes. Suddenly a child jumps up, a stammerer, with sparkling eyes, like one possessed by the holy spirit, his mouth stammering with excessive inspiration: "I-I-I know . . . " "Speak, speak," the teacher encourages him. "C-C-C-T-T . . . " "Cut off his thumb!" another child interrupts him. The cleverer children burst out laughing and the teacher too smiles. The stammerer is ashamed. Silence again.

"Nu?" the teacher asks with his eyelids. . . . "Bind a rag round it," someone suggests cautiously. "Cane him," another one proposes. "No!" the teacher shakes his head, "You don't know. A child who sucks his thumb . . . has this done to him." And the teacher begins showing the children, calmly and without haste, adding deed to word, how the matter is done: "You take pitch . . ." And the teacher takes some pitch. "And smear it on the thumb . . ." And the teacher smears it. "Afterwards you take snuff . . ." And the teacher takes that too. "And you sprinkle it on the pitch . . ." And the teacher sprinkles it. "And now"—the teacher concludes in a voice of thunder—"let him go and suck." On that day I was weaned from thumb sucking; but when the spirit moved me, I used to bite my fingernails.

5

A Good Idea and Its Reward

"Would you believe it, Pessi, he's talking to the wall!" . . . Such was my father's remark one winter's night, when he suddenly lifted his eyes from his account book and saw me standing in front of the wall grimacing and making strange movements with my head and tongue, with my hands and my ten fingers. His words were followed as usual with a smack. Truth to tell, I wasn't talking to the wall, but I was playing and talking with my shadow on the wall. And what should a child do in the long winter nights, sitting alone, shut up in the house? But Father was a martinet and could not abide either me or my game, and whatever I did was anathema to him and brought him to boiling point, resulting in smacking and kicking and shouting: "Pessi!" he shouted and kicked, "get him out of my sight—or I'll kill him!" And at that moment it really seemed as though I, Shmulik, had in fact committed some terrible wrong against Father at some time, a wrong too great to bear, for which I could not atone, as though, God forbid, I had made his life a misery or endangered his soul, Lord save us. God in heaven, when had I done him wrong? And what wrong had I done him?

So I began to keep out of Father's way and to stay out of view; when he was in the dining room, I was in the bedroom; when he was in the bedroom, I was in the kitchen, finding a place for myself in a corner, sitting alone and doing whatever caught my fancy. . . .

At that time a small matter had taken my fancy. I wanted to milk the wall. . . . I had heard from my classmates in ḥeder that there are wonder-workers in the world who attempt such things—and they are successful. I immediately fixed my eye on a certain wall in Father's house. From its midpoint downward, that wall was wet and mildewed, exuding a kind of green sweat, and it had already attracted my attention. During rainy days I used to sit facing it for hours on end, examining the strange shapes that the damp had imposed on it. I could see in the green spots whatever my eye desired: mountains and hills, fields and forests, castles and palaces. . . . "This wall," I said to myself, "was definitely made for milking," and all my free time I hung around it, examining it from every angle, and seeking the most suitable place for it. I found what I was looking for, at the bottom of the wall, close to the corner, where I noticed a swollen place, a kind of nipple—that must be the exact spot. All I needed to do was to make a little incision and stick a tube in it—and the milk would flow and pour out like a fountain. And in order to contain the full flow, without losing a single drop, I hastened to prepare in advance, before the milking, all kinds of receptacles: a neckless flask, the bottom of a broken bottle, a cracked pot for melting clay, part of a collection box for Rabbi Meir the Wonder-Worker, a tin can, perforated and rusting, a squashed funnel, closed at the bottom, a dirty skullcap, a dried-up sandal, a "widower" without a mate, and all manner of vessels and fragments of vessels of similar kinds, lying on the rubbish heap, in the attic, or under the bed. Nor did I forget to bring a cork! And why a cork? In order to cork the mouth of the nipple, namely, the hole in the wall, between one milking and the next. Surrounded by these vessels and armed with a nail and the pestle from the mortar, I sat on the ground and began to make a hole. The pestle went, "Bang!" and the nail sank in. My heart leaped, a little more, one more moment—and out of the aperture a white warm jet would flow—"*Tizz* . . . "—and here, just at the critical moment, my cheek was suddenly slapped from behind:

"The child is mad. Stop damaging the walls!"

The slap—was Father's slap. I could recognize it even in the dark and with my eyes closed. It was a sharp, polished slap, which appeared suddenly like lightning and departed rounded, sharp, and smooth, burning and ringing almost offhandedly. You hear the sound afterwards, after contact. . . . Father was a wonderful craftsman in this art, a master slapper. He understood the artistic economy of the process. One might even say that he used to slap with "divine inspiration," so to speak . . . and surely that isn't hard to understand. For forty years in succession, ever since he became "Father," he was wont to slap. . . . Somehow or other, the plan was ruined, sinner that I am, and the wall remained unmilked to this day. A pity! God is my witness that I had intended it only for the good. I saw my father's poverty, and I wanted to help him to the best of my ability. . . . The truth is that I couldn't bear to look upon his sorrow, when he came home in the evening and sat straining his eyelids over the account book, chewing his beard, and reckoning, and reckoning, and reckoning. . . . What connection can there be between an account book and anger? And yet nevertheless—beware of Father when he is concentrating on his accounts! It is a time of danger, and your life hangs by a thread. . . . Indeed my plan was certainly well meant. I thought, moreover, that I might, perhaps, win over Father's heart by these means and that he would look upon me with favor and not slap me anymore. But what could I do? Satan intervened, and Father destroyed his livelihood with his own hand.

6

MYSELF AND THE MOUTH OF THE STOVE

Consequently, I abandoned milking the wall and teamed up with the mouth of the stove. In winter Father's house was dark and desolate, and at twilight when I returned from the heder, it seemed to me seven times dark and desolate. Dampness, dirt, mold. A damp coldness exuded from the walls and the floor, penetrating to the bone. The air was heavy with the smell of pitch, cheap cigarette smoke, and some other foul smell—the odor of peasants during the day (my father had dealings with peasants and they had entry to our house). The simple furnishings—which always seemed lost and orphaned in the large void—were now merging into the twilight darkness and were swallowed up entirely. For that reason the void became particularly empty and sad. My mother sighed quietly in a corner, and the cat came toward me from some dark place, looking up at me and howling piteously. Cruelty to animals! . . .

Only in one corner in the wall of the recess, near the floor, there is a kind of little window—the square and sooty mouth of the stove two handbreadths square, which is stuffed up all day, but with the darkness, between the afternoon and evening prayer, when the windows grow blind and the house is filled with dread—the hump of the wall opposite would take on a reddish, yellowish hue and begin quivering and dancing. It is a sign that the mouth of the stove is alight and well . . . and at once—I am in the recess, near the mouth of the stove. With bent knees I sit in front of it on the remains of the heap of wood lying there, holding my knees in my hands, bowing my head, and looking. . . . The logs inside are hard, damp, cold. Most of them have thorns covered with dry snow and wrapped in trembling barklike wisps of beard. . . . The little flame of the dry splinters under the logs is still weak and feeble, and whenever it quivers and flickers, my heart throbs, afraid that it might die away, God forbid, before it takes hold of the logs. My eyes keep track of every lick and flicker of the golden flame, and I urge it on with everything in my power. "Climb up, climb up, onto that splinter"— I whisper to myself. "From the side, get it from the side, climb up higher, higher, onto its back. That's right, that's the way, take hold of its beard, its beard." . . . And the little flame listens to me, spreads out, twists about, doubles over, and wraps itself round about the logs, feeling and seeking a suitable place to get a hold. . . . Above in the sooty window—a howling of wind and a rattling of chains, terrify body and soul. I shake all over with cold, which penetrates my bones from below, from where I sit on the remains of the pile; a gust of wind, torn from the window of the stove falls downward, into the mouth of the stove, scattering a handful of yesterday's cold soot on my face—but I do not move from my place. My eyes and my heart are on the flame. I sit and watch how the fire flares up. And at the moment when the fire flares—I devote myself heart and soul to the conflagration. . . . I look at it and I listen to it in a way that no words can express. I hear a kind of tune, a mysterious tune, very light, moaning from the depths, rising from the glowing coals, stretching from within like the extrusion of thousands of fine, hid-

den threads, beautifully strung out . . . and I see a kind of dance, a
wild unruly dance of little tongues of flame, alive and dancing
rapidly. A great host of reddish, bluish, purplish, golden flames . . . a
riot of incandescent lights, rising in countless threads and straps,
wrestling and writhing, licking and flickering, embracing and clinging . . . the hissing of heaps of glowing coals and the winking of living eyes of carbuncles and rubies. *"Ts-ss"*—the tip of a brand hisses
on a turbid boiling drop bubbling upon it. *"Pok!"* answers a glowing coal that has suddenly split and splattered into fragments. And
once again a quiet, drawn-out groaning is dragged out, a fine, sharp,
thread of sound—*"Hm-m!"* . . . And suddenly—*"Prrr!"* A pile of
burnt brands bursts into fragments and is scattered like flecks of
gold. . . . The mouth of the stove is filled with heaps and heaps of
burning coals, its empty space—white-hot iron. It seems as though
at any moment a salamander will burst forth, a creature that, according to the lore of some of my companions in the ḥeder, is born
of fire and is all horrible and red like a boiled crab . . . and it seems,
too, that at the moment it emerges from the fire it will rear upright
on its two hind legs—with its eight legs leaping at your eyes.
. . . Quaking and terror take hold of me. I close my eyes and feel the
heat of the fire on my face and on my knees and listen in terror to
the rattling of chains in the chimney stack—*"Drrr."* I am afraid to
turn my head round. Some devil is standing at my back; actually
bent over my neck. "Mama, Mama!"—my heart cries out inside me,
but no sound comes out. It is stifled in my throat. A terrible fear of
death grips me. My teeth chatter and my knees knock and my heart
languishes from hidden dread. The howling of the stove comes to
me from a very distant place . . . and here, at this moment of peril,
there pops up in my brain the "charm," which the teacher entrusted
to me to keep me safe from the fiend pursuing me whenever I go
home from the ḥeder. In haste I thrust my two thumbs in my trouser
belt and at the same time cry out with tremendous devotion, "Hear
O Israel." The charm works, my fright evaporates, and I sit down
once again and peer into the mouth of the stove. The brands fall
apart into separate pieces. The glowing coals grow dark. The hot
ash increases. One brand, all velvet glows in its blackness and full of
checkered fissures and rifts, lies toward the side and sends blue puffs
spiraling up from between the cracks, like small, thin columns of
smoke. The howling in the stove increases. It is muffled and inter-
mittent, but repetitive and cyclical, without strength and without

rest . . . Yavdoha, our old servant, comes to rake the stove clean. My eyelids close of their own accord. . . . *"Hoy-ye, hay-ye!"*—*"Drrr, Drrr, Drrr!"*—I still hear howling in the distance and rattling near by, in my sleep. . . .

The whole night, I see in my dreams all kinds of black creatures, sooty faces, like chimney sweeps standing at night in the darkness of the world, scattered about a sandy, desolate plain, each bent over a heap of glowing coals and scraping away and scraping away with their shovels, each by himself. The heaps of coals cast no light except on the spot and on the angry faces of the people shoveling them. And the void of the world round about, above and below, in front and behind, remains just as dark as it was. And there, on top of the heaps, there stand dancing upright all kinds of many-legged salamanders, pushing their fat bellies and their putrid faces upward and waving their hideous wet abominable legs in the void of the world.

7

LOKSH

Meanwhile, in ḥeder I had progressed to the class of "readers' explanations."[4] From now on I was obliged, together with the other children in the class, to chant in unison, loudly and in tune, all sorts of words by heart, which were joined at the teacher's command to the end of each biblical verse. Where the teacher brought these words from, who invented them for him, and what connection they had to the biblical verses themselves—I neither knew nor had any intention of knowing. For truth to tell, I saw no difficulty in it. It was just the same as the letter bet with a u-vowel being *bu,* or like the word *rak* translated as *niyart* and like the word *ahu* translated as *gemusicht.* In sum, it was all an edict, and one doesn't question an edict. And so I accepted the edict, swaying back and forth with all my might, joining my voice to the throng, and shouting. . . . The important thing was not to be left alone. For as long as I sing and shout in unison—no

---

[4]The class of children reaching the level of being able to combine words into sentences and interpreting them. The Hebrew text was translated into an archaic Yiddish that was frequently incomprehensible.

great harm can come of it. On the contrary! . . . But if the class suddenly stops and my voice trills out alone even by a hairbreadth—I might just as well be dead . . . and I suspect the rest of my classmates to be in similar straits. What did my classmates and I resemble at that time? A group of blind people walking along together, holding and supporting each other, tripping along on floes of ice bobbing about on the river. Each one half-trusting his classmates, all moving and being moved at the edge of an abyss. . . . Nevertheless, on Thursday, the day of judgment in the ḥeder, some of the children could apparently chant the "exercise" properly in unison—something miraculous. I, Shmulik, scarcely ever understood the "oral explanation" of the "exercise." My mind was riveted on the *gemusicht* and the *niyart* and the *bayshtidl* and other strange classroom words, which my ear had never previously heard. I didn't know what they meant, and the teacher made no attempt to explain them to me. They must be the stuff of learning—I said to myself—and they must contain the very essence of "oral Yiddish explanation," and the rest less so. These meaningless words remained hidden in my heart, and in my free time, when I sat alone in the corridor behind the water barrel, there would burst forth from them, like summer butterflies bursting from the chrysalis, lovely figments of imagination, which entertained my spirit in its loneliness. . . . I would talk with them, laugh over them, and take comfort in them. . . . Some of them lasted only a moment. They came, peeked out, and by the time I noticed them— were gone! Here no longer. But some of them were regular guests or constant classmates. I had only to close my eyes and they were with me. With some of them I had considerable dealings and we shared a number of remarkable interests, which I could not reveal to a single creature in the world, nobody, not even my classmates in school. I couldn't, even though I wanted to. They, the children, were not worthy. They would laugh and mock me and call me "thumb sucker" and other nicknames and epithets. In addition, who knows whether they would believe me. I am sure they wouldn't believe me. They would only find a new disparaging nickname for me.

I already had names and nicknames, thank God, enough and to spare. Each nickname related to an episode and each name—had its own reason. Apart from "thumb sucker" and "pipe man" mentioned above, I had also acquired for a time such names as the following: Dolt, Dreamer, Useless, Nonperson, Animal, et cetera, et

cetera; and last but not least: *Loksh!* In another version: *Lekshele*—
by way of an affectionate diminutive.

And why *Loksh?* Because of an episode. One Friday at noon I was
sitting in class before the teacher reciting alone the weekly portion
from a worn-out, tattered Bible. And the teacher at that moment
was sitting, as was his habit every Friday, with a large, chipped
earthenware vessel in front of him from which he was attempting to
swallow, with the aid of a wooden ladle, warm food in the shape of
tasty strands of *lokshen* made of flour (the teacher loved this dish
beyond the love of women and he was willing to kill and be killed
for it). As he swallowed, I repeated a passage, and as I repeated, he
swallowed. Suddenly—*"Tfrr!"* The word *vayitmahmeah* (the portion was *Vayera*) stood before me like a Satan barring the way.
What was this long, strange word? Not only had I suddenly forgotten its translation, but its very essence now appeared to me as a
strange new creature. It had only just leaped out of the Bible and I
didn't know what it was. The cause was partly the little squiggle
suspended over it. I had never paid any attention to it until now. As
true as I am standing here, this squiggle appeared just like a grass
snake, like the one that Mitka, our neighbor Trochim's son, had dis-
turbed on the roof of his house only yesterday. And meantime there
flashed across my vision a kind of white thread in the teacher's
sparse beard, flashed and disappeared. My wandering eyes became
riveted, so to speak, on the Bible, but my attention was divided.
Suddenly, without realizing it, I raised a thin finger toward the
teacher's beard, and with a kind of strange joy I announced my find,
"Oy, of course, a *loksh!*" On my honor, the word escaped from my
mouth of its own accord, quite innocently, and without any evil intent, God forbid. In the act of swallowing, a *loksh* had actually
fallen from the spoon and got caught in my teacher's beard, a white
twisted *loksh* like a chain; that was the thread that flashed before
me when I was reciting I don't know what, and when in my innocence I saw it caught in the thicket, my eyes lit up from sheer delight. . . . But the teacher and his pupils saw it differently. They, the
pupils, suddenly burst out laughing at me, "Ha, ha, ha—*Loksh.*"
While he, the teacher, leaped from his seat as though stung by a
scorpion and fell upon me with the ladle like a robber. He rained
murderous blows on me, exclaiming as he did so, "There's a *loksh*
for you, there's a *loksh* for you!" All credit to the teacher's wife, for

had she not leaped from the stove to my aid, shovel in hand, they would have carried me out from the ḥeder in a shroud.

As a result of this episode I fell ill for about two weeks and in delirium I would mutter, "*Loksh,* snuff, *vayitmahmeah,* salamander . . ." and when I rose from my sickbed and regarded myself as something of a "privileged person," under no circumstances would I agree to return to the ḥeder of Reb Gershon (that was the name of my teacher during that "term"). So where did I want to go?—To the ḥeder of Reb Meir, the one in the little valley, beyond the suburb. And why just there?—I don't know. I had once passed by that valley, and it had caught my fancy. I had seen sandhills there, a sparkling water channel, and many, many plants—a sea of plants. Amid the plants an old ruin stood out, from which grew bushes and grass. My companions used to talk a lot about this valley and relate tall stories about it and the ruin in its midst. At night—they used to say—it was very dangerous to go into the valley because of ghosts and evil spirits. And it was said that Yehiel, the ragman, once entered the ruin with his sack in search of rags and found there old Reb Kohat, the one who killed his wife and died a year ago, sitting in a corner on an upturned barrel and examining his underclothes for lice. . . . This whole matter with the danger involved attracted me very strongly to that valley, and now that a window of opportunity had opened for me—I determined not to miss it. Come what may! I would go only to the ḥeder of Reb Meir!

My mother was agreeable, and Father—he, too, was not adamant on this occasion. In front of me, admittedly, he justified the sentence and beating by Reb Gershon. "He deserved it"—he would say, namely, that I, Shmulik, deserved to be killed . . . but when I was not there, he did admit in part that "Reb Gershon had overdone it a bit! The devil take his grandfather!" . . . And so I heard explicitly from behind the door. In short—the merits of my forefathers ensured that I became a pupil of Reb Meir.

The relief afforded me by my father on this occasion I regarded as an omen that my luck would improve from then on. In the quarter in which we lived—the pitch-makers' quarter—Reb Meir's ḥeder, I will have you know, was the pinnacle of learning. It had no superior! Reb Meir himself was quite unlike the other *melamdim;* as for all the other *melamdim*—"The devil take their grandfathers," in Father's parlance. But Reb Meir—Reb Meir was different! He was a handsome, elegant man with a fine beard and a fine forehead; his speech was measured and his gait dignified; even his black topcoat proclaimed: dignity. Women accepted his blessing and children hurried willingly to his ḥeder. His pupils were few, and they regarded themselves as especially privileged. Among them was an "advanced" group who, apart from Pentateuch with Rashi's commentaries, learned other books of the Bible and a little Talmud; if so, I too could be "advanced." . . .

At twilight on that happy day, when my joy overwhelmed me and I could not restrain it, I ran outside to noise my greatness abroad. I found a band of children, my former classmates, sitting sunk in sand, playing with pebbles, and throwing dust up into the air: they were bringing down "rain." I stood behind them, at a little distance, and folding my arms behind me in the manner of a grown-up, I stuck out my tongue at them and said: "Eh, I am in Reb Meir's ḥeder, I am." . . .

"*Loksh*!"—the whole band shouted at me, and a cloud of dust rose between us—"*Loksh, Lekshele!*" . . .

8

IN THE VALLEY

On the first morning, my mother moistened my side-locks with spittle on her fingers, cleaned my nose, tucked my shirttails into the opening in my trousers, put "provisions" in my hand—and off I went to Reb Meir's ḥeder.

My heart had not deceived me. A new ḥeder—a new world. Everyday, after the morning nose-clean, I would take my provisions and set off for Reb Meir's ḥeder—and I could not get enough of it. Beyond the suburb at the very beginning of the valley's slope, just near its edge, stood Reb Meir's lonely little home, slightly lopsided, with a shed at its end, and at its side a tree with a vegetable garden in front of it. Most of the house was sunk into the valley under the canopy of the tree, but the top of its roof and chimney, sparkling white amid the tree's green foliage, announced its presence to passersby above. It seemed as though the chimney had originally climbed on top of the roof to catch a glimpse from there through the network of branches of what was happening beyond, on the crossroads. . . . The exterior part of the house shone hap-

pily; all of it white as snow, but below the windows a blue strip
flecked with orange surrounded it like a girdle. The windows, too,
were adorned with a painted framework of blue buds and flowers
like swallows in flight. . . . The arch below, in the foundations of
the house, was all green as if new. At the edge of the house on the
right stood a propped-up ladder by which one could climb to the
attic through a dark and somewhat frightening hole. Above the
hole, at the very top of the roof, a little wheel like a windmill ro-
tated ceaselessly on its axle, humming as it spun, and reducing the
fear of the hole a little. . . . Reb Meir had made and fashioned the
wheel with his own hands. He was a fine craftsman and made
everything himself. Little bone cups, ear cleaners, toothpicks, and
other similar tiny objects for ornament or use. He had two snuff-
boxes, one of oak for weekday use and one of ram's horn for the
Sabbath—both his own handiwork. The symbolic painting of
Jerusalem on the east wall and the pictures of Mordechai and
Haman on another wall of his house—they too were his own
work. When he reached the description of the Tabernacle, he
would show his pupils a scale model of the Tabernacle and its furnishings; the priestly vestments, the menorah, and the table, the
cleaning tools and the goblets, and the other implements. Reb
Meir had labored on them with a knife for a number of "terms,"
and they were kept from year to year in a triangular cupboard
fixed in a corner. It was said that he was also a *mehokek,* but I did
not know what that was. Or rather I knew that *mehokek* was
translated into old Yiddish as *kritzler,* but I did not know what
was the function of a *kritzler.* Nor did any of my companions
know, and I was too ashamed to ask Reb Meir himself because it
was a personal matter. Reb Meir's shed, the one at the end of the
house, was the best and finest of all the sheds in the world. It
stood from year to year just as it was, and Reb Meir employed it
for many purposes. It served him consecutively in a number of
ways, each according to its season: a wood store, a goat pen, a
coop for fattening geese, a space for potatoes and cucumbers, and
in the hot season—even as a schoolroom for the pupils. A slight
chill and a welcome shade were always present, and through the
branches on the roof, the sun shed drops of golden light on the
pages of the Bibles. When Reb Meir was in a good mood and
wanted to please us, he would, toward evening, bring the table
and chair and two long benches outside the shed and we would

take our places and study Bible under the tree between house and garden. Believe me, that was my favorite time. The tree covered us with its green canopy, full of the chirping of birds and the flutter of unseen wings. To the right, the valley sloped downward, together with its sea of plants. Down at the bottom, a silver water channel twisted and sparkled; gurgling and bubbling, it ran on and on until it disappeared under a covering of grass. Opposite—a lofty yellow hill of sand with a green grove on top. A great red sun was fixed between the trees, setting them aflame. "A Burning Bush"—flashed through my mind. Sparks of fire and rods of gold radiated between the network of branches, setting our eyes on fire and making Reb Meir's pale forehead and black beard glow. Each single hair sparkled by itself. To me he seemed like one of the ancient sages, Rabbi Shimon Bar-Yochai, for example, sitting at the head of his pupils in some desert beneath a carob tree, while students from all over the world engaged in "the mysteries of the Torah." A moment of delight, of yearning and outpouring of the spirit. The sun was close to setting. The air was heavy with scent. And we were reading and intoning psalms before the teacher: "Happy is the man that has not walked in the counsel of the wicked . . . but his delight is in the law of the Lord and in His law does he meditate day and night. And he shall be like a tree planted by streams of water." . . . or: "The Lord is my shepherd; I shall not want. He makes me lie down in green pastures, He leads me beside the still waters, He restores my soul. Yea, though I walk through the valley of the shadow of death, I will fear no evil." . . . The translation of the words became superfluous, almost detrimental. The words flowed and flowed from the heart with the meaning bound up inside them. The gate of understanding was opened of its own accord, "like a tree planted"—quite literally, that was the tree under whose shade we were sitting. "By streams of water"— plainly, this was the water channel below. "The valley of the shadow of death"—that was the ruin, where evil spirits lurked, and the teacher had forbidden us to enter it. "You prepare a table before me"—this was surely the table that we were sitting at now, engaged in "God's Torah." "In the presence of my enemies"—who are these enemies if not the "hooligans," the young shepherds, a curse upon them, who sometimes appear with their staffs and packs on top of the hill, showing us from the distance "pigs' ears" and mocking us with their *"geer, geer, geer"*? . . . Surely they are those very same "wicked" in the psalm, who are destined, God willing, to be "like chaff which the wind drives away," one puff— and they are gone. . . .

Sometimes a cluster of light clouds, white angels, would appear above the little valley. It would hover for a little while on its path— and suddenly it would float away, just as it came. Only one of the clouds, the purest and loveliest of all, sometimes attached itself to the top of the hills opposite and remained there alone. It looked down upon us from on high, on the little community sitting in the valley and studying Torah. "Who shall ascend the mountain of the Lord and who shall stand in His holy place?" . . .

And at sunset, as I climbed out of the valley, I lingered at its edge above, my heart full and my eyes fixed on the ends of the earth. Mountain, grove, the skirts of heaven, torches, a river of fire, Gehenna . . .

9

REB MEIR'S ḤEDER

The ḥeder of Reb Meir (as his Hebrew name implies[5]) really lit up my eyes. It helped me see to the ends of the earth, and I could not get my fill of it. I, little Shmulik, a day-old chick, of no account to anyone, would sit bent and huddled on a hard bench in a narrow little room of a small clay house, all dark and rickety, sunk in a valley at the end of the earth, and my spirit would soar high over thousands of years and tens of thousands of leagues to the ends of faraway distant worlds. From the crabbed letters of worn-out books— Pentateuch, Rashi, Bible—all of which I learned in a fragmentary, disconnected manner, with great disorderly leaps, emerged for me in confused and inverted form: generations and jubilees, peoples and lands, deeds and adventures, which had long disappeared without trace from the book of life. I conversed with men of old and took part in their lives and actions. Nor did I even need complete chapters. I could build their long-gone world even from fragments of verses and allusions of word segments: a strange name, a word with

---

[5]Meir and the word for "light" and "one who makes light" have the same Hebrew root.

a different spelling, and a little letter kaf, a suspended letter ayin, an inverted letter nun, the musical notation known as cow horn, or chain, jots and tittles—were all excellent building materials. In the hour of need, Rashi would come along and add a comment—and all would become happily clear. Capital. I learned how to derive the hidden from the explicit meaning, and my power of imagination filled in whatever was unclear in the stated text. The things that were made known to me in Reb Meir's heder—were really very wonderful. Just imagine: from India to Ethiopia alone there were 127 countries. Exactly the same as the years of Sarah's life, neither more nor less. And Nineveh was a great city of the Lord, with a circumference of three days' walk precisely. And the Gibeonites[6] *hitztayru* (meaning "disguised themselves") and *hitztaydu* (meaning "provided themselves")—two strange words, which I suspected were not quite Hebrew in form—and went to the trouble of seeming to come with worn-out garments and patched shoes, loads of moldy bread in their packs, and split wineskins on their shoulders. And the spies came to great cities, fortified to the skies, and when they saw in the streets the sons of giants, a people tall and mighty, including three brothers, violent men of great renown, Ahiman, Sheshai, and Talmai[7] (these three brothers, stout as cedars, with flowing locks and caps askew, the middle one playing a harmonica, always apparently walking together and spreading fear all around them), the spies at once regarded themselves as grasshoppers—like the grasshoppers that jumped and chirped in the fields around the suburb—and rapidly fled for their lives, each to his own hiding place: Nahbi son of Vophsi—behind the gate; Gaddi son of Susi—in a hut in the cucumber field; Gamaliel son of Pedahzur—among the vineyards or among the cabbage stalks. . . . There all of them lay hidden, peeking outside fearfully. . . . And in Ham, that is to say, in the famous city Ham, the Zuzim[8] dwell, as is well known—what, you don't know who they are? They are the people that the Ammonites call Zamzumim,[9] who are different from the Emim: the latter, you should know, inhabited Shave Kiryatayim. And in the land of Elam reigned a terrible man of great and fearsome name: Chedarlaomer! A veritable savage. For all

---

[6]Joshua 9:3–4 and 13.
[7]Numbers 13:28.
[8]Genesis 14:5.
[9]Deuteronomy 2:20.

his searchings he could not find for himself a better name than Chedarlaomer! Different from them all were the Kaphtorites, who came from Kaphtor, together with the people of Pathros with the men of Naphtah and Kasluh[10] at their side. As for them, I have no clear idea of what to make of them, but my heart told me that they were only little people and their men were tiny, round creatures, like dwarfs, who always dwelt together in one bunch like ants in their holes, doing all their work in common. And how did I know that? Perhaps because their names always came in the plural.

Apart from this, I also had some acquaintance among the "Princes of Edom"—petty monarchs, not unlike our local "squires"—"The Prince of Kenaz, the Prince of Gatam, the Prince of Shobal, Prince Jeush.[11] Of similar kind was a certain remarkable personage, a very successful man by the name of Anah—the same Anah who found the *yemim* in the wilderness.[12] Lucky man! Sometimes I wander for hours on end around the outskirts of the suburb and poke about among the bushes, ditches, and rubbish heaps to extract a broken pot or a horn from a dead cow, whereas he, fortunate man, went out to graze the asses of his father Zibeon—and at once found the *yemim*. What kind of creatures are these *yemim?*—I am blessed if I know! My teacher explained it to me: "mules," that is to say, a strange kind of creature that is neither horse nor ass, but a mixture of them both together. From which I infer that the *yem* is made up of two parts; from its head to its navel, a horse; and from its navel to its tail, an ass. There is also room for another combination: the whole length of its right side is a horse, and its left side an ass. It was a fine point and hard for me to decide. It would appear that the *yem* was closely related to the family of Ahashtaranites, sons of the Ramachites, who were, as is well known, endowed with eight legs, four for running and four for resting. . . . At any rate Anah made a worthy find, since Scripture reports it and not everyone merits that.

Og, King of Bashan,[13] was one of the last remaining sons of the Rephaim. At the time of the flood, Noah the Righteous took pity on him and found him a place on top of the ark, and Noah handed him

---

[10]Genesis 10:13.

[11]All in Genesis 36.

[12]Genesis Chapter 14.

[13]Deuteronomy 3:2. The legends referring to the *yem, yemim,* and Og are taken from Rabbinic literature.

out his food through the window everyday. Og used to sit on top,
with his forehead continually brushing the clouds and his feet dangling several miles down in the water. There he sat, stuffing whole
loaves into his throat and gulping down from a large, dirty pot all
the leavings and remains of the table of Noah and his sons. And
how did that villain reward Israel? Finally, when Israel left Egypt, he
uprooted a mountain and wanted to throw it down on them. They
would have been completely flattened had not Moses entered the
breach by leaping with his battle ax more than ten cubits into the air
and smiting him on his ankle so that he died. So may they all perish!
Now all that remains of him is his iron bed,[14] nine cubits long and
four cubits wide, "by the cubit of a man": a wonderful precision,
which leaves not a shadow of doubt in the world. Admittedly, for a
man whose height reached the orb of the sun and whose ankle was
more than thirty cubits—such a small measure for a bed is a little
restrictive and serves to lessen the terrifying form of the giant in my
eyes to a considerable degree, but the holy Rashi, may his memory
be blessed, hastened to add a little comment to rescue the honor of
Og, which was not diminished in the slightest. "By the cubit of a
man"—that means by the cubit of Og himself—and the cubit of Og,
as is well known, was several miles long. In which case the bed was
in keeping with Og's dignity and henceforth there is no reason for
regret. Indeed, the bed, with its pillow and cushions, remains at
Rabbat Amon until this day, and if you are not too lazy, why not
go and see it for yourself? It's big enough for a whole regiment to
sleep on.

10

My Way Home and My Journey
Through Wilderness and Sea

Overflowing with clear and precise information of such kind, I used
to leave for home each day at sunset. My companions scattered happily and noisily to their homes or to their pleasures while I remained
alone along the way. My father's house stood apart at some distance
from the suburb, near a grove, and to get there I had to walk alone

---

[14]Deuteronomy 3:11.

along a path heavy with sand, which wound its way between rows
of trees, across a desolate stretch of land without a house, and cross
en route another place of danger: a little bridge arching over a canal
where, as rumor had it, a little devil from a company of imps had
taken up residence. This little devil, however, was well disposed to
children, so tradition maintained, and meant them no harm.
Nevertheless, when I saw the golden halo of the setting sun disappearing beyond the treetops—my heart skipped a beat. Across the
river, from behind the grove, a hidden "cuckoo" reached me and
frightened me a little, as I slowly made my way, alone and forsaken,
between the rows of trees at the sides of the path. Reddish drops of
light flickered above me, my feet sank into the sand, and my mournful spirit carried me away into the distance. . . .

I was not walking to my home, but I was a traveler, a wayfarer,
with staff and pack, crossing land and sea. Countless days had
passed since—I had forgotten when—I had set out to wander about
the earth, and thus far, alack-a-day, I had found no rest. I had
climbed mountains, I had descended valleys, I had wandered from
city to city and from village to village, and nobody knew who I was,
from whence I came, or whither I was going.

On the way I had joined a caravan of Ishmaelites or a convoy of
Dodanites.[15] I would not move from their side. Wherever they went,
I went, and wherever they camped, I camped. . . .

By day we passed through deserts, a dry and thirsty land, a place
of serpents, snakes, and scorpions. The young men walked beside
their camels laden with roll upon roll of silk, satin, embroidery, purple and scarlet, and piled high with aromatic gums and resins, bal-
sam, and all kinds of spices; while the old men, white bearded and
wrapped in turbans, rode at the head in splendid raiment, on bright
she-asses, with their slippered and sandaled feet almost dragging on
the ground and tracing grooves in the sand.

At night we would turn aside to camp in the woods, and there we
would light bonfires and sleep around them on the ground, completely encircled with a curved wall of stones to protect us from wild
beasts, in the manner, according to Rashi, of our ancestor Jacob. . . .

At one place we were joined by Gibeonites, those cunning peasants
with their ragged garments and patched-up shoes, and their cracked,
worn-out wineskins. Throughout the journey they walked to one

---

[15]Isaiah 21:13.

side, a self-contained company, with sad countenance and frightened eyes, as though nursing some secret. No one in the caravan knows who they are and what they intend, except for me, Shmulik, because I know all their subterfuges in advance from the Book of Joshua. . . .

If God had led me that way—I would have turned aside to spend a night in the study house of Shem and Eber, a place where our ancestor Jacob hid for no less than fourteen years when he fled from his brother Esau. I am convinced that I would still have found the lectern at which Jacob studied and the bench on which he slept, standing behind the stove until this day. . . .

And thus passed days, weeks, months. . . . We traversed the wilderness of Zin, we covered the desert of Paran—and still no end. Our feet were swollen, our shoes and garments worn out, our bread had become dry and moldy, and our water skins, without a drop of moisture left, had all split. We were almost at the end of our tether, when suddenly—hurray!—our eyes beheld Hazazon-Tamar![16] The men of the caravan revived! The legs of the asses and camels perked up like those of royal steeds, and before the sun set and the Sabbath arrived we all reached the place of rest. There, in Hazazon-Tamar the caravan found twelve springs[17] of cool, sweet water and seventy date palms, and they spent the Sabbath there at the water. From Hazazon-Tamar onward the way became much easier, a positive pleasure; from Rimmon-Perez to Mithkah,[18] from Mithkah to Hor-hagidgad,[19] and from Hor-hagidgad to Jotbathah.[20] Towns and villages passed like flocks of sheep. All the journeys of the forty years in the wilderness passed by in no time.

And suddenly—I am in a ship. It is bound for Ophir. The sea—the Sea of Tarshish.[21] Sea and sky. At the side of the ship an old man lies dozing on his bundle. Is that not the prophet Jonah? . . . If we reach our destination safely—we shall not lack booty! Gold is as common as stones! We will fill the ship's hold with gold. If we stir ourselves, we will turn aside to visit the land of Havilah, which is surrounded by the river Pishon.[22] The gold of that land is of the highest quality,

---

[16]Exodus 15:27 and Numbers 33:9.
[17]Numbers 33:9.
[18]Numbers 33:20–28.
[19]Numbers 33:29–32.
[20]Numbers 33:33.
[21]Jonah 1.
[22]Genesis 2:12–13.

of the very best, 96 percent pure. And there is also crystal and onyx. And in my estimation, the river Sambation[23] too must surely be not far from there, from those places.

When I awoke from my reveries—the sun had already gone down behind the grove across the river. Golden threads from the bright setting sun played among the trees, constantly slipping and falling from one leaf to the next. . . . A moment later—and the sun was swallowed into its sheath. Amid the trees in the distant grove, just as on previous days at this time, a tall and upright shape appeared again, head and shoulders above all the rest, peering angrily over the whole plain. Who was this? A tree? A giant? An armed robber? "An evil man watching a righteous man and seeking to kill him . . ."

And here too is the little bridge and the canal beneath. The water has lost its sparkle and flows weeping silently with hidden longing and the grief of twilight. . . . Even blind Ochrim, who sits here on a stone all day with his pack and his bowl begging for alms in a hoarse, quavering voice, he too has disappeared. Desolation and sorrow. The imp . . .

And I close my eyes in an orgy of fear, and with choking throat I run and run for home.

11

THE PITCH-MAKERS' QUARTER
AND ITS SURROUNDINGS

In Ham, the great city Ham, dwelt the Zuzim. Nineveh was a mighty city of God, containing many men and beasts. Bethar,[24] which the enemy destroyed, had four hundred marketplaces, and in each marketplace there were four hundred stalls, and on one side there was slaughter and mayhem, and on the other, weddings and celebrations, without either knowing what was happening elsewhere. And across the river Sambation are the huge, red-headed Jews, and if any one of our people happens to find his way there, they put him in a coat pocket like a nut, for example, or a handker-

---

[23] A legendary river. See next section.
[24] A large city in Judaea destroyed during the Bar Kochba revolt, c. 135 C.E.

chief, because of his small stature, and pay no more attention to him.

In the pitch-makers' quarter there were none of these wonders. Not even in the slightest. The pitch-makers' quarter was only a small residential area, quiet and poverty-stricken. If anyone sneezes at one end—somebody at the other end would say, "Bless you." If a cock crows at noon in one of the courtyards in its center—the sound echoes right across the river. . . . I only had to climb on the roof of our Sukkah or the fork of the hollow sumac tree in front of our house— and the whole quarter and its surroundings lay stretched out before me like a garment. I see in front of me about thirty clay houses and low wooden huts, all of them with low crooked walls, small windows, and patched roofs. The lower ones were crowded into the valley, peeking humbly out of the ground alongside the grass and hugging the shade of lonely trees, chestnuts and hazelnuts, planted beside them; the upper ones stood comfortably on both sides of the road, looking as though they had got there by deliberately escaping from the valley in order to relieve their crookedness a little and to ease their twisted limbs. Two or three of these laggard houses, including that of my teacher, had delayed their ascent and remained standing precariously and hesitantly in the middle of the slope—unwilling to descend and not daring to reach the top. On summer days the valley was full of tall, wild plants: thorns and thistles; and in winter—a layer of deep snow, so that the houses were reduced to half their height. And there were times when the chimneys were all that could be seen. . . .

Throughout the year the quarter seemed half-asleep. An air of slumber engulfed it on every side: from the wide, sandy track, which reached out to it from the forest, cutting it in half; from the solitary oxcart that sometimes crawled along that track, its wheels half-buried in the sand; from the peasant in broad linen breeches, gum boots, and cap, driving the cart with a pipe between his teeth, and from the lazy "gee-up" unconsciously escaping the peasant's lips toward the slow-moving horned oxen; from the silent groves and fields; from the tall golden corn waving in the nearby meadows in the quiet daytime wind, and from the chirping and humming emerging uninterruptedly from the grass, dulling all the senses, and making the eyelids droop; from the low, worn-out wooden crosses planted on the mounds in the gentile cemetery and peeking with quiet grief beyond the rickety fence; from the sandy plain stretching like an endless desert from behind that cemetery. . . .

The inhabitants of the quarter are equally unlike the Zuzim or the Zamzumim. They belong to the humble of the earth, poor, quiet men, lowly of spirit, and feckless. They seek no greatness nor aspire to wonders beyond them. They deal in pennies, and their merchandise are leftovers and remnants. In summer, an important part of their livelihood derives from tar and pitch, a dumb fluid, which drips silently from one vessel to another, making no noise and uncomplaining. A man will place in the little open space in front of the door of his house or the door of his shop a tub and a pot from which he sells measures of pitch and tar to peasants passing along the road with their wagons. Between one customer and the next, the sun hangs idly in the heavens—and the pitch lies quietly for hours on end, motionless in the tubs and pots, gleaming in perfect tranquillity and rich blackness and idly serving as a free mirror, a black, round mirror for the sun, the sky, light clouds, a passing girl, or a wandering bird.

The river that flows round the pitch-makers' quarter is called Titirov, and not Pishon; nor does it really "flow round" it, but for most of the year it proceeds innocently in a straight line without excessive twists or turns. Quietly and almost casually, it accepts as additional income all kinds of gifts offered both openly and in secret, effluents and rainwater and water from the depths, carried to it unceasingly from streams and rivulets, fountains and drains, but its surface is always facing upward innocently, as if to say, "Do with me what you will, O Father in heaven, behold, I am in your hand." In the hot season there were times when it gradually contracted in all humility and modesty—until it almost dried up altogether. Then sandbanks and protuberances were revealed in its midst, like little islands, covered with reeds and sedge, and in the heat of the day Children of Israel from the suburb would come and camp in groups, naked as on the day they were born, stretched out on the sand, hidden by the reeds and bushes, eating lentils together or cracking hazelnuts in company. Sometimes they would light a fire there and boil a kettle. At such a time, they seemed to me like the men of the caravan of Rabba bar bar Hanna,[25] who thoughtlessly landed on the back of a great fish, baking and cooking on it, and who were almost drowned in the depths.

---

[25] A Talmudic sage noted for his exaggerated tales.

Some of the lads were stouthearted, bold, and brave and risked their lives by crossing to the far bank of the river, where they wallowed in the sand and, without fear or shame, danced naked like wild goats, between the trees and thickets of the forest, filling it with noise and shouting. I wondered whether they would return from there in safety. They could be in peril from a bear bereft or a wolf from the steppes, which might suddenly pounce upon them and carry one of them off to its lair. . . .

But once a year, when the snows began to melt, even the river Titirov would overflow its channels and become somewhat turbulent. Then, from afar, it would carry to the suburb on its waves and ice floes pieces of board, an overturned bowl, barrels, logs of wood, a dismantled door, a watchman's hut, and sometimes even live geese and hens in their coops, cackling bitterly, or a pile of fodder with a dog on top barking bewilderedly. But no matter how mischievous, the river remained in good spirits and kindly. Its waves clapped hands, laughing and winking as though beckoning and calling to everyone: "Help yourselves! First come, first served!" And the Children of Israel would suddenly take heart and risk their lives hurrying to the river with pitchforks to loot and pillage. Fathers and sons would roll up their coattails and trouser cuffs and wade in up to their waists, snatching what booty they could with their rakes. The story goes that Mordechai-Aaron caught with his rake a perfect one-year-old calf tied to its crib. He put it in a pen and raised it until it became a cow, and now it supports him and his family comfortably and honorably.

12

THE GROVE THAT LIES BEYOND
THE RIVER TITIROV

The grove on both sides of the river contained neither the lofty cedars of Lebanon nor the tall oaks of Bashan. So what was there? Humble bushes, low thickets of reeds, willow branches for the *Hosanna* celebrations,[26] pine thickets for roofing the booths on

---

[26]On the seventh day of Sukkot it is customary to walk in procession in the synagogue bearing willow branches.

Sukkot, and thin, pliable twigs from which to make birches for the bathhouse. The elders of the quarter would point at sawn-off tree stumps of astonishing dimensions but now broken and rotting, which protrude from the ground to this day and bear silent witness to a generation of mighty giants that had been removed from the world to make way for a corrupt and worthless generation. Among these sawn-off stumps were those that remained moist and fresh for many days, and from year to year with the coming of spring their severed veins would ooze a reddish juice like tears mixed with blood. They weep and mourn away their very essence and refuse to be comforted for the glory of their strength that had been cut off from the world in its prime and before its time. The voice of their blood calls out from the ground: "Why was a hand stretched out against us?" According to the experts, this juice could not be used, because it was like the tears of the dead. Of that generation of patriarchs, nothing remained but individual trees, wretched cripples afflicted by God and stricken with sickness, twisted and humpbacked, with torn bellies and cleft skulls, with triple trunks and dried-up boughs; outcast trees without proper shape or form, resembling strange creatures of the animal kingdom such as monkeys, apes, camels, leopards, and sirens, or like demons, devils, and centaurs of impish kind who had been transmogrified into trees planted in place like nails forever to astonish folk and cast dread on night wayfarers through the forest.

These wretches, whom the ax had spared and left for a life of scorn and shame after their time, were the particular favorites of my friends and myself, and many of them were known to us by nicknames according to their strange shape; on holidays they served us as meeting places for games and capers.

One of them I knew, a bent old willow, with a split trunk and two empty holes facing each other at the top—hollows that had once held boughs, now fallen off the tree from dryness and old age like decaying teeth—looked like a big, dry fish, with a torn back and both eyes gouged out, standing upright on its tail, its belly like an open grave with a gaping mouth—ready to swallow alive anything approaching it. . . . Another one, a crooked, twisted pine, was like a flying serpent with a rider on its back raising a whip above it. Yet another was remarkably like a menorah with five branches, which everyone called: Menorah.

One hump-backed elm, mindlessly shaming its old age, had turned turtle, like a mischievous imp, and stood on its head with its legs shamelessly stretched out toward heaven. A fat old poplar bent itself to the ground like a bow, and from its back a young, thin poplar, white as pure silver, rose upright like a suckling with green foliage, treading on its father's back and reaching for the sky. . . .

One might imagine that many of these strange trees are the sole idolatrous remnants of sacred groves, the abominations of ancient peoples, whose forms the Holy One, blessed be He, had altered and left as a memorial for a later generation to see. . . .

From among the bushes their bare dry trunks sometimes thrust themselves aloft, their branches stretching into the air like arms. These were the skeletons of dead mummified trees, which had never been buried but remain attached to their pile of roots fixed in the "world of chaos," with hard, shrunken bodies, their bones dry and blackened by drought and rain, all full of holes on the outside and hollow within.

The young hooligans of the quarter, pasturing the pigs and calves of their father Ivan in the grove, or the heder children coming on Lag be-Omer to shoot bows and arrows, even if they were to search with candles, would find there—I can guarantee—neither the *yemim* nor the badger nor the buffalo nor the roebuck. So what would they find? Toadstools and fungi and the jawbone of a dead horse, pigs' feet, and miraculously even cloud-fall mushrooms, which look like egg-white from the Book of Job, or a kind of congealed and quivering fish jelly for the last meal of the Sabbath. . . . The women call this kind of concoction: "Mother Rachel's Tears," and according to them, it is helpful for women who have difficulty in bearing children. Any boy who was lucky enough to alight on this delicacy—once in a blue moon—would dash home joyfully to his mother, who would present drops of it to her pregnant neighbors to hang in little bags round their necks as a charm.

I have also heard tell that hazelnuts grow in the grove and Kol Nidre pears. And some people testify that they have found apples from the land of Israel there. Believe it if you wish. I have not been fortunate enough to see them with my own eyes. At some suitable time it might be worth entering the forest and scouring its thickets. It ought to be investigated. Who knows what might await me there? I often ponder about the forest.

13

THE PITCH-MAKERS' QUARTER
AND TALES OF OLDEN TIMES

For all that the pitch-makers' quarter was small, serene, and poor, in my eyes it was the very hub of the world. The essential tales of creation were told about it. Here, above the roofs were hung the luminaries of the six days of creation; here, in the gardens and allotments and in the grove, the earth brought forth grass and plants and produced fruit trees and shade trees; in the river Titirov and in the ponds of the quarter the water swarmed with living creatures, fish, whales, frogs, crabs, and leeches and various kinds of winged creatures.

The Holy One, Blessed be He, surely fills the whole world with His glory—but He chose his fixed abode in the sky at a place directly above the suburb, and He concentrated the power of His Divine Presence in the Holy Ark of our synagogue, between the wings of the cherubim hovering above the curtain.

The great events related in the Pentateuch and in Rashi and in the other holy books, which I studied in Reb Meir's heder, could all be properly confirmed in the suburb and its surroundings. And there are many matters that I find hard to determine where they were first revealed to me and from whence they first came into my mind, whether from the written page or from somewhere outside it. I could point my finger to the place in the field where the sale of Joseph took place. The pit into which he was cast could still be found in its exact form, just as it was in ancient days, right down to the present. It was the very same pit as in the Pentateuch, with all the obvious signs, not one of which was missing. Just as the pit in the Pentateuch was empty, without water, so was mine. Moreover, it contained, in my opinion, both snakes and scorpions, just as did Joseph's pit.

If I had wanted to take the risk of crossing that field alone, I am certain that I would at once have met a caravan of Ishmaelites. And the cows that Pharaoh saw in a dream were the very same as those grazing in the meadow on the banks of the river Titirov, or the descendants of their descendants; and that humble river, crawling slowly and quietly as always alongside our suburb, would never guess that these cows walking innocently along its banks, chewing their cud, were of such fine pedigree.

Nor was I unaware of the path on which Bathyah, Pharaoh's daughter, and her handmaids descended to bathe in the river. Throughout the summer days it stretched out from the suburb to the river like an extended tongue and reached down to the water. The day was burning like an oven. The path wound its way brightly between little grassy mounds and hollows, at times disappearing and swallowed up among bushes and standing corn. The princess walked with mincing gait in front, with her handmaidens behind, her head covered with blue silk edged with silver; she was clad in a fine white robe, with light badger-skin shoes embroidered in gold on her feet; her handmaidens walked after her barefoot, the soles of their feet pleasantly scorched in the glowing sand of the path. While walking, they stretch out their hands to the corn and the bushes to pluck ripe ears of wheat and red currants, their robes rustling against the stalks and ears of corn with a faint and pleasant sound. Colorful butterflies dart about in the air in front of them, while golden bees and blue flies buzz in their ears. And among the reeds and rushes on the banks of the river Titirov, in a tracery of sweet, light shadows, at that very hour, the infant Moses lies fastened in his little ark mewling and crying, *"Ahoo, ahoo!"* Nor does the little fellow know that his sister, Miriam, namely, Zlata, daughter of the widow Deborah, stands at some distance hidden behind a Kol Nidre pear tree, wrapped in a kerchief and shading her eyes with her palm, looking anxiously and fearfully toward the river, with beating heart. . . . Our forefathers of old, Terah, father of Abraham and father of Nahor, always dwelt beyond the river, on the other side of the Titirov. There they sat within the grove, carving wood and making idols. And on market days, when old man Terah had to bring his wares for sale, he would put the idols in sacks and baskets, ferry them across the river in a boat, bring them to the market, and set up a stall there among the other merchants near the gentile cemetery, close to Baal Peor, that is, the great idol fixed on a high wooden cross, planted in the middle of a square, a place that serves as a market for the peasants and their wagons from the nearby villages. I imagined that on the great sandy plain that stretches out behind the cemetery, far, far away from the suburb, the Children of Israel who left Egypt settled in their tribes. There, in that great and terrible wilderness, "their tents were spread out like the brooks," and each man stayed in his camp, by his flag, according to their hosts and their insignia, exactly like the camps of our army, which pitches its tents on this plain every summer.

I was sure too that the episode of Balaam also took place on the broad road that passes before our house and runs on between the corn and the plowed land until it finally disappears in the forest. Here Balaam passed, riding on his she-ass, his two lads with him on his way to curse Israel, and here on the crown of the road by Trochim's barley field, the Angel of the Lord stood in front of him like a Satan with a drawn sword in hand flashing in the sun. It all happened very suddenly, as though the angel had sprung from the ground or jumped from one of the pits among the barley. Balaam, of course, was not aware of him, and continued riding on his way, but the she-ass suddenly turned off the road and continued through the field between the stalks of barley. Later she turned aside again and came to a narrow place, the little alley between Yanka's garden and the cucumber patch of deaf Matthew, with a fence of canes and poles on one side and a hedge of interwoven branches on the other. There is no choice, Reb Balaam. You are caught in a trap. Get down, if you will be so kind, from the she-ass and take hold of her tail and pull her backwards; you can turn neither right nor left. . . .

Everyone knows how it ended. For all the wicked man's efforts, his evil design was not fulfilled—so he went and proclaimed a fair! A great fair, like the one that took place last year at one of the gentile festivals in the cemetery square around the cross. All the Midianites and the *katsap*s of the villages and settlements both near and far converged on this fair and brought with them in their wagons the daughters of Midian: plump, red-cheeked wenches, veiled and wrapped in fringed kerchiefs, in bright, embroidered dresses, weighed down with coral necklaces and glass beads, ornaments on their throats, bracelets of bronze and glass nose rings and ears adorned with earrings. Resplendent in all this finery, a delight to behold, the daughters of Midian wandered about the market by the booths and the stalls of the Jewish peddlers and merchants of those desert days, drinking *kvass* and cracking sunflower seeds, and, in general, behaving wantonly. At first these sons of Israel paid no heed to them. What concern was it of theirs? Let the daughters of the uncircumcised rejoice! They might be defiled, but their money was good. But toward evening, when the youths of the neighboring quarter each caught hold of his girl and the dancing commenced all

round the cross to the sound of flute and hurdy-gurdy and to the
noise of cymbal and drum—at that very hour, alas, Satan's wiles
succeeded, and the sons of Israel, woe to their shame, went whoring
after the daughters of Midian and were joined to Baal Peor. . . . And
the image of abomination was stuck in the middle of the square to
this day, and every passerby spits three times and whispers a well-
known verse.

There are many lofty mountains in the world: Mount Ararat,
Mount Sinai, Mount Hor, Mount Nebo; but the loftiest of them all
was none other than this mountain that rises beyond the valley, with
its cleft summit high in the sky. That is the top of Pisgah, which
looks over the face of the wilderness. Light clouds meet it as they
pass by, leaving strands of themselves attached to its boulders and
hillocks; and if any man should climb it and live, he would find fragments lying abandoned all over the mountain for anyone to claim,
but no one does so. On its exposed flank, some sections had been
detached by a rockfall or by digging, and the exposed places looked
in their reddish color like living flesh of the mountain, with holes
and caves in which the Moabites certainly lay hidden, lying in ambush for Israel in the desert at the waterfall of Arnon. The
Moabites—it stands to reason—certainly took their share! They
were sitting in their hideouts waiting for the Israelites to pass
through the valley, in order to fall upon them from behind—when
suddenly the two mountains from both sides of the valley pressed
together and the projections on one side entered the hollows on the
other, like genies in their bottles, and all the Moabites were crushed
like bugs! And the Holy One, Blessed be He, was not satisfied until
he had brought up the well of Miriam—that beloved well!—which
meanders here murmuring at the bottom of the valley below; and it
washed skulls and torn-off limbs out of the valley, floating them
away before the eyes of all Israel into the river Titirov, namely the
Brook of Arnon. . . .

The quarter was indeed a remarkable place, a kind of miniature
hub of the world. All the works of creation and history since the
first generations were enfolded within it like the legendary garment
in a nutshell. And there was nothing in the Torah that did not have
a corresponding explicit example or near-parallel in the quarter.
Which borrowed from which? An unsolved question. Perhaps the
Holy One, Blessed be He, looked into the Pentateuch and Rashi and
created the quarter on that basis; but the opposite is also possible:

He may have looked at the quarter and its surroundings and then written the Pentateuch and Rashi from them. Or perhaps they have been intertwined from the very beginning of time, with neither of them preceding the other.

14

NATURAL HISTORY AND ART

Quite apart from all this, Reb Meir's valley provided us with suitable material for the study of natural history, the various species of plant and animal life, as well as all kinds of art. On summer days when Reb Meir took his midday nap, my classmates and I would go out to sit behind the house on the valley slope, a handy place for games and idle chatter. There we were at liberty to do whatever our hearts desired, each one according to God's wish. Micah and Gadi, the liveliest of all, ran ahead into the thickets and bushes that grew on the hill slopes, climbing assiduously from one thicket to the next in search of red currants. According to the tradition that the pupils handed down to one another, those bushes were supposed to bear red currants every year, except that not one of these lively lads had ever come back with currants in his hand. Apparently there were others more lively still who got there first. They said the goats were to blame.

Velvele, a young imp, at once climbed up to the top of the tree, where he sat hidden and threw stones at every peasant passing with his cart along the track at the top of the valley. A kind of David and Goliath.

Nahum and Todi, both brave and active hunters—experts on flies and grasshoppers and locusts and every kind of wasp as well as gnats and butterflies—produced the tools of their trade, various kinds of needles, tubes, stings, piercing hooks, and pincers and all kinds of thin and delicate instruments of destruction, and immediately set about their work performing various "experiments" on the tiny, wretched creatures that fell into their hands. A few moments later—a small but very beautiful coach, made of folded paper, started out, harnessed to a pair of shining locusts, with a merry band of flies, wasps, and butterflies of various shapes and hues: golden, blue, red, spotted, sitting enthroned inside in pairs and

dancing in groups roundabout outside. They were fixed to their
seats or to one another by means of thin, sharp thorns thrust
through their insides and backs, all of them with quivering bodies
and tiny legs, praying in terror as they hovered between life and
death, and piercing the sky with their buzzing. But our two natural-
ists, Nahum and Todi, were not at all concerned and concentrated
on their work with philosophic calm.

Hershele, a pot-bellied child as round as a barrel, sat among the
tall grass secretly fixing a butterfly known as "dead man's skull" on
a small copper coin, in the hope and perfect faith that on the next
day he would wake up and find beneath it two coins. . . . This secret
was revealed to him in a whisper and at the cost of two buttons and
a slice of apple by Netka the thief, who, immediately after receiving
his reward, took to his heels and disappeared behind the ruin to
hunt for Spanish flies.

One group of pupils was gathering in the grass and stringing together "pearls," namely, fine, rounded, flattish grains, like small
dried figs; and another group was busy planting and weeding or
making bridges and sailing ships across "Miriam's Well," the canal
at the bottom of the valley.

At first I was attracted to the activities of one of these groups, but
soon enough and without my knowing quite how, I found myself
outside. . . . Unwittingly like a weak link in a chain, I slipped out of
the playing group and nobody noticed my absence. Like a discarded
and forgotten object, I lay among the grass, hidden by stalks and
leaves, with no one to see me or know about me. That was how I
wanted it. I had no need of them or their commotion. Seeing but unseen, I would lie by myself to one side, concealed in the bosom of
the world, left to myself and my dreams, watching, listening, and
keeping silent.

Here comes a crawling ant, climbing up a grass stalk, falling, and
climbing again. This tiny little creature was wandering in a thicket
of shade with no way out. And here is a ladybug, the horse of our
master Moses.[27] It is stuck to the back of my hand like half a lentil:
round, reddish with black spots, hard, smooth and gleaming, as
though clad in polished armor. It looks as though it should be fixed
like a ruby in a signet ring. Suddenly the armor is parted in the mid-

---

[27]The "cow of Moshe Rabbeinu" is a Hebrew translation of the Yiddish for "ladybug": "Moshe Rabbeinus Ki'ile."

dle. Slender flanks gleam, and the little creature is gone! The red in-
sect has flown away! May God be with it and may it fly in peace. I
shall do it no harm. It is a creature like me, fashioned by the Holy
One, Blessed be He. And who knows, perhaps it is just now going
on a mission for the Omnipresent. The Holy One, Blessed be He,
makes use of everything for His missions, even a frog or a gnat—
apart from the spider, which is anathema to heaven and the creatures of the earth because it brought fire into the Temple.

The same applies to the blades of grass. Each one of them has an
angel appointed in heaven who slaps it and orders it: "Grow!" And
that is why blades of grass sometimes waken from their sleep in
great haste, as fear and trembling takes hold of them, and they en-
courage each other in a whisper: "Grow, grow, the angel is slapping
and saying, 'Grow.'" It would have been nice to know what he slaps
them with: his middle finger or a little strap.

Hush! Right at my ear—and perhaps inside it—the sound of a hidden melody, drawn out in a still, small voice, smaller than small, a
mere hairbreadth. . . . A gnat is playing! The nearby voices of my
happy classmates suddenly seem absolutely remote, reaching me as
though from the other side of a thick wall or through pillows and
cushions, and swallowed up and negated by the sound of the sun
cutting through the heavens and ruling the world with its might. And
the faint melody still reverberates in my ear, in my innermost soul.
Why do you vibrate above me, melody, and why do you come down
to me? Stretch your strings, my mosquitoes, extend them well, strike
a deeper note. That's what I like, that is, nice and sweet. . . . Now I
am floating and melting into the tiny, pure cloud in the brightness of
the sky. Peace upon you, my comrades! Peace upon you, my mother
and my sisters! Peace, peace to far and near! . . . I am leaving you
now on a long, long road. . . . I am going to Feigele. . . .

15

In My Native Village

The melody continues, my eyes close of their own accord—and I am
in my native village:

. . . A bright morning. Sun and a glowing sky. Clay houses with
thatched roofs gleam between the green grass and the dew-flecked

trees. Each house has its garden, its courtyard, and its paddock. Pots and earthenware jars hang like hats on pegs and on fence palings and on the branches of trees. Cherry trees and sunflowers peek through the fences and railings. Every fence and every railing has its own cool shade alongside it. The pump handles of the wells creak haughtily up and down, and the buckets drip pure, live drops of silver and crystal. The voice of a housewife and the voice of a servant girl. The neighing of horses, grunting of pigs, lowing of cattle, and bleating of sheep—the pleasing sounds of animal husbandry. The wafting smell of manure and the warm scent of milk. The roofs spread incense to the skies from their chimneys and send up pillars of smoke. On a lofty field in the distance a windmill spreads its sails. And there beyond the windmill, at the end of the world—are undulating stretches of field, tracks, paths, forest, pure white mists. . . .

At the end of the village on both sides, a little green hill slants upward. It has a house and courtyard at the top and a house and courtyard at the bottom, gate facing gate. A yellow path divides the foliage of the hill stretching from one gate to the other. Hens and their tender chicks go out in families for their morning pickings. Swallows dart through the air like arrows. Twittering, chirping, gurgling, and tweet-tweeting—the delightful sounds of morning. Suddenly at the open window of the bottom house a thin, pale child appears, apparently about five years old, wearing a white shirt. It is I. I stand at the windowsill clad only in my shirt, my eyes half-closed against the flood of light, and the joy of morning in my face and in my bones. My head is lifted up to the top of the hill, and my eyes are fixed thirstily on the open window. My eyes seek only for *her,* my one companion and my "bride," for Feigele. A moment later she appears in the window above. Warm, sweet, and radiant, she stands there in her white shift and her golden curls, her face bright and shining, and all of her as fresh as the morning, all radiance and charm.

"Feigele!"—I shout toward her with outstretched arms as though ready to fly, and a wave too sweet to bear floods my heart.

"Shmulik!" She chirrups from on high, stretching out her little hands toward me. . . .

The vision disappears. The melody continues still. Another scene appears.

. . . The village after rain. The clouds have dispersed and the sun is shining. A great blessing has descended on the earth and a fresh, polished light shines upon it. The world is pure, pure. Everything looks renewed—from the blue of the sky to the green of garden and field. The mighty oak, with its wide top and heavy branches, stands on its mound in the middle of the village, fresh and more splendid than ever. The earth has drunk its fill and to spare, and it proclaims abundant joy to all both near and far in the song of running streams of water and in the trembling and sparkling rills. Roofs and trees drip gold, while buds and blossoms don necklaces of pearls and weep with happiness. There on the wet sand of the hill path lies a fragment of glass sparkling and sparkling as though it had suddenly achieved greatness. God in Heaven! How many suns! How many skies! Every pond has its own sun within it, every puddle reflects its own heaven. Fragments of worlds upside down and shreds of new heavens beneath the water beyond counting—310 worlds![28] Birds among the branches and tender chicks within the grass are wild with delight, opening their throats, spreading their wings, stretching wide their little mouths, and singing for all they are worth. . . . Song and praise above, melody and jubilation below. Suddenly two children, Feigele and I, barefoot and shirts blowing, emerge hand in hand from the house. They walk together, upright, keeping in step, with throats outstretched, heads high, mouths open—and they, too, sing for all they are worth. Without tune or words—only sound and exaltation. Like the song of the crane on a treetop in the forest, at the top of its voice. "La-la" and "la-la-la" and again "la-la" and "la-la-la"! One great joy, divine joy, has seized them all, the streams of water, birds, trees, grasses, the fragment of glass, and the two children, sweeping them away in the multitude of its waves. One happiness, the happiness of all the world, is above them, and one sound in all their throats—song and praise to the Lord of all worlds. . . .

And the melody continues and again I have a vision:

. . . Toward evening. She and I are alone in the village square. The sun is about to set behind a hill, and the whole square with its blossoms and flowers is all bathed in a reddish glow, the gold of the setting sun. The leaves and grass are transparent and drenched with light and the white geese feeding there are faintly tinged with gold— gilded silver! The sides of the solitary trees drip blood, and their shadows keep lengthening, lengthening. All about there is great si-

---

[28]A Talmudic figure of speech meaning many worlds.

lence. A sweet dread and wondrous grief. The butterflies spread their wings and flutter slowly over the plants. One can hear the grinding teeth of calves and colts scattered across the common, chewing in silent contemplation. . . . Feigele in her white dress flutters like a bird from bush to bush, gathering flowers, and I follow her. How much she has managed to gather today! She is holding a complete bunch! Suddenly she draws back: she has seen a dead house snake in the grass. "Don't be afraid!"—I calm her confidently—"It's dead, look!"—and I pick up the snake in my hand. I am quite familiar with snakes. They are to be found in our garden, and I am not afraid of them. "Drop it, drop it!" she cries in terror and draws back—"Throw it away!" A spirit of bravado takes hold of me and I shake the snake toward her, as though it were a whip. She flees, frightened and screaming, and I, cruel fellow, pursue her. As she runs, the flowers fall from her hand one by one and lie scattered behind her—blue, yellow, white; the strong radiance of sunset filters through her thin dress and earlobes, and I chase after her, snake in hand. Suddenly, I don't know how it occurred, Feigele has disappeared. She has slipped aside and gone. But the spirit of bravado has not deserted me and I continue to run on regardless, not after Feigele, but toward the setting sun. How near it is. Just beyond that hill. I shall pursue and reach it. I shall get there and see. A hand takes hold of me and carries me forward—and I am at the top of the hill. I lift my eyes—and turn to stone: fire, fire! All the corners of heaven and earth are consumed with fire. Streams of fire and mountains of fire. Palaces of fire and forests of fire. Fire burns within the fire, and fire consumes fire. Red fire, white fire, and green fire. A chariot of fire and horses of fire stampede, and burning lions pursue them hotfoot. And behold, the dread and glorious God descending in fire. . . .

My heart has grown faint with the fear of God, and I hide my face and flee. . . .

The melody continues in wondrous fashion, and once again I see a vision:

. . . It is noon, at the height of summer. The light is too strong to bear, and the day cannot contain its brightness. I am sitting alone in the middle of a path covered with burning sand, with my eyes fixed on the forest. I can see only one flank, a corner's edge adjoining the village, but I cannot see it all. I sit facing it in wonder. As always in the past, it confronts me with its dark secret from afar, but I am

small and ignorant and I cannot understand it. There is no one
round about, only heat and silence. The wafting scent of dry dust.
The stones in the field are scorched by the sun, and the fences burn
like an oven. Trees and bushes are too weary to weave the threads
of their shadows beneath them. All strength is dissipated, all spirit
drained. Dried-up fields and gardens pant with their last moisture
and appear to smoke and quiver, stray dogs with confused eyes and
drooping tails drag along like shadows, with swollen bellies and
lolling tongues. Shade, shade! My kingdom for a shade. They reach
a path and stop for a moment, lifting their bleary eyes to the hills, to
the forest—and turn back hopeless. Heat and silence. Suddenly the
edge of the forest facing me trembles, trembles and moves. From its
thick darkness three fine young head of cattle suddenly emerge: a
lovely red heifer and two young bulls, black as ravens. One of them
has a star shining on his forehead. As the heifer comes out of the
forest, she stops, but the bulls without relaxing their pace start running round her in a circle. Their movement is light and graceful. At
first nothing is seen of them except a patch of black, shining, quivering skin, legs galloping swiftly and rhythmically, scarcely touching
the ground, the graceful curve of their necks held downward as
though about to make a bow, while light flecks of dust rise from beneath their hooves, turning yellow for a moment and melting away.
Meanwhile the heifer stands quietly as though considering which is
better. But the competitors grow less patient by the minute, and
their excitement grows. Their muscles swell, their nostrils widen
and quiver, and their breath becomes more rapid and seized with desire. Their bloodshot eyes gleam madly. The dust beneath their
hooves increases, and their necks descend steeply toward the
ground. "Something dreadful is going to happen," my heart warns
me. At that moment the one with the star suddenly turns and stands
with forehead and horns inclined toward the other, who is still rushing round, charges him with murderous fury—and strikes! A savage
bellow, a terrible bitter roar arises from a cloud of dust, and the
ground round about trembles mightily. My heart leaps and my eyes
grow dark at the sight. And as the dust clears, I see one of the bulls
running, running across the plain, with blood streaming glittering to
the ground, and his bellowing splitting the heavens; while the second, with the star, together with the heifer, disappears again at a
light and easy pace into the forest. The scene ends. Nothing remains
except the crazy traces of hooves on the dust of the "arena" at the

edge of the forest and a great amazement in the heart of a little child, sitting alone and wondering in the sand opposite. . . .

And the melody goes on to the end humming very quietly . . . and I dream and once again, I see:

. . . A full moon on a summer's night, completely blue, and stars. The whole village is asleep, bathed in mysterious light, and no one is out of doors but me. I am standing alone outside the yard by the gate, not at all surprised that I, a little child, should be standing here alone at this hour. My eyes are fixed on the green hill, Feigele's hill, sloping up in front of me. The moon stands high above the roof of Feigele's house, and the slope of the hill is sown with clear silver light and drops of dew. The single house at the top, Feigele's house, now seems in its whiteness as though it, too, were cast in silver. The other houses in the village dream down below, each in its own place, in the shadows of the trees, sometimes glistening as the moonlight catches the pane of an attic window or the blade of a sickle hanging outside on a wall or on a fence. At the end of the village on my right, the high wall of the forest edge is silhouetted to its full width and height, black without and flecked inside with silver. Not a sound, not a whisper round about. No crowing of cocks, no barking of dogs, no croaking of frogs; the world dreams silently and I within it like a dream within a dream. Suddenly I see—I do not know whether with eyes of flesh or spirit—two short lines, like two black necklaces, of tiny little dwarfs, no higher than a finger, passing hand in hand in front of me on the hill slope, all of them dressed in black and wearing black hats. And all are walking slowly and solemnly, as though on a holiday stroll, and while walking, shaking glittering drops of dew from the grass and singing very quietly. They sing not with their mouths, but from within, inside their very souls, and without sound, like the music of the stars; I did not hear the song with my ears, but in my heart and in my flesh and in all my bones. Nevertheless the song surely came to me in its full innocence, clear and explicit, not even a semiquaver failing to reach me. My heart melted with sweetness, and my spirit trembled with secret dread. "Mama!" I wanted to cry out, but my throat was blocked and my voice choked. I do not remember the end of the vision. But for many days afterwards I remained quite silent and walked in a daze with wonderment. The magic melody, embroidered with moonlight sweet enough for the soul to languish, reverberated in my very depths and no one knew. . . .

. . . And the melody grows more distant, dying away, and its echo—ever fainter, until it can no longer be caught. Sweet as death with a kiss . . . finished! The melody has ceased, the sound has gone. My physical sight has returned to me, and I am still lying alone in the grass behind Reb Meir's house—prone with open eyes. From the bottom of the valley the voices of my playmates reach me again. . . .

And I turn this way and that, quietly and fearfully like a thief, and when I see that there is no child near me, I furtively bring out from my pocket all my magical treasures, my colored glass marbles, four in number—green, yellow, blue, and red—and one by one I hold them in front of my eyes and look at the world. These fragments of glass have a wonderful power to cast their light over everything my eyes see and lead me at will into four marvelous worlds, which no man has imagined nor any eye beheld but mine. Each world has its special light, a strange and wondrous light, emanating from some hidden source and penetrating everything. How great is your goodness, Lord, which you have stored away for those who revere You . . . but let not the charm be known to anyone else. God forbid! Those worlds are mine alone, mine alone.

An Additional Chapter

When angry, my father calls me "the lad," stressing the definite article, and when he speaks to me, a wave of hatred seethes and ferments in his bowels.[29] It is quite clear to me that is a mortal hatred. Why? I do not know. There must be something in my face, in my walk, and in my very being that brings him to boiling point. He regards me as a tarnished instrument, utterly tarnished: from the little forelock peeking out from under my hat to the slit in the back of my overcoat, and from the faint pockmarks on my face to the thin cigarette between my teeth. Even my hidden thoughts, which his eye has never seen, he supposes to be impure. In his eyes they are as suspi-

---

[29]Discovered among Bialik's posthumous papers, this chapter belongs to *Random Harvest,* but was written before the published section. Having decided to begin his autobiographical story with the earliest childhood days, he put this chapter aside until he might reach it in the course of the story.

cious as a brothel, the shutters of whose windows are closed to the world.

When Father passes behind me, my back immediately contracts. ... I can feel his gaze upon me even from behind. A kind of faint shudder passes through my spinal cord and spreads all over my skin like cold, sharp needles. My blood congeals, my body becomes paralyzed, and I cannot turn my head or move from my place.

And when Father and I sometimes happen to meet face to face—we immediately draw weapons from their scabbards: namely, our eyes. And this meeting of the eyes is dangerous!

For the moment Father is silent—and that is a bad sign. Father's silence is all cruelty and snake venom: it is an eighth division of hell,[30] which he has designed particularly for me. A hundred deaths are preferable to Father's silence. He began to apply this exquisite quality of silence to me when I became "the lad" with the definite article. Previously, when I was just an ordinary lad, he used to favor me with the quality of "speech"; and when he came across me in the house, he would present me with half a shoulder, turn his face to my mother, and say something like this in a strange and disparaging tone:

—Pessi! (That was my mother's name.) Might it be proper, perhaps, to ask, for example, how long a lad will remain idle?

At this point I too would turn half a shoulder toward my mother and mouth in exactly the same tone:

—Might Father, perhaps, advise what, for example, a lad might do? "He-he-he," Father would cackle in a queer voice, turning burning eyes upon me. He could go and become a "teacherling."
. . .

He deliberately stressed the diminutive "teacherling." Into this one word he injected all the poison of his lips and all the scorn and delight at someone's misfortune, which appeared in his eyes, thrusting them like a needle into my very heart.

Sometimes my father would add a sharp spice to his words in the form of a "slap across the face," and that was a third and different kind of penalty, a reminder of what he had used when I was still a heder boy. Now Father condemned and executed me by silence—and that, as said, was a very bad sign.

---

[30]Rabbinic tradition speaks of seven divisions of hell.

I was then about seventeen, with the first signs of mustache and beard, and nevertheless let me reveal a secret to you—there were times when I was as full of sins as a pomegranate has seeds and remorse would gnaw at my flesh like worms. I would yearn for a slap across the face, indeed, the sharp, polished slap, which appears suddenly like lightning and departs rounded, sharp, and smooth, burning and ringing. Such a slap across the face delivered at the right time is like a hot bath to a dirty body. Father was a wonderful craftsman in this art, a master slapper.

He understood the artistic economy of the process; one might even say that he used to slap with "divine inspiration," so to speak. That had been his custom in my childhood: when he felt that I deserved a slap and wanted it (there are such moments in a child's life)—he would immediately fall silent. . . . I would try to put myself in his hands when he was angry, acknowledging my sin, with my whole face declaring: "Slap me!"—and he would remain silent. "Since you are a wicked rodent, and want it—I won't give it to you. . . . When shall I give it to you? Unexpectedly, and when you think yourself to be perfectly innocent." . . . And when he did slap, far from closing the account or detailing the sin, he slapped and left something over on account, using any excuse that would serve his purpose; meanwhile you were again left in doubt whether innocent or guilty, so that your mind would never be at rest. . . .

Now he had changed his habit, and he fought me with other weapons—his eyes. When our eyes sometimes met—it seemed to me as though our fangs were being thrust into each other's heart, and each of us was biting and being bitten at the same time. The biting was silent, but passionate, prolonged, venomous, like a tidal wave of bitter enmity and suppressed loathing, like a vampire, which prolongs its bite until it has sucked out the last drop of blood. . . . I can feel his gaze even from behind. . . . A kind of faint shudder passing through my spinal cord and spreading throughout my back like cold, sharp needles. My blood congeals. I am afraid to turn my head or move from my place. . . . And so I remain congealed within myself until Father goes away.

I forgot the essential thing. The matchmakers give me no rest.

Father, it seems, has already despaired of me or is trying to show that he has. For some days now he has not, apparently, paid any attention to me. He looks at me as though I don't exist—and that is all. This morning when he finished his prayers, my mother began to speak to him about me for some reason. He waved his hand in a gesture of complete dismissal and said, "The lad—No!" meaning, let him feed until he bursts—and immediately after the final prayer he spat quickly and deliberately, hurriedly rolled up his tefillin, pulled down his sleeve, fled to the shop—and vanished. Mother started wiping her nose on her apron, a sign that she was about to cry, while I sat down as was my habit at such a time on the thread-bare sofa, my eyes fixed firmly on the ceiling as though I could see an angel there or was contemplating the heavens. . . . Afterwards I fixed my gaze on the tip of my shoes, rotating the sole of my foot and allowing a sort of prolonged *s-s-s-* sound to escape from be-tween my teeth. . . . My thoughts at the time were something of this sort: "So what do they think? That I would become a great teacher in Israel? What a thought! Or perhaps they would like me to go and serve in the shop and preside over empty boxes—I wouldn't be sur-prised." . . .

And once again the word *purpose* floated in the air before me in italics. For two years now I have been trying to avoid that cruel word, and, alas, I return to it every single day. Disturbing and trou-bling, it stands before me, chilling my blood and dimming the light of my life. . . . It was flung from Father's mouth in anger—and an evil angel was created from it to afflict me. On one occasion, Father and I were seated at the table for a hasty, noonday meal. Both of us were sitting as usual and eating in angry silence. I was chewing away and meanwhile glancing through a novel, and Father was also chewing away, sharpening his eyes on me in silence, and cutting out my bowels without a knife. . . . Suddenly his hand stretched out—and the book flew into the stove opposite.

—"Father"—I shouted as though bitten by a snake—"what do you want?"

—"I want you to choke on the crust of bread that you are stealing from me, bastard, apostate, sponger, I want you to be a proper Jew, a person like everyone else, go and find *a purpose, a purpose!*"

He pronounced the word "purpose" with his whole body shaking and through gnashing teeth: p-u-r-p-o-s-e!!! At that moment he seemed to me like an armed bandit with a flashing knife pointed straight at my heart. . . . Indeed, I realized that he was right, but I simply had no idea how this "purpose" could be achieved or where I could even begin. Everyday I made a vow: "Tomorrow, God willing, at sunrise I will begin. . . . I will certainly begin . . . a man must be as strong as a lion . . . a man must be as firm as a cedar." . . . But the next day when I wake up from my sleep and open my eyes, the clock points to a quarter to ten—and my vow has been broken . . . I wrap myself comfortably in my sheet and willingly yield my whole body into the power of morning daydreams. Gently, gently they come to me one after the other, gentle and light, soft and clear, and my soul floats, swaying on them like a boat carried along on its own without sailors, on tiny, warm waves. . . . The cat lies curled up at my feet warming itself, and the sun pats my face with its fringes. The sounds of morning arise from the street, and from the next room comes the song of our young servant girl as she beats the pillows. . . . The body becomes soft and pliable, the mind clear, and the heart yearning. . . . I light a thin cigarette and my eyes wander through the smoke as I scan the lines of some novel. . . . Upon my soul, I know of no more pleasant time than this. Everything is swallowed in the sun's glory and caught in the rings of fine, blue smoke; and everything is joined to a world that is small and light as a feather, a world that is all forgetfulness and rest, brightness and passing dream . . . a passage to a world in which there is no "purpose" . . . but where all creatures grow like plants in a field and pass by like morning clouds without any beginning and without "purpose." . . .

But at such a time my father's mere entrance is enough to destroy all my beautiful world. . . . One morning I was lying on my couch, wrapped up in my sheet and half asleep, listening with closed eyes to the singing of our young servant girl; and the song seemed to me to be very sad and very sweet, sweet to the point of swooning. Suddenly the voice stopped: "he" had entered the house. I peeked through a little hole in the sheet, and there he was coming straight toward me with his hands stretched out to the mirror hanging over my bed. My heart died. I lay like a stone beneath the outstretched arm covering me like a kind of sword, and on my own back, across my loins, I could feel the strap of its shadow. . . . Just as the neck must feel the sharpness of a sword hanging in the air for a moment before slaughter. . . . I had only one desire—to disappear. . . . I wanted to hide inside myself, like a chameleon in its sheath, so long as he didn't notice me . . . and "he" took the shop's account book from behind the mirror, slammed the door and hurried away. . . . Blessed be He who has set me free. Our young servant girl returned to her song, and I to my thoughts: about a servant girl and so on.

Why am I so afraid of Father? I do not know. It is a kind of pain left over from my childhood. It is not physical fear but something else, for which I have no name. Perhaps it is shame or anxiety lest I be hurt by his gaze. It is as though there is in my soul some small, hidden spot, and when Father fixes his eye on me—the spot burns up and vanishes. . . .

However that may be, it is difficult for Father and me to breathe the air of one house, difficult to the point of choking . . . and on every occasion when he rushes out of the house—I feel around me and within me a greater space, like a person suddenly emerging from an alley into a broad avenue. . . .

2

Behind the Fence

❖　❖　❖

$\mathcal{B}$*ehind the Fence* is a modern story wherein reality and symbol are interwoven. The plot is itself stereotypical: Romeo and Juliet transposed to a provincial Russian town. The lovers not only are the children of rival families but belong to different religious and social classes: the son of a small-scale Jewish lumber merchant and a Christian foundling oppressed by a cruel and grim Russian peasant woman.

But beyond this stock plot is an ingenious story, an educational novella. Noah, the protagonist, evolves from childhood to adolescence and finally to maturity. In contrast, Marinka is a flat character. She remains the passive, beautiful girl craving for a handful of love and tormented by a hardened elderly peasant.

The author is at home in Noah's world. (The name Noah is composed of the initials of his own two personal names Ḥayyim Naḥman—reversed to *Noaḥ*).[1]

Noah, the child and the adolescent, is not totally oblivious to the realities of his Jewish milieu and the wide cultural gap that separates the two lovers. He knows that the fruit trees, the fruit, and the vegetables of Marinka's world are alien to the Jewish world of lumberyards piled with dead wood of once-flourishing trees, or the market stalls peddling plucked fruit and vegetables. Marinka, the child of love, is unencumbered by the stern taboos of the Jewish ethic. The reactions of the two chil-

---

[1] The Hebrew version of "Noah" is "Noaḥ."

dren when they encounter a snake poignantly stresses the cultural gap between them. Noah wants to kill the snake (symbol
of the Eros), the mythological tempter of Eve. The snake
caused the original sin that led to the expulsion from Eden.
Marinka protests, "You must not kill a snake!"

The narrator's sympathies are with the young peasant girl.
She is an uncomplicated child of nature, hardly governed by
the restrictive Jewish inhibitions. The shtetl shuns the vitality,
the spontaneity, the passions of life, suppresses the wonderment of childhood, fences off the child from the living contact
with forest and field. Noah is instinctively drawn to the natu-
ralness and vitality of the peasantry. They seem to represent the
lost Eden of his childhood. He prefers their world to the
gloomy, puritanical world of the Jewish community, represented by his stern father. Both his parents fail to bind his
hands with the thick straps of phylacteries and the stern discipline of the Hebrew schoolroom.

The fence separates the homes of Noah's father and Marinka's
witchlike guardian, separates Jew from gentile. It also represents
the Halacha (Jewish law), around which Jews are expected to
erect barriers to prevent the slightest violation of God's commandments. It separates Noah from Marinka. Noah is impelled
to breach the fence to meet Marinka. Other erotic symbols are
noted throughout the story. "Apples" not only allude to the fruit
forbidden in the story of Adam and Eve but are also metaphors
for Marinka's beauty and appeal. Before Noah leaps into the
garden to consummate his love, two apples dangle before his
eyes. The enclosed garden itself is an erotic biblical metaphor:
"My beloved is an enclosed garden" (Song of Songs 4:12). So
are the trees, fruit, and vegetables associated with the gentile
peasantry. The Jewish merchants chop down the trees and turn
them into lumber. Noah longs for the fruit. His first encounter
with Marinka occurs after he plants his own vegetable patch on
his side of the fence. Marinka chides him: the garden will not
grow, because it stands in the shade.

Noah is attracted by the beauties of nature, the brawn and
bravado of his peasant friends. He nostalgically recalls the
country village where he was born, its forests, its glowing sunshine, its lush fields. For him, leaving the village for Zhitomir's

crowded streets is a falling from grace, an exile from a lost Eden.

The two lovers are innocents who relish the verdant vegetation of the garden and the fields. They are in the Garden of Eden before the Fall. However, as they mature, their love ripens (like the fruit Noah has stored away in the stable loft) into physical love. Images from the animal world now replace those of the vegetable world—for example, Noah's mature cravings for Marinka are symbolized by the raging sexuality of a horse in heat.

Noah's yard is almost treeless. The surviving battered oak serves a variety of literary functions: it is a symbol of the degeneration of Jewish vitality. However, it also suggests the possibility of regeneration. It enables Noah to leap from the stable loft into Marinka's garden.

The story concludes in a realistic, ironic vein. Noah will grow up to be Harry. He is about to marry a "nice" Jewish girl. Marinka, still innocent, clutches Noah's child as she watches her former lover and his Jewish fiancee. She remains in the garden on the other side of the fence.

❖　　❖　　❖

1

Twenty or thirty years ago, the lumber district had been a small but spacious farming community inhabited by well-to-do *katsaps,* who owned groves, orchards, and vegetable and pumpkin patches. Nowadays, it has changed completely into a large, crowded Jewish quarter, whose inhabitants traffic in all the bits and pieces of the denuded groves as well as in uprooted vegetables and fruits. Everything has turned Jewish: the homes, the farmyards and their uneven fences, the chickens pecking in the garbage, the very air and the fowl flying in it. The *katsap*s, with their groves, orchards, and vegetable patches, have all been pushed back far beyond the quarter, spreading out freely under God's sky. They sow and plant; lead their horses to pasture; kindle golden bonfires at night; raise cattle and sheep, little goyim, and dogs. They reap the benefits, and so do even the Jews—a little. Often a Jew would rise at dawn, drive his wagon into the forest beyond the quarter, and return at noon laden with God's blessed produce, exuding the good smells of fields and gardens: green onions, radishes, heads of cabbage, a bunch of mushrooms, a bale of still-moist hay, and, sometimes, hidden beneath it, red apples or a small jug overflowing with wild strawberries or gooseberries.

Only Shakoripinshchika, a stubborn elderly shiksah, a childless widow who had raised a foundling in her home and a big dog and puppies in her yard, only she of all the former *katsap*s clung to her patrimony: yard, orchards, trees, and vegetables. She held on with both hands. She'd be damned if she would move. Year after year rolled by. Her neighbors tried to drive her away either with sweet reasonableness or harsh words. They laid siege to her yard by erecting barns and buildings all around its fences, piling mounds of garbage, manure, and stones against them. Finally, they began channeling their sewage into her yard, flinging their refuse into it, and tearing its fence apart for kindling. They performed all manner of outrage against her. But she held her ground: "Come hell or high water, Jews, I won't budge from here." Not a day passed without

some sort of noisome quarrel erupting; not a week without a summons to court. They poured ashes and burning coals into her yard.
She retaliated with smoking logs that once almost started a fire.
They plucked geese, sending the feathers flying into her yard. She
roasted a pig and filled their windows with its stench. They used the
slats of her fence to reinforce their outhouses. She raised her fence
by a span or two up to the level of their windows, blocking out the
noonday sun. They let their sons loose in her orchards; she turned
her dogs on them.

"A tough nut, she won't crack quickly." Her neighbors gave up
for the time being in despair: "Her day will come!"

The siege, in the meantime, grew more intense year after year.
Shakoripinshchika continued to barricade herself against it. She
raised her fences foot by foot and added new hounds to her pack of
watchdogs. She locked and barred her gate and the small portal
that led onto the street facing the Jewish quarter, thus cutting herself off from it completely. When she or Marinka, her foundling,
had to go to market or to town, they would use a small door at the
rear of the courtyard. From there, they would take the narrow
path, trodden down by their own feet, climb over a low fence and
enclosure by way of areas that Jews hardly ever frequented. They
would disappear into the shadows cast by the bushes and trees lining the road.

Shakoripinshchika rarely ventured into the quarter itself except
when she drove her produce to market. At such times, the outer gate
would swing open with a loud creak. A two-wheeled cart would
emerge pulled by a pony called Gootsy. Laden with fruit, the cart
would emerge from her yard with Shakoripinshchika perched on
top and holding the reins. The apprentice wagoners, who usually
stood opposite the gate waiting for her exit as if for the Messiah,
would make way for her, greeting her with hurrahs. As part of the
fun, they would quickly snatch a large, green cucumber, a red apple,
or a beautiful pear from the cart and, within sight of their victim,
sink their healthy teeth into it.

To make matters worse, Shakoripinshchika's house had to border
the alley that led to the synagogue. On Friday evenings when Jews
left the synagogue dressed in satin clothes and velvet hats and
padded through the alley, three escorts accompanied them along
the full length of the wall: Shakoripin, the largest of Shakoripinsh-

chika's dogs, who bore his mistress's name (or, the other way round, she, the mistress, bore his) and two "ministering angels."[2] The dog himself was hidden from sight. He was in the courtyard behind the fence. Only his growling bark, reinforced by the clank of his chain, rose from the courtyard, scaring the devil out of all who passed.

On the street side, Shakoripinshchika's house protruded a little beyond the house line, assuming an odd, abnormal stance. The house faced the yard, windows and all, showing its windowless back to the public thoroughfare, as if in defiance: "Jews—I turn my back on you!"

This architectural affront alone was enough to bring down the wrath of the neighbors. "Look, Jews, she's ruined the house line," they would say and shake their helpless fists at its backside. But the house had another and worse fault. It was a downright hazard.

How much damage can roofs and boards inflict? But out of the far corner of Shakoripinshchika's house a long pole protruded onto the alley; from afar the pole looked like a thumb extending from a fist. All Shakoripin had to do was to bark at the Jews walking by— "bow wow wow"—and that pole, placed exactly at a man's height, would really hurt.

When a Jew passed through the alley at night and turned left, all of a sudden—crack! A round, egg-sized protuberance would rise on his forehead. "Damn it to hell," the victim cursed, as he rushed home to press down the bump with the blade of a knife.

All the neighbors' shouting about the pole was to no avail; you might as well talk to the wall. The offending pole reached out from the house and furtively did its job: which was to lay eggs on Jewish foreheads. You might say that it did it with malice aforethought. Lurking behind the corner, the devil, as soon as he saw a Jew coming—crack!

There were hotheads who vowed "to break windows," but when they reached the house itself, they ran out of steam. Before them stood a dumb, blind wall with not a trace of a window. "Damn it to hell," and off the victim would run to his home to press the lump down with a knife.

---

[2]According to folk tradition, five ministering angels descend on the Sabbath and accompany the pious to their homes.

On the other hand, the house had a pretty—if somewhat queer—roof. Actually, it wasn't a roof but a heap of thatched earth, slanted on either side. In the summer, it sprouted all sorts of vegetables, grasses, and thistles. The entire house looked like a hairy creature standing bareheaded under the vault of the sky; the chimney was practically invisible, its smoke rising through the grass.

Whatever went on within the yard was beyond the range of human eyes. The little door was, after all, always closed, and Jews, even the closest neighbors, were not allowed to set foot in the yard. Then there was Shakoripin. The Lord preserve us from even getting near that confounded dog. You took your very life in your hands. He wasn't just a dog; he was a veritable panther. He tore people apart. He had a blood-curdling bark and was always in an ugly mood. He just had to smell a man walking in the nearby alley and at once, "grrrrr bow wow wow." It was a *wow* with a long "o." Dogs who bark in long "o's" are worse than wolves.

And how clever was Shakoripin! When necessary, he would hide in his kennel, curled up in feigned silence. And then suddenly—in a flash—he came out of nowhere. He went only for your throat. Once a thief foolishly entered his yard; he was found the next morning laid out in front of Shakoripin in a pool of blood, his throat in shreds. And Shakoripin hadn't barked once that whole night!

And since all the Jews of the neighborhood valued their throats, you could not find a single one willing to risk poking his head or neck into the yard even out of curiosity. But small boys, as they walked to the synagogue through the alley or when they purposely came there to tease the dog, would peek into the yard through some hole in the fence at what was inside. The yard was square and spacious; its surface was thoroughly swept, neat as a pin, with not a thing out of place. In front of the house lay an open grassy area fringed by a tall row of branching trees. A long clothesline was drawn from trunk to trunk. On the lower fence hung several jars. A black row of overturned jugs lined the green coping of the house. On the opposite wing was a large shed, half of which served as a stable for Gootsy, the pony, and the other half as a pigpen; a small barn for the single cow; and a woodstove. Near the shed was the two-wheeled cart, a pile of refuse and manure, Shakoripin's kennel, and Shakoripin, himself, secured by his chain. At the far end of the yard began the orchard—its verdant foliage could always be seen through the open windows of the synagogue, and the smell of its apples and the rustling of its branches mingled with the sounds of the Sabbath morning prayers. This was the very garden in which Marinka used to sleep alone on summer nights, guarded by Shakoripin.

At this point, one of Shakoripin's adversaries would shove a stick through a hole in the gate, dangling it before the dog's very eyes, and the battle would begin. They, the heroes behind the gate, would growl—"*grrrr . . . grrrr . . . grrrr . . .*," that is to say, burn in hell—and the dog, tied to his chain, would roar and rumble "grrrr . . . grrrr . . . ," straining at his chain, while every one of his bones would stiffen for combat.

Who knows how far the battle would have progressed had Shakoripinshchika not emerged and put the heroes to flight? Not that they were afraid of Shakoripinshchika. What harm could a woman do, even a *goyah?* What was it then that frightened them? Her voice!

To tell the truth, she hardly had a voice. It was lost forever as a result of the shouting bouts she had had with her neighbors. Nothing survived except a fuzzy shadow of a voice reinforced by shattered fragments of shrill shrieks. A sort of a long hiss of Slavic syllables that poured from her throat and spat at your face like searing sand. What she said or screamed no one really heard, but one sensed that the *goyah* shrieked out of the depths of her heart and with her very last breath. It was as if a wheel were turning in her throat sharpening a knife: a hissing, a shriek, flying sparks. Your nose smelled sulfur and your teeth were set slightly on edge, as if watching somebody eat a sour apple.

And imagine! This hissing alone had the power to drive away the devil himself. Better the hissing of snakes, the howling of cats on a May night, or the rolling of thunder than the hissing of Shakoripinshchika's throat. The neighbors swore that they could not sleep at night. The hissing of the old *goyah* would saw through the boards of house and yard, reaching their bedrooms—all night long, "tss . . . tss . . . tss!" Why did she hiss the whole night long? It seemed that she beat "the bastard" and ordered her to be silent. Nahum Yosi heard the lashes and the girl's screams. The bitch. It's not enough that she works the shiksah to the bone, she also has to beat her to death. It's cruelty to animals!

And "the bastard," Marinka, worked in the yard and in the house, growing taller by the day. She was whipped every night, but her cheeks reddened like poppies. Her long hair thickened and glistened, and her breasts were like autumn apples. The peasant boys and their dogs had started coming to town on spring and summer nights, hot on her scent, lying in wait for her where the yard ends and fields begin. But Marinka acted as if she were unaware of them. She slept alone on such nights in the little straw shack that stood in the middle of the orchard, with Shakoripin crouching at the doorway. The dog guarded the orchard and Marinka diligently.

Marinka rarely showed her face in the Jewish quarter on the street side. She would open the small door, stay out for a moment with her arms crossed at her chest, then withdraw at once and lock herself in. The eyes and mouths of the wagoners standing alongside their leprous horses would fall upon her and send her scuttling away.

But, every once in a while, one of the boys who go to synagogue— and are therefore well acquainted with the cracks and holes of the gate along the alleyway—would peek through a hole looking for Shakoripin, and his eye would accidentally alight upon Marinka. The ruddy and bosomy girl would be standing in the middle of the yard bent over the washing, for example, with her chest bared a little more than a handbreadth and her naked arms sunk to the elbows in the sudsy foam of the tub. Then his eye would suddenly become glued to the crack, immobile. In a moment, a second, a third, a fourth boy— all the cracks would now be filled with eyes, like flies piled on a honeycomb. They would stand, knees buried in the thorns, leaning behind the fence, heads glued to the clapboards, eyes on Marinka. Nobody would say a word. All was silence and concentration. Each one would have her for himself—all of her—nothing was left out.

Sometimes Marinka would show up bare-thighed on the roof; she would climb up there and, standing erect, would spread beans and sesame seeds to dry in the sun. Then the apprentice wagoners standing below in the square alongside their wagons, with their whips tucked under their arms, suddenly would lift their eyes upward in unison, and a pleasurable, sensual smile would light up their faces, baring their white, horsey teeth. The gang's clown would throw out some remark that would set Marinka's cheeks ablaze and force her to lower her head toward the grass and vegetables on the roof. The wagoners would burst into laughter: "ho, ho, ho, ha, ha, ha," and

Marinka would lower her head even more. A cat's leap and she would disappear in the courtyard.

2

Everything in this world has its double, and so too did Shakoripinshchika's home. Its counterpart was the double-gabled house that was second in the row and stood shoulder to shoulder with it, separated only by a high clapboard fence.

Relations between the pair were not neighborly. The very moment that the second house was transferred from the *katsap* Serafim's domain to that of Hanina Lippa, the Jew who had moved here a few years ago from the village with his fat wife, Tsipa Leah, and his only child, Noah, the quarreling immediately began. They bickered over a span of land, over a stray chicken, an obstructed view, a breach in the gate—as neighbors are wont to do. But Shakoripinshchika's chief complaint was about the stench. Ever since these Jews settled next to her, she complained as she sharpened the knife in her throat, she couldn't stand the stench. The geese, she said, on the Jews' roof—Tsipa Leah was fattening geese—they foul the air she breathes. What a bitch. An impure *goyah* who keeps a dozen pigs in her sty—she can't stand the stench! Things got to the point of face slapping and Hanina Lippa was—may it never happen to you—taken to court and made to pay a fine. He gritted his teeth and paid.

From then on, a silent battle began in which even the dumb wood and stones inside the neighbors' yards participated. It was like a continuous, exhausting, dreary rainfall made up of petty sub rosa hostile acts about which one doesn't protest but which penetrate one's guts like drops of boiling pitch. It was as if even the walls of the two homes nursed a deadly enmity toward each other through the tall gate lying between them. Each plotted against its neighbor, and each silently waited for its neighbor's imminent ruin and utter defeat.

In the meantime, the rotting roof of Hanina Lippa's house was torn into irreparable shreds. Its spine was bent and broken, and holes appeared along its sloping ribs. And when? Right in the middle of the rainy season, the season of the geese, when about ninety-five geese sat and cackled under his roof. Quickly and cleverly, Hanina Lippa fixed a slate roof as a kind of shelter atop the old straw roof. The former roof continued to exist for some considerable time, all the while deteriorating on its own. Tsipa Leah would pluck handfuls from it for the defeathering of geese and the scouring of earthenware. The new roof hangs in its place on four posts, as if by a miracle, like a creature in its own right, to this very day.

And so within the row of houses Shakoripinshchika's house and its counterpart stood shoulder to shoulder. One with its unkempt head and tousled hair, and the other with its new hat and its old yarmulke. Both sank into the earth from year to year—as in fact the ever-widening space between hat and yarmulke bore witness. A great enmity was bottled up deep within the hearts of both owners, an enmity that seethed quietly like a serpent's venom.

When the hatred grew so strong that it demanded action or reached a point of madness, when each was ready to set fire to the other's home and everything in it, the two owners would suddenly emerge from their homes into their respective yards and begin to vent their pointless anger by directing it at any piece of wood, stone, or dumb animal in their path. Both would suddenly become industrious to no purpose, dashing about from one corner of their properties to the other, seeking and finding all sorts of insignificant and unnecessary tasks to do, performing them for their own sake out of impatience as well as the repressed and shattering enmity between them. Shakoripinshchika starts examining the jugs lining the roof's coping; discovering that they had not been properly washed, she inflicts on them a second scouring. She soaps up and scrubs all the vessels with all her might and anger—swiftly, swiftly, and her busy elbow prances in the air while she works. Just as suddenly, she begins to remove all sorts of worn sacks from some hiding place. From inside her house, she tosses out the sacks until a large pile of rags lies outside her front door. The next moment, she scoops up the fallen sacks and returns them all to their original hiding place; the pile disappears as though it had never existed.

In the meantime, she runs into Marinka and gives her flesh a sharp pinch. If she comes across a sow, it gets a kick in the ribs. Shakoripin sees what is going on and silently retires to his kennel or squeezes behind the trash pile. And silence! Shakoripin is no more. That dog knows his mistress's mood when she is angry.

For his part, Hanina Lippa also suddenly becomes busy, driven to make order out of chaos. He dresses rapidly and sets to work. Some evil spirit drags him into the yard, where he toils—groaning, sweating, and finding no respite. His yard is topsy-turvy! Everything is in disorder; everything is where it should not be. "This barrel, God damn it," he mutters as he kicks the shattered and rickety barrel. "It belongs—the devil take it!—next to the stable and not here." Suddenly with a "pop!" the barrel splits and its sides fall apart, leaving Hanina Lippa with his leg hanging in midair as he prepares to deliver his next assault. Bursting with anger, Hanina Lippa begins hurling the barrel's boards at Shakoripinshchika's fence as he fumes: "A fire take you! A plague! Cholera!"

A moment later, bending his entire body and breaking his back, he drags out an old door, rolls a large stone, and then groans in agony as he tries to move a large beam that had been lying like a corpse in the middle of the yard. It can't be moved. Already bathed in sweat, he plots how to move the beam. He attacks it from every angle, trying to lift the beam as much as a hairbreadth. It's killing him.

Sometimes the exertions end well enough. Hanina Lippa, after removing his caftan, braces his hips, spits on both his palms, and— one, two, ready!—moves the beam ever so little. He is pleased with himself. At other times, he toils in vain—and then the quarrel between the neighbors grows fierce. What has begun with curses, shouts, and invective in the yards on either side of the gate ends up with stones, shards of wood, and pottery being hurled from both rooftops. Like wrathful tigers, the two enemies suddenly appear, facing each other from the heights of the quarter—Hanina Lippa atop his double roof and opposite him, Shakoripinshchika, standing amid the onions, garlic clumps, and the high sunflowers atop her roof. To the distress of the birds above and the delight of the wagoners below, spatulas, rakes, jars, and wood shavings fly from roof to roof. Shakoripinshchika's yard is filled with the wailing and howling of dogs and the screeching of roosters. Shakoripin clangs his chain on one side, and Tsipa Leah whimpers on the other. The wagon men's apprentices on the street cry out in delight as the neighbors play out their aerial combat. An awesome terror pervades the entire Jewish quarter for many days.

3

Of all those living in both yards, only two did not get involved in the neighbors' dispute: Marinka, Shakoripinshchika's foundling, and Noah, Hanina Lippa's only son of the same age. During a quarrel they would stand silently on the sidelines. Even as children, during the first years they were neighbors, the two became good friends. In those days, Marinka was lonely and felt abandoned. At first, when "Uncle" Serafim still lived in the neighborhood, things were not so bad. She would go to his home on some errand for her aunt, to borrow a pot or a sieve, and sometimes she would play in the sand with his little son, Makarka. The "uncle" himself treated her kindly. On holidays he would bring her a bagel from the marketplace, and when her "aunt" beat her to excess, he would come to her rescue. But when the "uncle" moved away and the adjacent yard was empty, her world turned dark. Now there was no "uncle," no Makarka, nothing but her wrathful and miserly "aunt," and beatings and hunger and imprisonment in the courtyard. Those were spring days, a time of lively and energetic work in the vegetable garden and in the orchard. "Auntie" would rise early and go out to the vegetable garden at dawn to join her women workers, and she would return after dark. She would leave the yard with a hoarse but severe warning, "Don't go out and about," which was directed only at little Marinka. Marinka obeyed and did not go out or about. All day long she sat imprisoned within the four barriers guarding the enclosed yard. Were it not for Shakoripin, the little dog, who joined her at that time and became attached to her, she would have died of sheer boredom. She carried a single, hidden treasure in her lap, a string of hard little bagels, which "Uncle" had left her as a present before he departed. For many days she refrained from eating them, and when she remained alone, she would take them from her lap and play with them. Each day they appeared new to her and she would discover a different and special quality in them: they were yellow, round as rings, and rattled like gravel. True, they were little, but so thick, so thick that they almost had no holes at all. She would count them one by one with her fingers several times a day—and imagine what a miracle!—they always added up to nine, no more and no less. Once, however, when overcome with hunger, she was unable to withstand the temptation and ate them. From then on all she had left in the world was her dog Shakoripin and the memory of her "uncle." She especially remembered "Uncle's" last words. He had entered wearing high boots, whip in hand, to take his leave from "Auntie," and before he left, he said to her: "Look here, old woman, don't beat the child too much. She's a pitiful thing, fear the Lord." These lovely sweet words she, Marinka, had heard with her own ears, as she sat on the threshold cutting up pumpkins for the pigs. Her heart melted with gratitude, and when "Uncle" went out and crossed the threshold, she quickly crawled on all fours and kissed him on the back of his boot. It was a quick, furtive kiss without his knowledge. True, "Auntie" did not fulfill his command and did not stop beating her, but Marinka, too, never stopped repeating to herself the very same words day after day, "Look here, old woman . . . "

Once when she was tempted to violate "Auntie's" warning, her heart drew her to "Uncle" Serafim's house. She got up, left the court-yard like a thief, and entered. When she came in, she was overcome by a great sadness. The house was empty, desolate, and strange look-ing. Her aunt said it was sold to Yids. Who are those Yids who will be coming here? Where had "Uncle" Serafim gone? She sat on the floor silently in a corner and began to cry. Crying was so sweet, sweet, bursting from the heart spontaneously. She wanted to sit in this corner crying as long as she lived. All of a sudden two odd crea-tures entered the house. One was a short, hairy, fat man wearing a *kapota* and holding a whip in his hand. The other had red fingernails and held a builder's rod in his hand. Through the tears that welled up and quivered in her eyes, their faces appeared to her strange and very threatening. Marinka was frightened; she shrank into the corner and was silent. The creatures spent some time in the house, examin-ing the ceiling and the windows, and left. Marinka immediately re-sumed her crying, but it had been disrupted midway. It was now tasteless and without flavor. In the evening "Auntie" found her there asleep in the darkness—and she dragged her home by the hair. Since then, she no longer took even a single step outside the yard. Every day, alone and sad, she would sit by herself on the bench between the row of trees and the house. At her feet crouched Shakoripin, who was also small and free, with no chain around his neck—the only one who was attached to her and understood her. The little creature would lie before Marinka, watching her mouth with unblinking gaze. In the distance, from the direction of the orchard and the veg-etable patches, fragments of the song of women workers rose, their clear voices fresh and springlike. Both Marinka and the dog would suddenly perk up their ears. The dog would begin to tremble and suddenly would shake himself, jump to his feet, wag his tail, and stare at Marinka impatiently, as if to say, "Let's go Marinka, right now." And she would lift him to her knees and press him to her: "We mustn't, Shakoripin, we mustn't. 'Auntie' will beat me."

One day, the second yard was filled with tumult. "The Yids have arrived," said "Auntie." From that day on, "Auntie's" warnings as she went out became more severe and her pinches were sharper than before. To her tight security measures she added even more stringent precautions. Whatever could be hidden or put under lock and key, she hid or locked away. She put locks on the cellar, on the attic, on the woodshed. She brought a new dog into the yard. "Watch with seven eyes," "Auntie" would caution her over and over again. "Do you hear me: Jews and gypsies are all thieves. Do you hear? If a Jew sticks his snout in here, set the dogs on him. Do you hear? The dogs—Jews are afraid of them. Do you hear? Here's a slice of bread and an onion; don't wander about outside. Do you hear? If anything at all is missing from the yard, I'll skin you alive. Do you hear?"

"Do you hear, do you hear?" Oh, how Marinka hated this sputtered and grating phrase. On the upper part of her heart, near the shoulder, there was—so Marinka imagined—some sensitive round scab about the size of a coin, which that phrase had irritated with its constant rubbing. The expression constantly scratched the scab and was exclusively directed at it: "Do you hear, do you hear?"

And Marinka would lower her head and listen. The very moment the small backdoor at the rear of the orchard creaked twice and slammed behind "Auntie," she would stand beside the fence between the two yards. Ever since the Jews had come here she would stand day after day behind the fence, her neck bowed, her little head in the palms of her hand, her eyes fixed upon a crack in the fence. She preferred standing like this to the boredom of sitting on the bench. She would see new faces and hear strange things—"*Ghe, ghe, ghir, ghir*"—without understanding a word. On the ground lay scattered and neatly arranged heaps and stacks of beams, boards, sticks, poles, shavings, and plain wooden utensils. Some were old and black, others new and damp, still shining white and glistening with live and pungent drops of resin. Wagons would come in and depart—wagoners and other people. Among the stacks a short, fat man with a *kapota* and a head of hair walked about, doing business, groaning and sweating. Where had she seen this man? It seems she had seen him before. "Yes, yes, it's him, him!" It's the very creature that frightened her at twilight when she sat in the corner and cried. "And he's the Yid!" Marinka concluded fearfully and kept on peering. At the Yid's feet a dark, curly-haired boy was darting about, climbing up one stack after the other. He jumped on the beams, skipped on the poles, sat on the driver's seat, and cracked a whip in the air, shouting, "hoah, hoah!" The hairy old man in his *kapota* scolded him, pulled him down from the stack, pushed him with his knee, and sent him off. The little boy turned away and ran home crying. Immediately, a screaming voice resounded in the yard. It was a woman's voice calling from the direction of the house: "Nina Lippa, Nina Lippa . . ." and a few other shrill words that Marinka did not understand. Little Shakoripin, who was with her, began to prance about opposite the fence, very quickly, and bow-wowing. Marinka broke away from the fence in terror and fled with Shakoripin to her usual place on the bench.

"A pretty, lively boy," thought Marinka. "Is he a Yid too?" Marinka passed several days working and assisting Shakoripinsh-chika with housework and yard chores. In the orchard at the back of the yard, trees were being trimmed. The little girl was harried and driven from place to place. She would go down to the cellar and climb up to the attic, running errands, feeding the chickens, and preparing the mix for the hogs. And above all getting pinched. The noise of loading and unloading resounded all day long: heaving and unloading, unloading and heaving. And Shakoripinshchika would seethe and pinch, pinch and seethe.

Some time later, Marinka was left alone once again and returned to the crack. She saw nothing. A large stack of beams piled high close to the fence blocked her view. The conversation that reached her from beyond the beams was muffled and unclear, even very crude—"la-la, la-la." She cocked her ears trying to pick out the boy's voice from among the others, but she couldn't.

On Monday morning, immediately after "Auntie" had left the yard, Marinka examined the full length of the fence. She found a round, open knothole shaped like a bull's eye. It was low, close to the ground, and faced the edge of the neighbor's wall. She crouched down and peered through it. Darkness and silence. Along the border beneath the low-hanging edges of the neighbor's roof stretched a small black strip of plowed earth. It was made up of several small patches with a shovel stuck in their midst. There was no one to be seen. "Who's doing the planting here?" Marinka wondered. Footsteps! Shakoripin shook himself and got ready to bark. "Shush," Marinka silenced him and cocked her ear. Not footsteps but skipping, skipping like a pony galloping. The skipping came from the side, getting closer and closer.

A minute later, a dark, curly-haired boy arrived, hopping and skipping into the small alley between the fence and the neighbor's wall. "It's him, him." Marinka recognized him and held her breath. The boy was aglow with joy, lifting his cupped hands on high as he danced and shouted: "Everything, everything; there's everything here!" Through his fingers, beans, lentils, and sunflower seeds spilled to the ground. "Crazy," she thought, as a repressed laugh bubbled in her throat. She covered her mouth with one hand and Shakoripin's with the other. She felt his body shuddering. He, too, could hardly contain himself and was about to bark. "What's wrong?" she suddenly cried through the knothole, immediately regretting that she had spoken.

The boy was shaken for a moment and looked about him, somewhat taken aback. He hurriedly hid the seeds in his pockets. Then he spotted the knothole. Quietly he bent his knees and with frightened eyes peeked through the knothole. His eye met a bright, alert, and pleasant eye on the other side. There was a moment of silence and confusion. "Who are you?" he finally asked the eye. "I'm Marinka." "And I'm Noah." A lengthy silence. Marinka backed away a little. Noah stared at her for a minute and said somewhat angrily, "What are you peeking at?" "Nothing. I just wanted to see what you were doing here." "Me, I am planting seeds." "Ha, ha, ha," laughed Marinka, lowering her head between her shoulders. "You there, why are you laughing?" Noah was irritated and insulted.

At that very minute, the dog barked. Noah was immediately placated and began to talk to her. He asked her about the dog, and she replied. The talk drifted from one subject to another, and he started urging her to come over to his side, to the alleyway. "You see," he tried to entice her, "I'm planting a garden. Come here and we will plant it together. I've got everything, thank God: beans, peas, and sunflower seeds." And he emptied one pocket after the other. "You won't tell anyone," he suddenly asked in a whisper. "I took some of my mother's seeds secretly; mother will never know anything; when they grow I'll return them ten times over. I swear. Nu. Marinka, would you like some?" Marinka shook her head: "No." "Why?" He was disappointed. "Because. The sun doesn't shine in the alley." "So what?" Noah was surprised and perturbed. "The plants will grow wild. You're wasting your time." "Liar!"

Noah was irritated again and almost cried. "They will grow, they will, and they will become vegetables. The sun gets here before sunset. I've seen it with my own eyes. I really know."

Marinka did not reply. She put the dog in her lap, patted his head, and blew behind his ear. Noah wanted to say something else to her, but at that moment a screeching voice rang through the yard, a woman's voice calling from the direction of the house, "Noah, Noah!" Noah jumped up and disappeared from the alley.

4

From that morning, the two children became friends. When Shakoripinshchika was not in the yard, they would meet furtively at the knothole and reveal all their secrets to each other. As the weeks passed, Noah talked a great deal, always with feeling and enthusiasm, cheeks flushed and eyes burning. His warm breath would flow through the knothole and meet Marinka's eyelid. He would talk about the village he had come from, the friends he had left behind, and the pretty little dogs that he had there. My, my—he would shut his eyes, deeply moved—so little, so pretty. And he would also talk about a certain forest, a very, very big forest—big as the whole world, by God. The trees were so tall—tremendous! He himself had crossed that forest, by God, when he left the village with his parents, crossed it in a wagon. They rode and rode and the forest still didn't end. He fell asleep on top of the bedding on the wagon. When he awoke he no longer saw the forest, and he cried, by God. He cried and cried. Even Mintsa, their cow, cried. She walked behind the wagon tied to it with a rope, and from time to time she would turn her head back and bleat tearfully, lonesome for the calf left behind in the village. Oh how pretty that calf was. He was reddish with a white patch on his head. He would skip about all day long like this, hop, skip, and jump. Petra bought him for five rubles, by God. Cosma bought the pony, who also skipped about, but he was black and kicked. In the village they had many cows and horses, and now all they have is a single cow, Minsta, and a single horse, Shmargaz, and he's in the stable. Eh, Marinka doesn't have a Shmargaz!

Marinka would tell Noah about her chores in the yard and the orchard, about the fruit in the orchard and how she spent dark nights there. She would sleep in the shack and was so scared. All night long, a ghost used to walk along the pathways and stalk among the trees. He would walk about quietly back and forth, back and forth. Even Shakoripin was afraid of him. He would lie beside her on a straw stack and close his eyes, pretending that he heard nothing. Marinka would whisper about this, as if she were telling a secret, and her whisper was suffused with a mysterious terror that chilled Noah's blood for a moment. During one of their talks, Noah asked her where her mother was. "I don't know," she said in a whisper. "And your father?" Marinka was silent. "Is he dead? Are you an orphan?" "I have no father," said Marinka and lowered her head.

Noah was full of pity. In the days that followed, he would share with her all the delicacies his mother gave him. During the fruiting season they would swap things. He would throw a piece of white Sabbath ḥallah over the gate, and she would throw him a lovely apple or a beautiful pear. At times he would break off a piece of gizzard his mother had given him and pass it to Marinka through the knothole. Sometimes he felt the urge to climb down into her yard—but was unable to do so. It was hermetically closed off on every side. Once when Noah talked about horses, Marinka told him quietly, as was her way, that there was a little pony in "Auntie's" stable called Gootsy. "Auntie" used him to transport her into the city. Noah became excited, "Really, a pony? Oh please, Marinka, show me Gootsy. Take me to the stable." "No, no, no." Marinka was afraid. "It's forbidden." "Yes, yes," Noah insisted. "It's permitted."

And as he was talking, he climbed the fence. Marinka shook with fear, jumped away, and spread her hands. "Get down, Noy, get down! 'Auntie' will kill me, oy, oy, get down."

And Noah got down. "Why is she so afraid of her 'Auntie'?" he would later ponder, out of pity for Marinka and hatred of the old "witch." How did Marinka get here? His compassion increased on Sabbaths and holidays, when he would go out to the yard happy and in good spirits, well dressed and well fed, and find Marinka sitting or standing on the other side at work, with her clothes and her whole mien as before—all profane. It was then that she appeared to him to be so forlorn and unfortunate. "Why wasn't she Jewish?" Noah was so sorry, and timing his action for when the "Auntie" was not looking, he would hastily throw Sabbath delicacies to her

over the fence—a honeyed wafer and the like—whatever he had earlier hidden for her in his pocket.

Once, when he went behind the house, a suppressed scream
reached him from the other side—a sort of broken, stifled cry. He
peered through the knothole into the yard. No one. The cry had
come from the house. It was Marinka's. "Auntie" is beating her, he
thought, and cocked his ear. The cry was muffled and fragmented,
but it came from the very soul and pierced the brain, like the cry of
someone burned by a hot brand while gagged. It seemed to Noah
that she was screaming from the very pit of her stomach, crying
from her very toenails, from the very hairs on her head. Noah
couldn't stand that cry; his face writhed with pain and be began
hammering his little fist against the fence, hammering and crying,
hammering and gritting his teeth. "Oy, oy, stop it, stop it." The
hammering had no effect on the other side, it seemed, because the
crying did not cease. On this side, Tsipa Leah sensed what had happened and came running quickly. Only with great difficulty was she
able to detach him from the gate. His face was pale and his entire
body trembled with anger. "Oy, oy," he cried and stamped his feet.
"She's going to kill her, to kill her." Tsipa Leah dragged him away,
whispering an incantation against bad dreams.

"Tuf, Tuf!" she spat on the ground, wiping Noah's nose with her
apron. "The child's gone mad through sheer idleness. Can you
imagine? When the witch beats the little shiksah, he hammers on the
gate and cries. "Have you ever seen such a thing in your life? Woe to
his mother, he has turned quite blue."

When he went to bed that night, he couldn't sleep. He was in bed,
but his heart was behind the gate. The same dreadful crying rose re-
peatedly to his ears, piercing his brain. It no longer reached him
from outside, from some other place, but from within himself. His
very being was shaken. Noah got out of bed and placed his ear
against the wall facing the side of the gate and fell asleep. The wall
shrieked and shrieked. "What does the witch do to her?" The
thought seared his brain. "What does she do to her?"

When they next met, he asked her about it. Marinka did not respond but stood up and bared her arm above the elbow.
"Look . . ." The arm was totally bruised, swollen, and scarred. Red
gashes and blue marks were scattered all over it, one beside the
other, outnumbering the white areas. "What are they, Marinka?"
"Pinches." Noah's chin trembled. He wanted to hold Marinka's

hand, to run his palm over it, to caress it—but the gate lay between them. "Does your arm hurt Marinitchka, hurt a lot?" Marinka shook her head. "No. It only hurts when it's pinched. Oh how it hurt! But not now." "But why does she torture you?" he cried, hitting the fence with his fist. "Marinitchka, why does she torture you, huh?" "I'm a foundling, Noy, without mother or father," Marinka responded, sobbing quietly. "A foundling? What's a foundling? Why do folks call her a bastard? What does it mean having no father and mother? Did they die?" But Marinka says that she doesn't know where they are.

Once he came and asked his mother, "What's a foundling, Mom?" Tsipa Leah was very busy at the moment frying pancakes with her maid and did not fully hear her son's question. "Oh, a foundling?" Tsipa Leah said with her eyes on the open stove, completely absorbed with the pancakes sizzling in butter. "A foundling, you say. A foundling is, is . . . O my God, the pancakes are burning!" And Tsipa Leah quickly withdrew the pancakes from the stove. "Mom, Mom," Noah did not let up. "What's a foundling? Huh, Mom?" "If you don't get out of here you little devil . . . Hanina Lippa!"

So Noah didn't know what a foundling was. He learned what it meant in the course of time, but by then Noah was already meeting Marinka without any barrier between them.

5

At the rear of Hanina Lippa's yard and Shakoripinshchika's orchard, behind the Jewish quarter and beyond, there was a sort of mysterious world—a desolate and spacious fallow field. It was completely surrounded by vegetable and squash patches and was enclosed by fences on every side. You reached it by a narrow pathway running between two fences and entered it through a breach. All winter long it was abandoned to deep layers of white snow rising to the height of half the fence—all kinds of grasses and wild plants quietly flourished there, with a lone calf or single hog grazing. The distant crow of a cock or the sound of a man's voice would reach this place as though from another world. Everything would appear like a dream. Once in a while, a gentile would come to scorch a pig and skin its carcass. The only ragpicker of the area, a taciturn old man who was slightly crazy and suspected of witchcraft, would stand there alone for hours at a time with his stick and bag, silently poking at the refuse. He would poke as he moved his worn lips and seemed to be whispering incantations. Along with the dried-out skulls, the white skeletons, and the cows' horns lying in the darkness, in the thick grass, and in hidden pits, there were also many heavy and silent stumps of uprooted trees still buried in the soil. Here and there one could even see the round, broad tops of felled tree trunks looking like ancient monuments in memory of trees that once existed but are no more. In the past, so they say, a verdant grove of trees rustled in the area. Now a great silence prevails, the silence of a graveyard. From this former glory only two trees survived: an ancient, superannuated oak tree, a mighty burgeoning citizen planted in the middle of the field, with its top towering over the roofs of the quarter; and a single, low, half-desiccated pear tree standing apart on its little mound and rotting in the sun. In addition, there was a thick, canopied sumac tree. This old tree stood isolated outside the field near the breach, leaning with its branchy treetop against the gate, looking all those years from afar at the oak—its mighty and older companion.

After Noah felt comfortable in the quarter, he would often go to the field and pick wild pears or look for reeds. When he entered the place alone, he was overcome by a silent fear of loneliness, as though he were going into a haunted house. He did not go in all at once, but stealthily, bit by bit. First he poked his head through the breach, peering to and fro, and then he placed one foot inside. This he did cautiously and furtively. Hush! Any slight movement, such as a rabbit leaping from one of the holes, would make his heart throb with a kind of sweet, hidden terror. He did not understand why he was frightened, but fear came over him as soon as he put in his head. That field exerted some mysterious, threatening, and, at the same time, tempting power. It was as if it had a hidden living soul in all its lairs and pits that drew one toward it.

One July day, Noah entered the lot. It was as hot as a furnace; the very thorns in the field gave off sparks of fire. Noah climbed a tree and sat in it. For some days, he had not found Marinka at the knothole. She was guarding the orchard's ripe fruit, and his soul pined for her. He scanned the area from the top of the oak and saw Shakoripinshchika's large orchard. One of its corners touched the field's fence and shared two or three of the fence's boards. The orchard's trees were laden with fruit; apples were ripe and pears had turned yellow—but they were far off, far away. Perhaps he might see Marinka from here and call her. But she was nowhere to be seen. Noah climbed down and went to the corner. The fence's boards were high, with sharp tops. It was impossible to climb over them. "If there was only some breach in the fence"—the happy thought flashed through his head—"I would be able to see Marinka without obstruction." He at once began to dig up the earth under a board, using his nails and a stick. After less than a quarter hour, a small tunnel large enough to accommodate a fist was excavated under the fence. He stuck his hand inside—ouch—the hand touched some briar and was scratched. All of a sudden he felt something like a mouth and a snout in the tunnel—Shakoripin! The dog began growling and sniffing. He poked both claws inside, his body straining—scratching and digging with nose, mouth, and claws, and trying with all his might to broaden the tunnel. He did not quite succeed and began to yelp quietly, as if to say—"Come help me." At that moment Marinka appeared between the trees. The dog withdrew his head and ran toward her, pulling her to the tunnel. "Marinka," Noah shouted gleefully. "Noy," Marinka was taken aback and stood aside. "What are you doing here?" "Please, Marinitchka." "Get out of here right now," Marinka interrupted him in a frightened whisper. "'Auntie's' in the orchard. Go away and come back tomorrow, in the morning." Marinka whistled to the dog and disappeared among the trees.

Noah returned home full of sorrow. All night long he searched his mind for some device to break down the fence that lay between Marinka and himself. The next morning he rose early and took the little ax from under his father's bed, hid it under his coat, and slipped out of the house. In the yard he ran into Hanina Lippa, who was standing at the well watering his horse from a bucket held slantwise in his hand. His father peered at him suspiciously and greeted him with a fatherly: "Good morning. Where are you going, you little imp?"

Noah, likewise, emitted a nondescript phrase and took off. "I haven't any time," he said as he dashed to the field. When he arrived, it was already suffused by a strong light, but the wild plants in the shadow of the fence alongside the tunnel were still wet with glistening dew. Noah sank down among them and immediately went to work. He inserted the ax head below the edge of the board nailed to the lower beam and leaned on the handle with all his strength. The board gave way a little, and a bit of the black head of a nail was exposed between board and beam. The space between the two had widened enough to allow a finger to be inserted. At that moment, Marinka and her dog emerged from between the rustling trees. Noah strained again. One, two, three—creak! The lower nail gave way completely, and the board dangled loosely from the upper nail like a curtain. Noah pushed the "curtain" to one side. The orchard's cool air sent a sweet wave across his flaming face. On the inside in front of the breach stood Marinka and her dog. "Come on out," Noah said to her, holding up the board he had pushed aside.

Marinka and her dog squeezed through. The sun beat down on Marinka's face blinding her eyes with its rays. In the strong light her heart leaped with a deep sense of relief. Every leaf and tangle of grass sparkled. She shaded her forehead with the palm of her hand as a quiet, grateful smile flushed her face. "Is it good, Marinka, good?" "Very good, Noy, very good," she responded, smiling and glowing like a bride. "And will you take me into the orchard, Marinitchka?" "I'll take you, Noy, I'll take you." "And will you give me some apples?" "As many as you want." "And pears and plums?" "Everything. I'll give you everything."

But Noah was no longer listening. He turned into a spinning wheel. Mad with joy and bursting with energy, he began turning somersaults like a four-spoke wheel, rolling along on its own. The dog too ran, rolled, and pranced after him. Suddenly the earth swallowed him. From below a peculiar whistling sounded. The dog turned his head back toward Marinka and stood astounded. His eyes asked, "What's this?" "Noy," Marinka shouted, a bit frightened. "Ha, ha, ha!" Noah emerged from a pit into which he had fallen as he rolled. "That was a good whistle, huh? Come and look, it's a hole, a hole."

Noah ran, pulling Marinka and the dog after him, and showed her the pits hidden under tangles of thorns and jumbled weeds. From inside came a rustling sound and a furtive crawling of unseen beings. In one of them a lizard flashed and immediately disappeared. Shakoripin suddenly deserted the group and started after a rabbit. "Catch it, catch it," Noah urged him on and ran alongside him. The rabbit skipped ahead, reached the fence, and disappeared. "Heck." Noah gave up and fell to the ground exhausted. "He's hiding in the grass. There's lots of rabbits here, hedgehogs and moles, too, even scorpions and snakes. They used to live at the base of the house, big, small, and tiny. Some were so beautiful. Father would go out with his ax and kill them off." "Killing snakes is forbidden!" Marinka said fearfully. "Silly girl, forbidden? We are commanded to kill them.[3] Their dead bodies were piled up in our yard. As sure as I'm standing here, I used to hang them like sausages along the gate, Marinka." Noah suddenly jumped to his feet. "And when shall we go to the orchard?" "Follow me," Marinka nodded her head at him. "Shakoripin!"

Shakoripin left the grass he had sniffed and explored, and ran after Marinka and Noah to the orchard. Beside the tunnel, the little ax still lay where Noah had abandoned it. Marinka pulled the "curtain" aside. "Come in."

The three of them were swallowed up by the orchard. Noah raced ahead, exploring and running among the bushes and in the shade of the trees. The joyous full-throated cries of morning birds rang out over his head like crystal sounds. He was enveloped in a sweet coolness. He ran—as round spots of light, swift and fleeting, like golden mice, flitted across his face, head, and clothes, up and down, up and down. He felt their warm, sweet caress on his cheeks. The dog ran ahead, looking as if he had rolled over and become tangled in the network of the intertwined light and shadow. Branches were weighed down by large apples; they hit Noah's head, knocking off his hat. Apples, apples, apples: apples above and apples below. Apples were scattered in the grass over the entire surface of the earth. Next to the hut, on a bed of straw, lay redolent piles of apples, large and small. Atop the cherry trees, isolated, blacker than black, forgotten cherries peered stealthily and craftily through the foliage. Among the low-lying bushes, behind a green leaf, a single, modest mulberry, bluish red and fine as silk, was still hiding—seeing but unseen.

Noah was intoxicated. The coolness of the shadows, the smell of the fruit, the song of the birds—all assailed him at once and made his head pound. He ran from one tree to another, plucking and eating, plucking and pocketing, plucking and trampling. Marinka did not scold him. On the contrary, she helped him choose the ripest and the best, showing him the choicest and tastiest fruit and filling his pockets and his lap with them.

When Noah finally returned to his home—worn, tired, and happy, out of breath and puffing, with his pockets heavy with apples, pears, and plums—he again encountered his father at the courtyard gate.

---

[3]Or killing them is a virtuous religious act (see Genesis 3:15).

But miraculously his father did not notice him; he was busy with some farmer who was to transport a wagon loaded down with timber that the horses found hard to move. Thank God! Noah slid peacefully into the house. He replaced the stolen ax under the bed, and no one was the wiser. He took the apples, pears, and plums up to the stable loft and hid them in a pile of hay, to await their time.

From then on, the field and the orchard became Noah's and Marinka's meeting place. At every opportunity they would come together there, stretch out in the shade of the trees or sink in the grass and play together. All this was done in secret because the neighbors' bickering had begun again. Shakoripin, who always stood guard over them, neither protested nor betrayed the secret. Marinka ordered him to keep silent and he did. In the end, he was drawn to Noah and would greet him with leaps and joy, groveling, and wagging his tail. He would wait with doggy eyes for Noah's hand. And Noah, when he came, would bring a nice slice of bread—half for Marinka and half for the dog.

On one such day, Marinka took Noah into her yard. This she did with great caution and trepidation. From the first minute he entered it, Noah felt he had come into a different environment. He ran at once to the stable, half of which served as the pigpen, to see Gootsy. Unfortunately for him, the stable was locked, and he peered inside it through a crack. A pungent smell of warm dung reached his nose, and when in the darkness his eye made out a pony standing at the trough munching away, he was unable to stir from there. "Oh, oh, Gootsinu,"[4] he implored like a small child as he stood peering in. From the stable, he quietly approached one of the cracks in the fence and peeked into his father's yard. It seemed so odd, standing on this side in the yard of the *goyah* and peeking into Papa's courtyard. Everything in it now appeared to him in a different light: a different color, a different order, everything in reverse. There's Papa himself. "Ha, Ha." Noah shrugged his head and smiled to himself furtively. Papa himself was standing there among the beams quite unaware. "Whenever I want to, I can make a face and stick my tongue out at him: cock-a-doodle-do, cock-a-doodle-do." Hanina Lippa turned his head around as if surprised. Noah was seized with terror and sidled off. Finally, he stole away and pressed his face to

---

[4]That is, little Gootsy. The suffix *nu* in Yiddish and some Slavic languages is a diminutive expressing affection.

the window pane of Shakoripinshchika's home. He shaded his eyes with his hands. Everything was quiet and asleep inside. The bed was spread with many pillows and bolsters piled high to the ceiling. Noah also saw a heavy, tin-plated, iron-clasped chest with a big lock suspended from it, a table and benches in white wood, and icons hanging on the walls. Noah turned his face from the window and his eyes searched for Marinka. She was sitting as usual on the bench, with Shakoripin crouching at her feet. "Marinka, do you go to church?" She shook her head: "No." "Why not?" "I guard the yard." "And where do you sleep in the winter?" "In the house." "*With her,* in the bed?" "On the floor."

Noah sat on the grass beside the dog at Marinka's bare feet and looked at her compassionately. He wanted to ask her something but did not. Tears filled Marinka's eyes. "Why are you crying Marinitchka? Does 'Auntie' beat you? Is she starving you?" Marinka's shoulders trembled as she suppressed her sobs. Tears ran down her cheeks. "Please don't, Marinitchka," Noah consoled her by placing his hands on her knees. "Don't cry. I'll come to see you everyday, I swear."

And Noah kept his promise. Everyday he would bring her part of his meal. Hour after hour Tsipa Leah would shout and scream through the quarter: "Noah! No-ah!" But Noah paid no attention. During these hours he sat with Marinka in one of their hiding places—even the birds of the air did not know where he was. Finally, their friendship was discovered, and a big quarrel ensued between the neighbors. Tsipa Leah raised the roof. Alas, poor mother. She sees the child wasting away like a wax candle, and why? Because of the witch's bastard, may her name be blotted out. Whatever we give the boy, the bastard gobbles up. God in heaven, may worms and maggots consume her. Hanina Lippa loosened his belt and wanted to lay Noah over the bench, but Tsipa Leah stood in the way. Shakoripinshchika dragged Marinka into the house, and nobody saw what she did to her there. From the house, one heard only the broken, suppressed cries that pierced the brain. Noah, lying in bed, heard the sobbing and almost went mad.

The two were separated for several days. Shakoripinshchika compounded her prohibitions. Marinka was again isolated, completely closeted. For days, Noah did not go to the field. Tsipa Leah guarded him, kept hold of his hand. The knothole was also blocked. In the narrow strip between the fences where Noah had his vegetable patch, they placed all sorts of planks. The entire area was filled in. Noah was furious. He lashed out and embittered his parents' lives. No one understood what had got into him: "My patch, my patch," he shouted and kicked. "Why did you ruin my patch?" Hanina Lippa stamped his feet and loosened his belt. "Shut up, you bastard, or I'll tan your hide and throw you to the dogs. Did you ever? He's fussing over vegetable patches!"

The season of rain and snow arrived. "Auntie" was in the house, and Marinka did not stir outside the yard. Fear of her "aunt's" angry eye restrained her. In "Auntie's" presence, she was afraid to approach the fence. Even when Noy's whispered voice sometimes reached her through the crack, she pretended not to hear it. The entrance to the field through the breach in the orchard was also blocked. The snow kept one out. The field, as usual, was blanketed with snow nearly half as high as the fence, and one couldn't wade through it. A sea of white.

In the meantime, the neighbors' quarrels became more frequent and more severe. For Marinka, these were days of constant hard labor. In the Yid's yard, the piles of wood grew ever higher. All day long, unloading and heaving, unloading and heaving. The fences separating the yards also became higher and higher. Now there wasn't even a crack. And if one existed, the tall trees along the length of the fence on the near side blocked the eye.

When spring came, Noah was entered in the local heder. Now he was busy with other matters. Days, weeks went by, and no Noah. Marinka waited for him in the orchard, looked for him in the field. He was nowhere. "Where is Noy? Why doesn't he come?" Marinka would ask herself.

Once again summer arrived. Shakoripinshchika had already lost her voice because of so much quarreling. But she did not deviate from her habits. Day after day during the season, she would rise early and go to the vegetable patch, returning to her yard after the stars were out. During those days, Marinka would once again sit alone and sad on the bench between the trees and the house. Shakoripin would lie on her knees, and she would stare silently into his eyes. At times when she looked at the high fences, she imagined that it was not that *they* had grown higher but that *she* herself had shrunk inside them. Sometimes when she sat there, with everything about her silent in the summer quiet, a screaming cry would ring out in the neighbors' yard—a woman's voice shouting in the distance: "Noah, No-ah." Then Marinka would quickly run toward the fence separating the yards. For the thousandth time, she would search for a mere crack, a hairbreadth of a crack. Shakoripin sympathized with her and helped her grope about. He ran and ran ahead of her, leaning his two front paws on the fence over and over again, scratching and digging with his nails, sniffing and sniffing. And after searching in vain, she would return quietly to the bench, raising Shakoripin to her knees, staring into his eyes and suddenly hugging him tightly to her bosom, hugging him and trembling all over: "Shakoripin, where is Noy?"

6

"Noy" was dragged off to the ḥeder everyday because he would not go willingly. Tsipa Leah, his mother, would supply him with all sorts of "royal delicacies" for a snack, such as gizzard, preserves, and the like, and yet he still didn't want to go. Tsipa Leah cried, and Hanina Lippa loosened his belt, but Noah was adamant: "I don't want to, I don't want to." He ran away from one ḥeder and again from another. "What could you do with a little runt like him? Quite a young man and still unable to distinguish between an aleph and a cross."

His heart was drawn to dogs, horses, orchards, and vegetable patches. Everyday he sowed all sorts of patches and planted all kinds of orchards. "Have you ever seen the likes of it?" They finally handed him over to Reuben Hirsch, the *melamed,* a man who at first glance seemed as sweet as a honey tart but turned out to be as bitter as horseradish. He was a murderous drunkard with a sparse mustache who mumbled "this" and "that" through his Adam's apple and crushed his pupils under his armpit until they almost died. "He, Reuben Hirsch," so the neighbors told Hanina Lippa, "will take care of him, he will."

At first, everything went smoothly. Every morning after removing his tefillin, Reuben Hirsch would habitually slap his Adam's apple, with a finger, cast a smiling, crafty wink at the sideboard in the corner, and then signal to the pupils that it was time for "this." That is, the bottle. After downing one, two, and three gulps, he would begin "that," namely squeezing his pupils, crushing them one after the other until tears flowed, all strength was drained, and they slumped to the ground. In less than five minutes not a single pupil was left

sitting at the teacher's table. One was under the table, another under
the bench, a third under the bed,[5] a fourth rolling behind the slop
barrel, and a fifth in the hollow under the stove. "That," the crushing, Reuben Hirsch would say, shrewdly squinting his small left eye,
is good for "this," namely, Torah.

When it came to Torah, Reuben Hirsch's wisdom faded. In no
way was Noah willing to accept the yoke of "this"—Reuben
Hirsch's Torah. During the two years that Noah studied Torah with
him, he fled the ḥeder and was returned to it about ten times. Once,
when Reuben Hirsch, after much "squeezing," tried to pull off
Noah's trousers and whip him, the boy gave his teacher a real kick,
straight in the stomach, and escaped. For a whole day and night,
Noah did not return either to his parents' home or to the ḥeder.
Reuben Hirsch and his pupils spread out everywhere to find him,
through the quarter and his usual haunts within and outside the
town's Sabbath limit[6] until they got as far as the dogs.[7] Tsipa Leah
almost went mad. As fierce as a tigress, she burst into Reuben
Hirsch's ḥeder, rake in hand. All the neighbors leaped out of her
way and gathered outside the window. "Where's that drunk?" she
shouted bitterly, shaking the rake at Reuben Hirsch, who was sitting
with his yarmulke on his head in front of his pupils, his eyes bulging
with sudden fear. "Where is my son's murderer? Let me kill him!
Children! I must kill him." The pupils were faint with fear, and the
Rebbe jumped up in terror: "Beh, meh," he was wordless. He
wasn't able to move a limb. The rake swung before his eyes as he
stood there trembling, backing away slowly, looking for a way out
and unable to find one. All of a sudden, he took courage and like a
lion, with a single leap, escaped through the window and hid in the
outhouse, where he clung onto its boards like someone holding onto
the horns of the altar in ancient days. It was what Reuben Hirsch
would often do in moments of great danger, when a policeman came
to the house and the like. The pupils were delighted! From time to
time, one of them went out to check on their teacher, who was sitting terror-stricken in his refuge. Each one wanted to see him in his
glory. "Is it all right to come out?" the teacher asked each of his vis-

---

[5]The traditional "classroom" was at the home of the teacher, which due to
poverty and the high birthrate had a bed in almost every room.

[6]The limit marking the 2,000 ells (about 1,000 yards) that one was permitted to
walk on the Sabbath.

[7]That is, until the homes of peasants whose watchdogs were fierce.

iting pupils in a whisper. "God forbid, it's dangerous, lie still, Rebbe, lie still!"

All day long Tsipa Leah roamed about the suburbs with her agents, looking for her son. In the evening, Hanina Lippa joined her. They searched the orchards and the empty fields; they probed the pits and trenches. They stirred up all the dogs of the neighborhood—all in vain.

About midnight, the good Lord opened their eyes. They found their darling son asleep in the alley behind the fence, holding in his hand a large, half-chewed cucumber!

After this incident, when Tsipa Leah made the rounds of all the teachers, none would take him on. "It's impossible, Tsipa Leah, in the middle of the term. We can't trespass on another teacher's preserves. God willing, things will be different after Sukkot, all being well." The teachers were afraid of her rake! Noah was hardly perturbed. He was, just then, busy raising pigeons, a task to which he devoted all his time and energy. His friend Makarka had brought him some pigeons from the peasants' suburb, and Noah was building a dovecote for them. Makarka specifically promised that he would eventually even find Noah a dog. And he was already casting his eye on one of Serafim's puppies.

Besides pigeons and dogs, there was one more object in Noah's world—Marinka. But when Noah began ḥeder, he firmly relegated her to the back of his mind. He knew that Marinka sometimes went out to pasture her pigs in the field, and he avoided going there. All day long he would wander about the quarter but would never go to the field. He was afraid and ashamed. Why and of whom? He himself did not know. Each time he had occasion to pass that field, his heart would pound, and he would glance at it sideways. It seemed that from every crack and hole the single eye of Natke Kambala, his former friend but now his deadly enemy, was watching him. This blind man, may his thieving father perish, had only one functioning eye in his head, but it was a sharp eye that could see through anything. It always lay in ambush behind your back and your very spine felt its presence. It was quite possible that he knew something about Marinka and the field. Alas! Where could he hide the shame?

But the field continued to tempt him. One idle day Noah could no longer restrain himself and entered it stealthily. Immediately upon entering he covered the breach with a piece of board and turned to and fro overcome by a sweet feeling of dread. The field was the same as before. The tall thorns and thistles grew there in a wild tangle as usual, luxuriating and glittering in the noonday sun. From the sea of vegetation, the back of a large pig protruded, and the squeals of little piglets could be heard. The big pig chomped and snorted. Weren't these Marinka's pigs? The underbrush rustled and trembled; a flight of black and white butterflies fluttered in the air. Noah cocked his ears. Some creature was hidden in the grass, rapidly making its way toward him. Noah stopped and waited. The tremor in the undergrowth moved closer and closer, and suddenly Shakoripin leaped out at him. The dog almost went crazy with delight. He began prancing on both legs, hopping, jumping, and bouncing like a rubber ball, reaching for Noah's face, intending to hug and kiss him. "Down, down," Noah waved him off with a light affectionate gesture. His heart leaped as well. He immediately began to cuddle him. He grabbed his two paws and looked into his eyes, "Nu, dog, where to?" The dog understood and began running ahead of him through the high grass, running and turning his head back from time to time until he reached the oak. Under the oak, on a bed of grass, Marinka lay asleep. Here the dog halted, as if to say—here's what belongs to you. Noah inclined toward her slightly and looked at her. She lay there, the poor girl, alone at midday in the deserted field, curled up in the grass, her tiny fist tucked under her head, and her eyes tightly shut. He bent down and touched her gently: "Marinka, Marinitchka . . . "

Marinka stirred and opened her eyes. "Noy?" Half asleep she lay dazed, her arms drawn up to his neck, as if of their own accord. Noah closed his eyes and abandoned his head to her enticing arms. His head grew faint with emotion. He did not notice that he was being drawn down to the ground.

An hour later—the high grass of the deserted field still covered the two little neighbors. True, both had grown taller than they were before their separation. Now the grass could no longer conceal them entirely: two heads, one dark and the other blonde, protruded. But never mind! Who would be mad enough to come here suddenly. Besides, Shakoripin was diligently watching over them. Any slight motion, any rustling, would immediately cause him to prick up his ears. In any real emergency, there was always the deep, dark pit, its entrance laced with branches and its interior always cool. There was also a small hollow whose floor was strewn with all kinds of jawbones, horses' hooves, and teeth; and on its slope lay a single, orphaned gourd. Large and swollen, it grew here summer after summer, miraculously, on its own. No one knew who tied it at its center here in the summer, and where it disappeared in the rainy season. And beyond it was a small mound, completely overgrown with thorns and bushes, and farther on, the trunks of the oak and pear trees. You could have no trustier hiding places than these. Once there, the entire quarter—all the world—seemed nonexistent, and you could do whatever you wished.

Noah became a regular visitor to that deserted field. The summer days were drawing to a close, and still no teacher could be found for him, so he had plenty of free time. He was also no longer wary of his friends. At noon, when Marinka and her pigs came out to the field, Noah also came there after wandering through field and forest. He was tired and his face was flushed. As soon as he arrived, he would spread-eagle himself in the deep grass or in some other hiding place, lying there alone for hours with Marinka. They would tell each other, as was their custom, whatever was in their hearts. He spoke to her with intense passion and flashing eyes, as if he had neither enough time nor energy to tell her a thousandth part of what he had in mind. And she spoke to him in slow and calm conversational tones, very, very quietly, stringing words together and unveiling secrets. The subjects of their conversation were also a little different from those in bygone days, before they had been separated. Instead of the village and its farmers about whom Noah used to talk longingly, he now spoke about the *katsaps'* suburb and its habitants; instead of swallows and ponies, he spoke of pigeons and horses—full-sized horses that he, Noah, had ridden. Like a bird flies, like a bird. No rider in the entire suburb could ride like him, not even Makarka, and without any saddle, no saddle, believe you me. When he mounts a horse and flies—gangway—whew! "And don't you go to the *shkola* any more?" Marinka interrupted in a whisper.

Shkola? When? Maybe next winter. For now, the teachers don't want to take him, drat them! Does Mom really think that he will go begging with her at the teacher's door and ask for pity? A fat chance of that. Not for any money in the world! In any case he's already become a byword to his former friends. And who is to blame, does she think? Reuben Hirsch, that drunken leper who gives him no reprieve. On the Sabbath, when Noah goes to the synagogue with Papa, Reuben Hirsch immediately sets his pupils on him. "Kurkivan son of Pultiel"—that's what they call him. Do you know Kambala, the blind man? You don't? Why he is a rotten scoundrel beyond compare. Whenever that blind man passes by him, by Noah, in the synagogue, he makes his blood boil. He'll knock his brains out, as sure is sure. You think that he passes you by chance, completely immersed in his prayer book, but really—a plague on his healthy eye— he only wants to provoke. If he ever meets him in the alleyway, he'll poke out his other eye, he will! Next Saturday, he, Noah, will no longer go to synagogue. No way! He will come here to the field, to look for reeds and pick pears. "On the Sabbath?"

Noah was slightly taken aback. "No, no, it was only a manner of speaking. But even so, even if it is the Sabbath, so what?" He'll tell her in a whisper; you're not going to tell anyone. When he goes to the *katsaps'* quarter, he engages in every kind of work on the Sabbath. He and Makarka. "And your Dad, what will he say?"

Dad? What can Dad do? He knows nothing. He, Noah, does whatever he pleases. Tomorrow, for example, he and Makarka are preparing to go to war, and against whom do you think? Against Reuben Hirsch and his pupils, no less! They will be going down to the river to bathe, and he and Makarka will lie in ambush, and as soon as they all undress, they'll come out of ambush and set the dogs—ha, ha, ha— set the dogs on them. Oh boy, all hell will break loose. "And you Marinitchka," Noah suddenly asked, "won't you go to the *katsaps'* suburb? Uncle Serafim always asks about you. When you grow up, he says, and you are able to work, he will take you in, he says, to his home. He pities you; the old woman, he says, will torture you to death. Marinitchka, would you like to go to Uncle Serafim?"

Marinka was silent.

"Why are you quiet, Marinka? You will be rid of 'Auntie' and her beatings, and I could visit you everyday in the suburb. No? Tell me the truth. Do you want to go to Uncle Serafim?" "When the time comes, you'll see," said Marinka, her eyes shining and lovingly caressing his face. "Great," shouted Noah gleefully, jumping up and climbing the oak tree. He grabbed the end of one of its branches, shook it, and showered acorns upon Marinka's pigs. The pigs rushed to the acorns, squealing and grunting, and Noah climbed higher to the top of the oak. From there, he could see all the surrounding country as if on the palm of his hand. On one side were the quarter's roofs, the yards with their timber piles, and the marketplace; and on the other, the vegetable patches, lines of fences, and yellow fields stretching as far as the eye could see; and yonder, in the distance, the suburb with its small white houses along the silvery river wending its way beside it, and over there the black copse across the river.

If Noah came to the field and did not find Marinka there, he would immediately look for some other occupation for himself. Above all, the pear tree. This low, very ancient tree was quite crippled; its roots were bared and its trunk bent in strange turns and twists, full of humps and protrusions. Although its branches were thin, they were twisted and crowded and heavier than the tree could bear. They appeared to tangle with each other in mortal combat. If a breeze passed through the tree, its tiny branches emitted a dry, rattling sound like the low clinking of jars. Nevertheless, this old, dry, hardened tree was very loath to die a natural death. Every seven years it girded its strength and bore some kind of fruit. This year, for example, after a desperate effort, it produced about a hundred sickle pears. Noah cast his eyes on these pears from mid-August to Rosh Hashanah. When they all ripened, they dropped one by one into his hands. Across a nearby fence was the synagogue, from which untrained blasts and screeches of a shofar that had fallen into the hands of the boys rent the air. Noah, sitting alone on the tree, picked pears that were no more than twice the size of a stone, as hard as gravel and sour as vinegar. They were also slightly salty, but this could be remedied. Noah used to bury them in the hayloft in the stable. There they remained until they rotted; once rotten, they would ripen and turn sweet.

Sometimes when he came to the field at eventide, the place was empty and frightening, and Marinka was nowhere to be seen. He would climb up and hide himself in the thick, aromatic top of the sumac tree and stealthily search for birds' nests. Suddenly, when he saw the sun setting and the skies were rivers of fire, a great awe overwhelmed him. He lay silently on a limb, pressing his cheeks against the cool, broad foliage. He rested his head upon it as if asleep, turning his flushed face toward the sinking sun. And then he imagined that long ago he had grown on that tree like one of its leaves. When he closed his eyes and was swallowed completely in the tree, a picture of an evening in his native village at once appeared before him. He, the child, was hidden in a little nut tree beside a thorn hedge. The rim of the sky was like a bonfire—the entire universe was aflame. His father's yard was all redness. In the midst of the yard stood some ten cows reddened by the sun, and between their legs sat peasant girls with feet, arms, and shoulders bare, holding tilted jugs in their hands. Thin, white streams of milk squirted from the cows' teats in sweet, warm jets. The white foam in the jugs rose ever higher. He was overcome with desire to plunge his finger in the milk and feel the warmth. The world was redolent with the smell of milk. And suddenly Mother appeared in the middle of the yard, her face turned to the sun, holding a pail of milk in one hand and shading her eyes with the other. She stood all flushed, and a voice was heard in the red void of the world: "No-ah, No-ah!"

7

The season of mists and rain had arrived; it was after Sukkot. The deserted field was even more desolate. The foot stumbled and sank in slippery mud. The leaves of the plants were trampled in the thick slime, and the smitten stalks lay stretched out atop each other like dead worms. The oak was completely stripped, and its branches appeared black and twisted like a mass of dragons and flying scorpions leaping to attack each other but paralyzed and petrified in mid-flight. The tall oak tree still held the remnants of leaves that beat against it like soiled rags. The tiny valley was filled with brackish waters, and the single gourd had suddenly disappeared as usual. Marinka grew taller. She was sent out daily to the fields wrapped in a shawl to dig holes for the potatoes—and Noah, Noah came under the authority of a new teacher.

Marinka was once again locked away in the dark recesses of his heart—for a long time.

The new teacher into whose hands Noah had fallen was by nature a gentle, kindly man, cheerful and imperturbable. The pupils took advantage of him, but no matter. "When there's no citron," Hanina Lippa said, "you can fulfill the commandment with a potato."[8]

Until the Torah reading of *Vayechi,*[9] the world went on as usual. One Torah portion came and the other went. The pupils would skate on the ice most of the time, and do battle with Reuben Hirsch's pupils. The teacher received his full tuition fee and a bonus at Hanukah and Purim. He would take a leisurely nap every day at

---

[8]On Sukkot Jews were commanded to bless the lulav (palm fronds) and the citron, both considered to be beautiful objects.

[9]Genesis 47:28–49:26, a weekly Torah portion that generally falls at the beginning of the winter.

noon. Once in a while Noah would sneak into the room when the teacher was asleep and, in the presence of the other pupils, tie a small bundle of snow wrapped in a rag over the teacher's bed exactly opposite his face. The snow in the bag would drip down on the Rebbe; drip, drop. The Rebbe, still half asleep, would slap his face as if chasing away a fly, and the pupils would squirm with laughter until the Rebbe woke up in fright. "Hoo, ha, who's there? What's going on? Get your *ḥumashim.*" During the goose-killing season Tsipa Leah would send, as a free bonus to the Rebbe, a generous portion of cracklings. So the world behaved itself until the *Vayechi* reading.

On Thursday evening of that week an accident occurred in connection with the phrase *va'ani.*[10] Instead of *"va'ani ya'akov"*—that is, "and I, Jacob"—as the Rebbe had taught him to chant and translate five days running, Noah suddenly intoned, *"va'ani vaani"* (and I, Vani).[11] This "goyish" error was a desecration of the sacred name of our father, Jacob, with the impure name of some Vani from the *katsaps'* suburb. The error kindled the fury of even the good and lenient teacher. "Can this be possible, can this be?" In short, he lost his temper and was about to slap Noah's face. Noah, anticipating the blow, hit him first—and fled.

He fled, but the name Vani pursued him all winter long and well into the beginning of the following summer. From now on all the boys called him Vani, and Noah would wait in ambush in the alleyways and attack them. When they went down with their teachers to bathe in the river, he and his gentile friends would set the suburb's dogs on them and stone them. Everybody realized that without a decisive battle things were impossible. One Sabbath day in summer, the battle broke out.

On the green field between the Jewish quarter and the *katsaps'* suburb—the usual battlefield—from two opposite sides the two camps came forth. The Israelite boys were headed by Natke the thief on the one side, and the suburban "goyim" were headed by "Vani"—that is, by Noah—and Makarka on the other.

The sun was about to set. The green field and its yellow flowers turned crimson. High in the air above the town a golden cross[12] was lit. The camps were ready for battle.

---

[10] "And I" (Genesis 48:7).
[11] Vani or Vanya is a shortening of the Gentile name Ivan or John.
[12] Atop the local church.

Suddenly the air trembled. The city's big bell sounded: "Boom, boom, boom . . . " "Hurrah!" a great shout arose from the enemy camp followed by a heavy hail of stones. "Be strong and of good courage," the camp of Israel roared on the opposite side and let fly gravel stones at the enemy.

The battle was long and heavy. Both sides fought with fierce enmity. Stones flew, sticks whistled, dogs barked, noses and skulls bled, and the bell kept on tolling all the while: "Boom, boom, boom . . . "

The camp of Israel held its ground. Everyone felt the importance of the hour. Most of the stones, according to a predetermined command, were aimed at Noah. "How come a Hebrew lad joined hands with the goyim? We'll kill the apostate this very day." And again stones flew into the air, and again the shouting of "Hurrah!" and "Be strong!" rose up in unison. The little children gathered stones, and the bigger ones did the throwing. Eyes burned, faces flushed, and hands never tired.

The sun was already resting on the treetops, but the bell still persisted: "Boom, boom, boom . . ." The field resounded with terror. Heavy, dull, and dark, the solid peal of the bell shattered into pieces, falling one by one into some dark abyss. But the atmosphere around the combatants was continuously shaken by a heavy, reddish, frightening, and alien roar that rolled on wave after wave and spread over the green fields and the reddening lots.

And the hands, the hands of Jacob[13] grew weak. Meanwhile the sun had set and the "apostate" was not killed. With the darkening of twilight the enemy camp grew larger and larger. From every side the irate barking of dogs drew closer and closer and increasingly surrounded them. The clink, clink of the dogs' little bells mingled with the booming of the big bell. The Jewish boys were terrified and fled to say their evening prayers in the synagogue in the alleyway, while Noah returned with the band of goyim to the *katsaps'* suburb.

All that evening he sat among the goyim like a mourner at a wedding, as though he were the one defeated. After *Havdalah* Hanina Lippa came there by cart to fetch Noah home. Noah did not refuse and went with him at once. During the entire way they both sat silently in the cart. When they arrived home, Hanina Lippa left the horse and cart in the yard just as they were and took Noah into the stable, locking the door from the inside. What he then did to him

---

[13]See Genesis 27:22.

only the walls of the stable, the wheels, and the pegs lying in the darkness knew. When the deed was completed, Hanina Lippa emerged with blood smeared on his hands and face. As he came out, his feet stumbled over Tsipa Leah's body, lying in front of the threshold where she had fainted. Noah was carried home by the neighbors, limbs broken and half dead.

8

Noah was bedridden for about two months. When he recovered and went outside one summer day, he found that he was totally isolated. His former friends avoided him; the teachers had totally given up on him. And Marinka—she too was not to be found in the yard. She worked in the fields as a female hand, and when she returned at night, there was no opportunity to talk to her. He was, after all, a "grown-up," and there were eyes that saw things. During the long, idle days of that summer, Noah roamed the fields and lots and went down to the vegetable patches. He rode horses, swam in the river, and sallied into the woods. In the evening, he would return, hair disheveled and face flushed, carrying the fruit and produce of the woods—truffles, mushrooms, wild walnuts, crab apples, sickle pears, all kinds of berries, and sometimes even a strange bird. He would bury the pears and apples under the hay in the stable to let them ripen. He had already several bushels stored away. All of Tsipa Leah's *tsimes*es contained them. He would place the birds in cages, which he hung from the high beams of his home. The entire building was filled with chirping and bird droppings; there was no escaping them. "You could go out of your mind," Tsipa Leah complained. "Almost a bar mitzvah boy and he plays with chicks. Hanina Lippa, why do you keep quiet? Are you a father or aren't you? How will it all end?"

Hanina Lippa took his wagon to town and returned with a private tutor for Noah—a silken young man who had just finished living with his in-laws.[14] He was a thin, desiccated creature, all skin and bones. "Do you see this gizzard?" Hanina Lippa said to Tsipa Leah immediately upon entering the house and pointing to the young man. "He cost me seventy bills plus his meals, a big deal, a

---

[14]It was customary for a newly wedded couple to live with the bride's family for several years, depending on the terms of the marriage contract.

kosher bargain, huh? Don't pay attention to his looks. He's little and emaciated but full of Torah like a bulging sack. We only have to feed him up a bit and he'll be a man. Where's our little jewel?"

The "jewel" was at that time sitting in the stable busy with a puppy that Makarka had given him as a gift the day before. He was a pretty, curly dog resembling a lamb covered in white wool and many, many curls. Only his tiny eyes and the tip of his nose shone through the whiteness like three deep purple spots. When Hanina Lippa stabled his horse and found his son dawdling in this fashion, he became very angry: "You bastard," he shouted. "You bring him a Rebbe and he plays around with a dog! Seventy bills I paid; seventy lashes I'll pay you on your body."

The new Rebbe sized up the creature before him and, seeing what he was worth, concentrated his efforts upon a single practical task: eating. Coincidentally he taught his pupil how to put on phylacteries, using Hanina Lippa's for that purpose. These were the size of a pair of boots, if you will pardon the comparison, and their straps were hard and thick as sandal leather. Everyday the young man would "harness," as he put it, "the donkey," that is, Noah—binding the straps on his arms and teaching him the rules by rule of thumb: "Tighten them, tight, tighten them properly and say 'Blessed art thou,' wrap and wrap them round again three, four, five . . . whoa stop! Now around the finger, one, two, three, and the head piece!"

Tsipa Leah saw the fruit of her womb decked out in phylacteries and almost wept for joy. How fortunate she was. She was pleased, and the Rebbe received his due. While he was still folding his prayer shawl and hardly finishing the "Aleinu"—on the table before him appeared one after the other: a lovely flask of vodka, a reddish plate of cherry preserves, a glorious gizzard, a handsome chicken thigh, the choicest of waffles, sweet-smelling cracklings fried with onions, a warm roll, and a pancake dancing in fat. "Taste them, Rebbe, do taste them," Tsipa Leah urged him. "A hearty appetite!" See here, my son, you must listen to the Rebbe. You're a bar mitzvah boy. Oh, the pain of it, the torments," and she wiped her eyes on her apron.

Several weeks went by. The young man carried out his duties faithfully; he stuffed his mouth with food, and the food likewise fulfilled its task. On one unbearably hot evening in June, he could no longer control himself and made a pass at the maid. He entered her room quietly, but as you can well imagine, emerged in an uproar—two slaps on the face and flaming cheeks—causing the entire household to jump out of their beds. The pupil hopped out of his bed with the rest and found the bewildered Rebbe in his underwear in the middle of the house, his right side-lock folded over his ear and his bared cheek aflame.

By sunrise, the young man had fled. Tsipa Leah rushed to examine her silver spoons and forks in the chest of drawers, and finding them all untouched, her mind was put to rest. She was not sorry, but her joy was mitigated: woe to the mother whose child becomes bar mitzvah without a Rebbe.

Noah was now permanently free of Rebbes. When he reached thirteen, the ceremony of donning phylacteries by the "only son" took place in the synagogue under the sole supervision of Hanina Lippa, but with the aid of some neighborly wagoners. The poor father had a hard time during the procedure. The task was a bit too delicate for his hands, and two outsize drops of perspiration formed on his forehead. The head piece would in no way "sit" on the skull. Berele, the old wagoner, fulfilled the commandment of "you shall surely help"[15] and rushed to his aid. "Tsk, the head piece is a-kicking; rein it in a bit."

After the prayers the wagoners and all the other guests joined in the bar mitzvah meal. The house became as noisy as a tavern. Tsipa Leah and her maid carried in platters of food. The wagoners poured glass after glass down their throats as they shouted, *"Le-ḥayim!"* They blew their noses like trumpets and put their teeth and jaws to hard labor. Spoons and forks dug into bowls, and plates and pitchers gave each other ringing kisses. Poor Hanina Lippa stood over the guests, responding with *"Le-ḥayims"* in all directions and sweating like a bear. Old Berele, who had polished his boots with resin for the occasion, suddenly rose from among the assembled guests, properly soused, thick-tongued, and unsteady on his feet, began banging with his fork, and calling out, full-throatedly, at the lady of the house, long life to her, that she Tsi-tsipa Leah'nu sh . . . should come over to him since he has to tell her s . . . s . . . something. *Le- le- le-ḥayim,* he wants to say to her. And Matty Funfy turned his snub-nosed face to the celebrant and asked in nasal tones: "Young fe-n-llow, do-n you-n want to-n ge-n-t marrie-n-d?" The young fellow stared at him with burning eyes and blushed. "Heh, heh, heh," snub-nosed Matty smiled and patted him on the shoulder, "you're quite a fellow!"

After the party, while Hanina Lippa lay snoring on his bed like a wooden plank and Tsipa Leah busied herself with clearing the dishes,

---

[15]Exodus 23:5.

Noah went out to the courtyard to get some fresh air. He was uncomfortable in his new suit and felt hemmed in. Unwittingly, he reached the alleyway between the house and the fence. It seemed that for a moment Marinka's blonde hair appeared above the fence. His heart leaped with veiled delight. She probably climbed up to see what our house was celebrating, but how did she do it? With a ladder?

Noah yearned to climb the fence and see for himself, but then he remembered the phylacteries and turned away. His body again felt the weight of his new clothes. All day long they had irritated him. That evening, when he finally rid himself of them and found himself at his bedside in his new underwear, his whole being felt pleasantly relieved. When he got into bed, he recalled the nasal question asked by Matty Funfy word for word, and its tone: "Young fe-n-llow do-n you-n want to-n . . . ?" Noah quickly wrapped himself tightly in his blanket but the dirty question penetrated even beneath the cover and became a hairy, pug-nosed face leering at him with yellow teeth. "Young fe-n-llow do-n you-n . . . ?" Next moment it distorted itself into the shape of the young Rebbe with his Adam's apple, standing abashed in his underclothes in the middle of the house. Noah writhed with repressed laughter, and from Shakoripinshchika's locked cellar Marinka poked her head out at intervals calling, "Cuckoo!"

One day, Noah rose early in the morning and went out without saying his prayers. Wherever he went, he did not return until mealtime. His new phylacteries with their resin smell were left untouched in their sack on that day, and for many days thereafter.

Gossip spread throughout the quarter. No one saw or heard anything. On the contrary, everyone knew that nothing had happened or could have happened—but nevertheless, everyone was gossiping. And word of what was being said reached the ears of both neighbors, although no one had told them. The two neighbors also knew that they were groundless. Nevertheless, a fresh quarrel was added to the others involving the two neighbors: a long and cruel battle between father and son and between "Auntie" and her foundling.

9

Some four more years elapsed. Hanina Lippa's house had sagged a little along one of its sides, but a new roof capped the old one. The yard had broadened at its rear and now reached as far as

Shakoripinshchika's orchard. At that spot, at the very border of the orchard, a new structure now stood, a sort of shack for the drying of lumber. Near the top of the shack was a small, square window, and one of the *goyah*'s trees rubbed against its back boarding. The shack was joined to the old stable, and both formed a single, long structure extending toward the orchard and crowding its fence. The piles of lumber in the yard also grew taller. Hanina Lippa, who had grown somewhat older and had a running ear stuffed with a piece of cotton wool, no longer knew his way around so well. Shakoripinshchika's house had sunken into the earth an additional span and the barriers between the two properties rose even higher of their own accord. The *goyah*'s back had also bent over, and her strength had declined. Shakoripin rattled his chain unhappily. Noah and Marinka, who had grown up in the meantime, yearned for each other and became more and more cautious in their ways.

Noah was now eighteen years old, a strapping young man. His large forelock was as black as pitch, and he wore his hat, with its shining black crown, tilted over his ear like a bold Cossack. His dark face and coal-black eyes were like a gypsy's. He was a frequent guest in the *katsaps*' suburb. When he returned from there on his steaming horse, he would burst into the Jewish quarter suddenly— "Hey there! Make way!" He would pass through the entire quarter in a flash, like a bolt of lightning. All the groups of wagoners who at that time were standing in the middle of the street would automatically split in half. Each burgher would flee in terror to his yard gate with a twisted smile on his lips: "that jewel." Through the windows the daughters of the burghers would stare breathlessly at the dust raised by the dashing horse and rider until both disappeared.

When Noah went out in his tall, shiny boots and his short jacket and stood at the yard gate, his appearance made an impression on the quarter. The apprentice wagoners, who lingered nearby chatting away together, lowered their voices a little. Boys and girls turned aside and passed by him hastily. There was something in his look, in his whole demeanor, some element, some kind of movement that set the hearts of the boys and girls aquiver. It was something that attracted and at the same time frightened them. Sometimes a single courageous girl would deliberately pass before his burning eyes, seeking to be stirred for a moment by a sweet and sharp sensation.

But Noah paid no attention to the girls of the quarter. He remained silent, and no one knew what he thought. He did not socialize with the people, nor did he do much talking with the wagoners. Once, a bachelor wagoner put himself at risk by hinting to him— "Eh, eh, to the *katsaps*' suburb, that is, to the shiksahs?" Noah eyed him sternly, and the latter's blood froze: "What did you say, leper?" "Eh, eh, nothing, I've said nothing," the fellow spluttered as he backed away, with his whip tucked under his armpit.

Most days, Noah did not show himself in the quarter, nor did he mix with its people. On Sabbaths and holidays he went to synagogue and stood to the side alone, looking at his prayer book silently without even moving his lips. During the intervals, he did not go out to the hallway. When his father returned home, he found him already there.

On other days, Noah went and did whatever he pleased; Hanina Lippa didn't check up on him. In the course of time, his father's authority had lost its sway; no one knew exactly when. Only Tsipa Leah still kept an eye on Noah from afar. She would darn a stocking and sigh furtively.

But Noah's wandering days were over. At the back of Hanina Lippa's house was a pile of planks, higher than the rest. From its top you could see everything in the *goyah*'s yard.

Noah spent most of the day there. No one else knew why he lay there all day long. From the top of this lookout his eyes spoke to Marinka's.

At sunrise, when the sunflowers and their garlands on the *goyah*'s roof turned golden, Marinka would leave her sleeping shack in the orchard and show up in her yard. At that hour, she would go out carrying her tools and her small bundle to the fields. At the same time, Noah stood straight up on top of the pile and greeted both the sun and Marinka with a smile. She stood below, healthy and pink, smiling at him and blushing, while he from up above, dark and with gleaming teeth, would smile at her as well and toss his forelock, "Good morning." His eyes would follow her until she disappeared.

After she left, Noah would stretch out on top of the pile and fix his eyes on the yard. He knew that Marinka would not be returning until the evening. Nevertheless, he would lie there, staring. The morning commotion was about to begin in Hanina Lippa's yard. The maid would milk the cow and send her out to pasture. The old man would pull the horse out of the stable by his mane toward the well, speaking goy-talk to it, as was his custom. Tsipa Leah would feed the chickens, crying, "*Tsip, tsip, tsip,*" and Noah would still not stir. When he finally rose to descend, the sun was already at its zenith, and among the lumber piles stood two or three wagoners with their planks half unloaded.

In the hot, dry hours of afternoon, while some of the shutters were bolted and boards would exude sap and creak because of the heat, while a swallow pursued its mate in midair before catching up with her, and while the world was satiated and weary with pleasure—at such times Noah would go out to the yard after the midday meal and wander about as if drunk among the high stacks of wood. His head was befogged, his body heavy, and his skin unable to contain its flesh. He would try to find a niche for himself but without success. He would go from one hiding place to another. Sometimes he would disappear into the alley, stretch out on the ground, and lie in the shade; and sometimes he would go behind a stack of beams. Finally he would again expose himself to the sun on top of the high stack. He would sprawl on his back and lie on his belly for an hour or two, his head propped up on both hands and his eyes focused on the neighbor's yard. He could now see everything inside it. Over there, lying on its side was a large keg from which two dirty and callused feet protruded—they were the feet of Shakoripinshchika who now stayed home to guard the yard instead of Marinka. She was taking her afternoon nap in the keg. Over there was the orphaned bench, and here was Shakoripin, crouching stealthily, curled up beside the shack as he caught flies with his mouth and growled. Once in a while, he would open one eye slightly, peering at Noah through the slit of his lids. "Dog, why are you angry with me?"

Sometimes Noah would slip away and suddenly disappear from the yard. Tsipa Leah, who sensed this, would go out in search of him because of some hidden concern. She would find him at last under the roof of the new stable. He would lie there in the dark, deep in the hay, peering through the little window at Shakoripinshchika's orchard or the deserted field. "What is he doing in the loft?" Tsipa Leah was worried and vaguely suspicious.

She decided not to take her eyes off him. It became clear to her that the "boy" should be carefully watched, especially when Marinka showed up in her yard or her orchard. Marinka was now fully grown and had become a beautiful and healthy young woman. At twilight, when she returned from the fields with her implements, with hoe or scythe on her shoulder, Noah would pop out and appear at the fence or at the corner of the roof or some other hidden place where he could talk to her. Tsipa Leah noticed this, and one afternoon, while sitting at the threshold darning a stocking, she suddenly said to her husband, who was sitting beside her, "You know, Hanina Lippa, I think we must marry him off." "Who?" "The boy! Noah!" "Mazel Tov! Have you run out of time, woman?" "You always have plenty of time. . . . "

Tsipa Leah shifted her knitting needle from hand to hand and sighed. At that moment Noah was lying in the hay under the roof of the stable in the dark, plucking small pieces of the remnants of the Sabbath *hallah* and throwing them through the little window into the orchard. There amid the bushes, Shakoripin was standing with head and eyes raised toward the window as he caught the pieces in midair. The orchard was silent in the midafternoon. The tree bordering the new stable's wall leaned its crest against the sloping roof and did not stir. Beneath the ceiling could be heard the dull stomping of hooves, together with the chomping of teeth and the swishing of a tail; the horse was standing there at his trough chewing oats in the dark and fighting off flies with his tail. Through the open holes, tiny windows to the sky, swallows came in and out as they chirped and cavorted gleefully, flying for a moment in the stable's dim and empty space: tweet, tweet, and again tweet, and then they would fly away. On the hay, stone chippings and round sunspots were strewn here and there like scattered coins, and slender golden strips spread out. In a corner, a thin spider's web trembled. From outside, from distant fields and patches, through orchards and meadows, endless strands of melodies and fragments of the melancholy songs of farmhands reached him—long and short, fierce and soft, near and distant—and penetrated the darkness of the loft through the small window. They were so stealthy and so sweet, filling the inner recesses of the heart. Noah sensed in all his limbs that at this hour, as he reclined all wrapped in the dusty and redolent hay and enveloped in this sad and shining darkness, something was ripening within him like the wild fruit he had stored here, like those plums on the trees that even now were bursting with juice. His heart swelled like dough in a mixing bowl. His body filled from within, and his blood cried out from his flesh. Suddenly his heart trembled, and a sweet wave flowed over him. In the strains of escaping sound, it seemed that a quick syllable, a short, powerful note from Marinka's song, flashed for a moment and was immediately extinguished. Noah pressed against the little window; the dog turned his head and froze. Both as one sensed her voice and waited silently with bated breath and trembling heart for an encore.

At times, Noah lay here in the loft, and his soul would go flying with the swallows through the little window over there to the fields and patches where Marinka was now standing with her companions amid the high corn and the ripe vegetables, or he would sit alone with Shakoripin, near the shack, standing guard over the earth's produce. He lay there, seeing but unseen, behind a fence, peering furtively at what was going on inside, devouring every part of her body with his eyes.

So he lay all day long, and in the evening when Marinka returned home, he might emerge from his ambush and suddenly appear before her in one of the alleys. Or he might not! Perhaps he might also follow her and hide in the orchard, and when she came to the shack at night, he too would come there.

When his blood reached boiling point, Noah would leap through the fence at the end of the yard, and his feet would at once be standing outside the Jewish quarter. He would walk along the shabby and damaged reed barrier as its shadow followed him and wound itself around him, strip by strip, in a cold and warm envelope of black and white, like a prayer shawl. Every summer, the crowded houses disappeared. The gardens and vegetable patches would emit their scents. The deserted field looked at him through the breach in its fence, winking at him like a living creature. Upon your life, he would actually see eyes blinking at him from there.

Suddenly, a sweet perfumed breeze covered his face. He was completely hidden in the heavy shadow of the sumac tree that stood with its thick foliage on the outside near the breach. At that moment, a golden shower poured over his head—the chirping of birds and grains of light streaming down from the top of the sumac tree. The birds themselves were unseen, but from their chirping you could infer that there were many thousands of them, as if the entire sumac rang with tinkling leaves—and it was magic. Once there he was unable to budge. A wave of sweetness swept over him, his eyes crusted over, and his limbs grew limp. The earth actually drew him to its bosom. He looked for a secret hideaway to be with her, and he entered the deserted field. There he found a hiding place, a round hollow shaped like a mortar, concealed in the darkness, and padded with grass and brush. Light filtered through the thatch drop by drop, and the wild plants inside shaded themselves in random fashion with their broad, thick leaves. He threw himself spread-eagle into the chill, dark void of the pit. The grasses screened him as he lay face down, pressing his cheeks against the earth and digging his nails into its moist, loose soil. At such a time, his soul would return to its roots and he would become one of the fruits of the earth, one of its plants. Each one of his hairs imbibed the scent of the soil, and all the blood of his youth cried from the earth: Marinka.

Marinka continued to grow, continued to dominate his thoughts. By now she was free to come and go as she pleased. Yet just now fortune did not bring them together to a single tryst. She no longer went out to the field. "Auntie" had noticed the breach and filled it in. Marinka was clearly avoiding him. In the morning, her eyes smiled at him with promise, but in the evening when she returned, her promise disappeared into the shack where she slept night after night. He knew what time she went to the *katsaps'* suburb, but he never met her there. Maybe he ought to lie in wait for her in one of the alleys.

10

One Sabbath eve, as darkness fell, Noah lay hidden among the thorns and thistles growing under the fences outside the quarter and waited. He knew that Marinka would be returning this way from her daily labor. It was a hideaway; fences and hedges stood on every side, and at this hour few people frequented it. Nearby was the small portal leading to the orchard.

Noah's heart beat wildly. All about him reigned a great silence, the quiet of a Sabbath eve outside the quarter. Stars flickered one after another, a large, round moon was cut in half by a pole across the way as it rose over a hedge. From beyond the fence behind him, the chanting of the Sabbath worshipers in synagogue rang out, pouring a mysterious sadness over the thorns . . . the sound of the congregation and then the cantor's voice.

A hushed sadness and a veiled fear invaded Noah's heart. There behind the fence, about forty or fifty paces away, in the big and many-windowed building filled with light and the voices of the worshippers greeting the Sabbath, his father would be standing dressed in his Sabbath *kapota* and hat and calling out aloud: "For forty years I was angry at a generation"[16] . . . and he a traitorous Jew lay in ambush behind some fence waiting for a shiksah.

The moon rose on high and in the meantime was caught between a tree and the chimney of a white house in one of the fields. In the foliage nearby, a strip of path leading to the orchard glistened white while crickets sawed away. Soft, hushed steps were heard. Noah raised his head a little and got ready.

In the light of the full moon, Marinka appeared with hoe on shoulder. As soon as she reached the hideaway and disappeared into its shadows, Noah took a single leap, and his hands clasped her hips like a vise. "Noy?" Marinka was terror-stricken. She dropped her hoe. "What are you doing? Let me go."

Noah did not release her. He was out of his mind. He clasped her to his heart, lifted her into the air, whispered in her ear, kissed and fondled her, mouthing all sorts of wild phrases: "Do you love me, Marinitchika, tell me do you love me? Why are you silent? Do you love me?"

Marinka struggled in the vise, pushing him away and drawing him to her simultaneously. She pressed herself against him more and more. Her whisperings finally became lower and softer, full of pain and entreaties. "Let me go, Noah, let go now, there's no need . . . " "When Marinitchika, when? Tonight in the orchard?" "No, no," Marinka whispered, but all her being was saying, "yes." And suddenly she stirred and called out in fear: "Let go, oy oy, do you hear? People are coming."

She pushed Noah away with all her might.

Noah released her. In the orchard, bushes and dried branches rustled. Marinka lifted her hoe without looking behind her. She ran toward the orchard. A moment later the little portal closed behind her. Noah remained alone between the hedges and the fence. The noise of prayer ceased. Was it the silent prayer, or was the service over? He hurriedly returned to the quarter.

The houses to his right and left had taken on the air of Sabbath. Window after window had its lit candles. Only the *goyah*'s home stood isolated as if under a ban, windowless and without candles. It seems that the rest of the quarter's homes stared at it from their lit

---

[16]Psalm 95:10.

windows with the delicate contempt of the privileged. Men's heads were not seen in the windows. If so, Noah consoled himself and turned into the synagogue's alleyway. "The silent prayer!"

In the alley he ran into those who were leaving the synagogue. He intermingled with them and tried to show himself to his father, greeting him uncharacteristically with "a peaceful Sabbath," and followed him home.

About an hour after dinner, when the full moon—the white moon of a hot July evening—was shining over the quarter, heavy-limbed Jews and Jewesses began to leave the porches and lock themselves into their bedrooms. Noah suddenly told his mother that tonight he was going to sleep up in the stable loft. "Why the stable loft?" his mother asked in worried tones, looking at her son's glistening eyes. "Because I want to." "I'll make up your bed in the hall." "No, in the stable." "*Pfft,*" his mother spat. "Crazy."

He climbed into the stable loft but did not take any pillow with him. All night long Tsipa Leah was unable to shut an eye. She imagined that there were thieves in the stable. Several times she wanted to wake Hanina Lippa but controlled herself. She was now afraid to let Hanina Lippa enter the stable.

The air of the stable reeked with the smell of warm sweat and dung beyond bearing. The horse stood in the total darkness of the lower level, weary and kicking incessantly with dull thuds. Noah lay in the loft turning and tossing impatiently. The same demon tormented them both.

Finally the quarter fell silent. Noah cocked his ear. It seemed as though the tree that leaned against the outside wall of the stable was secretly scratching its side. He got up and stuck his head out of the small window. The tree presented him with two ripe red apples hanging on a nearby branch, as if to say, "Take them, they're yours."

Noah stretched out his hand but couldn't reach them. A little more, a little more—but still he could not reach them.

His eyes sparkled. He took one leap and fell into a warm, inky bath, the sweltering darkness of the lower level. A kick at the door—and he was outside. Again he ascended—to the top of the stable's roof. Another leap and he was inside the orchard itself.

All the ascents and descents lasted no longer than the twinkling of an eye. The bushes in the orchard awoke from their slumber and shot sparks in the moonlight. In the shadows of the trees, Marinka and her dog appeared like a vision of the night. The shack swallowed the two neighbors' children. At the door Shakoripin stood guard.

11

And so did Noah get up one night and elope with Marinka?

You do not understand the mind of an inhabitant of the lumber quarter! On the Sabbath of Hanukah, Noah married a proper virgin, the daughter of a tax collector. The marriage was arranged by a marriage broker, with a *ḥupah* and religious vows. On Shavuot he and his new bride came to his parents' home in the lumber quarter amid great joy. After the dairy meal,[17] the young couple sat alone on a beam that lay behind the house. At that very moment Marinka stood peering through a crack, with the baby in her arms behind the fence.

---

[17]Traditionally eaten on the holiday.

3

Big Harry

❖　❖　❖

*B*ialik submitted *Aryeh Baal Guf (Big Harry)* to Asher Ginsburg, better known by his pseudonym Aḥad Ha-am, the editor of *Ha-Shiloaḥ,* in 1898. In his cover letter, he stated that "the main character of this sketch is a certain *baal guf.* This is the nickname bestowed by the masses of Volhynia (southwestern Russia) upon every vulgar ignoramus who had become wealthy and yet remained brutish." "Big Harry" despises the "soft" gentry of his town and despairs of ever being admitted into their circle. His wife, however, avidly strives to attain the status of a "fine lady" and entices him to erect an elegant home and invite the town's leading citizens to a sumptuous house-warming party. Their attempt at social climbing ends in a dismal failure. The couple becomes an object of derision to both rich and poor. Bialik explains to Aḥad Ha-am that the *baal guf* is a stock comic character in the lore of the backward towns of Volhynia, replacing the "tax farmer" of former generations as the butt of laughter. "He has not yet," he averred, been "adequately depicted in our literature."

Bialik aptly referred to the work as a "sketch" rather than a story. Harry, his wife, his sons, and the rest of its characters are "flat." They remain unchanged throughout the narrative. On the other hand, Bialik's keen descriptive powers and his sense of the grotesque are remarkable. He shows an uncanny ability to transform Harry's folksy Yiddish vulgarisms into Hebrew, despite the fact that Hebrew was not yet a spoken language. In his letter to Aḥad Ha-am, he expressed his disdain for the nouveaux riches and his regret that they had displaced the old learned and dignified "fine Jews" who once led the Jewish communities. However, the artist in him conveyed a certain admiration for the earthiness and pragmatism of this new type in contrast to the "soft" spirituality and subservience of its predecessors.

The paragraphs describing the housewarming, with its overladen tables, the crude gluttony of the guests, the "tragedy" of the sagging pudding, are hilarious. So, too, is Bialik's handling of the battle between Harry and his sons and Alter "Cockerel" over a customer, and the native cunning of Mitra, the gentile peasant, haggling with the rivals over the price of his wagonload of timber.

Bialik was in his mid-twenties when he wrote *Big Harry*. He was influenced by the social satirists who portrayed the life of the ordinary Russian rural folk (Gogol and Goncharov, for example). Some critics even discern the influence of Balzac's *Père Goriot*, a novel that Bialik might have read in a Russian translation. It is more likely that his literary mentors were Mendele Mocher Sefarim and Peretz Smolenskin. But in his masterful Hebrew, his tight structure, his deft symbolism, and above all his ironic humor, he surpasses the Yiddish and Hebrew writers of his period. (We should also note that Shalom Aleichem's Tevyeh had not yet been fully developed at this stage.)

The social milieu of the story is the world of the Jewish lumber dealers of the timber district of Zhitomir, in which Bialik was raised. It has been suggested that Harry's disordered lumberyard, with its tiered wood piles, serves as a symbol for the degeneration of Russian Jewish life at the close of the nineteenth century. The older, sturdy, heavy lumber in the tiered piles is buried under lighter and cheaper wood. When the heavy beams are excavated from beneath the poorer timber, however, they have been eaten away by rot. The house that Harry erects is built of these rotten beams. Other symbols of degeneration are the two beautiful apples that Harry proudly stores as showpieces, the contrast between the plebeian flutes that his sons play and the aristocratic strains of the violins of the sons of the "important" citizens. They underline the negative attitude toward the contemporary Jewish leaders that our author conveys. Bialik's co-option of the biblical language describing King Solomon's construction of the Temple of Jerusalem and the great banquet he held after its dedication to caricature the erection of Harry's rickety mansion and the plebeian meal is irony at its best.

Yet the celebration of the earthy, this worldly, Harry and his sons is not entirely one-sided. The artist in Bialik seems to relish the vitality of the new "folk type," as if to declare that in the age that was about to dawn, Jewry might be better off with a little more brawn and less brains.

❖　❖　❖

1

Early each morning as soon as sunlight sparkles on his window, Big Harry, "the goat," springs straight out of bed, clad only in white underpants and a shirt—and goes at once to the stable in his yard to visit his chestnut stallion.

He makes his way through the yard, which is piled up with wooden beams, great heaps of logs, stacks of wood, and all kinds of forest produce—Harry's trade—opens the stable door, and goes inside.

In the stable, to the right of the entrance, hidden in shade on a spread of hay, straw, and mingled dung, a chestnut stallion stands motionless like a dead, frozen corpse, its redness swallowed in black shadow, tethered to its crib. His little ears are folded, and he appears to be dozing or sunk in thought. Above his head a black raven hangs in the air, condemned to death by strangulation and attached to the ceiling with a fine cord to ward off evil spirits that afflict and weary horses during the night or tangle up or twist their manes.

Harry approaches the horse, laying his thick strong palm on its neck, at the same time saying, "Get up, Chestnut!" The stallion gives a start and retreats, ears erect and eyelids fluttering. But Harry rebukes him gently, saying: "Get up, rascal! Don't be afraid, for I am with you!" After which he takes hold of the horse's mane a second time, patting its full stomach, examining the crib to see whether the fodder has been eaten, and deriving great pleasure from the sight of the horse's belly, which has grown round and swollen during the night.

After passing his hand over all the horse's limbs, its ribs, its spine, and even its tail—he loosens the tether from the crib, takes the bucket from a peg fastened into the wall, and leads the horse to the well in his yard to water it.

And while the horse drinks from the bucket held slanting in Harry's hand—the latter stands whistling shrilly through his lips so that it may drink with relish. What the horse leaves over, he uses to swill his hands and face in morning ablutions, for it is acknowledged that such leftovers are good for the body. And as he turns his forelock under the cold jet, two reddish rings are exposed on the flesh of his neck—the traces of surgeons' cups: it is Harry's custom to let blood on the evening before the new moon, as that clears, in his own words, any impurity from the blood, and it is good for headaches.

The strong, thickset frame, with its iron sinews and bronze limbs and its full ruddy face—so that even though he has already reached the age of fifty, he is as strong as a thirty-year-old—returns wet and cold with manly stride, he and the horse with him, to the stable, and at every step his full, strong cheekbones move and shake.

Having returned the horse to its place, Harry turns to the cowshed, to see whether his cow has already gone to pasture in the meadow with the sheep. He then turns to the timber shed to make sure it hasn't been broken into during the night by one of his many neighbors, all of whom are suspect in his eyes of stealing wood. While walking, he casts a glance at all the piles of planks near the fence of his yard to see whether the marks, which he is accustomed to put in the evenings before going to bed, again because of fear of theft, are still in place. And only once his mind is satisfied by this inspection does he return to his house to waken his wife, Hannah, and his three sons and to finish dressing.

Clad in black clothes made of strong coarse fabric, which he favors, Harry soon leaves his house again, unlocks the gates of his yard facing the quiet street still sunk in slumber, and as he opens it he mutters his usual mantra in the vernacular whose meaning is, "Let every merchant, seller, and buyer—turn in here," and while doing so he indicates with his hand the "plain" in his yard (thus the wood merchants call the enclosures and fenced yards for forest produce and building wood), and his intention is, "Here, here, that is, to me, to Harry Goat, bring all the customers in the world, O Father in heaven!"

Whereupon Harry turns this way and that—and is content: all the other yards and enclosures are still shut, and he is the first of them all. The squeal of the gates of his yard was the first to disturb the silence of the street "because they are all hoity-toity Jews, pampered, so to speak, or simply lazy sleep lovers. But he is not lazy, thank God, and as people say—the early bird catches the worm. But why are his sons so late in coming into the yard?"

Harry comes back to the window of his sons' bedroom, taps on it noisily, and cries: "Shefil, Zelig, Moshe! Aren't you dressed yet? I'll be after you, you dogs! Hurry on out!" And only after that does Harry return—if it is not a market day—to his house to drink tea.

To this task—that is, the task of drinking tea—Harry applies himself only after taking off his coat and rolling up his shirtsleeves—only then does he sit down at table and cry, "Hannah, bring the samovar!"

A round, pot-bellied samovar, boiling and steaming, is set on the table right opposite Harry, who applies himself to the act of drinking deliberately, seriously, and with intent. Every single gulp makes a noticeable impression on the glass. And thus he drinks and empties glass after glass—and he does not move until he is bathed in sweat.

Once he is sweating, he puts on his coat and stands up to pray. And since Harry is "a simple man"—he does not make long supplications with his Maker and his prayer is brief: winding,[1] kissing, spitting—"Hannah! Bring the food!"

Once finished with the act of breakfast, composed of a mixture of sliced radish and onions—in which exercise all Harry's features are engaged like a mill working with all its wheels—his mind is at ease and he feels a need to go out to the gate of his yard to belch because of the radish and to yawn because of the idle chatter of a group of cart-drivers who have already begun to congregate near his property.

2

That solid, rugged body going out to stand at the gate of his yard facing the street—looked from afar, in its fullness and strength, in its form hewn from one block, a complete stone without lumps or hollows and without ups and downs and chiseled bones, like an oak that, even if all the winds in the world were to blow upon it, could not be moved from its place.

That body had not experienced the plagues and ailments of mankind. It had never been stricken with pain or suffered illness.

---

[1]The straps of the phylactery are wound around the arm during the morning prayer.

And even the pestilence that twice already has raged through the street and reaped a rich harvest—even that axman had not assailed this tree. It would appear that even the destroying angel drew back in the face of flesh and blood like this and skipped over him, just as the inhabitants of the street who were not on good terms with him drew back in fear when they passed within four feet of him, although he himself never used his strength to evil purpose except by way of sport and mockery, when the opportunity presented itself.

Harry was aware of this and regarded it as a virtue. A feeling that derived from a kind of confidence in his strength and the power of his arm always came over him when he saw fear descending on folk and the praise of his valor ringing in every mouth, even though he was well aware that the measure of his strength was constantly exaggerated, and that the praise was out of all proportion when people related tall stories of his prowess and the remarkable deeds that he had never done. These were mere butterflies released by Harry himself for people's amazement.

A similar feeling arose with respect to his wealth, which was also vastly overrated, because of Harry himself. But although we may cast doubt on the exaggerations, nevertheless, we are forced to admit that Harry is a "Big Man," not merely literally but also metaphorically: a man whose position is sure and who stands "fullsquare" on the ground, the owner of wealth and property, with wads of ready cash wrapped up and stuffed in his pocket and his strongbox.

Harry's main occupations are his lumberyard and collecting the large interest from small long-standing loans that he had made to poor *katsaps* who came from faraway places to settle on holdings surrounding the town. Through Harry's kindness they did, indeed, succeed in getting a foothold on the ground, except that they became his bondsmen with respect both to their labor and their wealth, providing a tithe for him, while he became a partner in all their activities to the present day. Once a week Harry would go out in his cart drawn by the chestnut to do the rounds of "the *katsaps*' quarter," his cucumber beds and fields of gourds, exacting taxes, whether willingly or unwillingly, from his bondsmen: in produce of the ground, like beans, cucumbers, gourds, and other vegetables or from living things such as hens, ducks, and a one-day-old calf, and he would not spurn living produce such as eggs or milk. At the same time a little cash might be collected or added to the account. All of this by virtue of the interest on the original loans charged to them. Harry set off with an empty cart, returning home at evening with his wagon full to the brim, loaded down with the good things of the *katsaps'* quarter and the fruits of the earth.

Such are his main occupations, but the major source of his wealth comes from his landed estates and his "bundles" of money. "Bundles"—that is Harry's favorite word, constantly on his tongue. "If there are no bundles"—Harry would say and pat the full and bulging pocket of his trousers to indicate the meaning of the word— "if there are no bundles, there is nothing; and if there are bundles, there is everything. The beginning of everything and the end of everything are bundles."

And the bundles are most comforting when they lie in his pocket next to his flesh; for that reason Harry was never inclined to deposit his bundles in a bank or turn them into bonds or income-bearing shares. He doesn't trust them, just as he doesn't trust other newfangled inventions of the present time, such as the telegraph, for example, even though he is not averse to using them in case of need.

"Banks shmanks, shares shmares"—Harry used to say—"all those fancy ideas are only trickery and cheating of those hoity-toity types, good-for-nothings and pigeon fanciers, who have nothing in the world except pi-pu-pa (Harry would wave his hand in the air, to indicate the meaning of pi-pu-pa), here today and gone tomorrow to the fair at Irkurtsk, singing 'A Soldier's Farewell.' . . . I wouldn't give you a penny for all their shares! They're only fit for wrappers on jars! But cash—that's a different matter entirely."

For this reason—for fear of trickery and cheating—Harry keeps well away from any even slightly complex deals that are based on suppositions and conjectures and complicated calculations beyond his grasp. Harry likes solid profit that is obvious and immediate, but if anyone proposes to him "pie in the sky," stuff and nonsense—No! Harry is not the man to be seduced.

In real estate he has the large fenced area for living and for business, with the house facing the street; storage sheds, barns, and stables, nestling among heaps of planks and tall piles of timber heaped on top of each other without order; apart from which he has a large stone house in one of the town's marketplaces, which came into his possession from the property of a certain gentleman that was publicly auctioned by his many creditors, including Harry; a large garden in the outskirts of the town, which he also took from what was owed him by one of the *katsap*s, a well-known drunkard, whom Harry had helped in time of need and lent a certain sum at unlimited interest. In addition he owned open spaces, uncultivated land acquired from various peasant farmers in the town's allotments, which since coming into his possession have remained fallow and uncultivated, lying under thorns and thistles, as pasture for oxen and horses. And if we add on to all this the cucumber and gourd patches and various kinds of vegetables of the "suburb" from which produce Harry takes a portion as a full partner on account of the interest—all this indeed gives Harry the right to be called the "Big Man," a term they use in this region for a coarse man who achieves wealth while remaining common and without refinement.

3

They call him "Goat" not because that is his surname but because it is impossible to be a resident of the town N. without a sobriquet or a nickname. Whenever a person comes to live there, the townsfolk at once apply a nickname to him derived from some personal or family dishonor, and this nickname is firmly attached to him until the end of time. If in other towns they are less particular about names and borrow nicknames from the whole range of creation and the natural world, in the town of N. they derive most of their nicknames from the animal kingdom: Alter Adder, Reuben-Hirsh Panther, Akiba Virgin, Shalom Turkey. And every nickname, of course, has its special reason, after those who impose the names have made a thorough and careful investigation of some shameful characteristic of the recipient or in the affairs of his family. Here too "Harry Goat"—because his father, may he rest in peace, an ignorant old tax farmer of the kind found in the previous generation, had throughout his life the lease on the "community goat" from the squire, and all who possessed nanny goats were dependent on him, obtaining his favor for a fixed sum. The father bequeathed this nickname to all his offspring, and the "Goat" family has not vanished until this day; and Harry Goat is among its most prominent members.

Of all Harry's possessions, he derives particular pleasure from the above-mentioned stone house and garden in the town square. "I am just going down to my property," or "I am just going to tour my es-

tate"—Harry would reply, while perched on his little wagon harnessed to the chestnut, to anyone who met him in the market who
might ask him in Jewish fashion, "Where have you come from and
where are you going, Mr. Harry?" To hear him talk, the garden was
unique and without compare in the district, a full day's walk, with
many trees and choice fruits whose taste and smell excel all other
fruits in the world; and the garden yields produce valued at five
thousand a year.

"Have you seen the autumn fruits on my estate?"—Harry would
boast about the fruit of his garden. "Alas, fool, haven't you seen
them! If so, you have never in your life seen autumn apples. Do you
think that they are ordinary apples, apples like all the other apples
in the world?—Of course not, you big fool! Apples like my apples
are not to be found even in the district governor's garden. . . . Do
you know what gourds look like?—That's the size of my apples.
Every apple—like an Egyptian gourd. And from a distance, you big
fool, they look like gourds hanging on a tree and peeking out from
between the leaves. Come and I will show you, idiot, so that you
won't say that Harry has deceived you."—And with that he would
haul the doubter after him to his house and show him two very
large coarse apples, admittedly excellent of their kind, and he would
go on recounting their praise and exaggerating their taste, appearance, and scent. And even though it eventually came to light that
these two apples "had not grown on Harry's patch," but had come
from the garden of the squire Lampidritski, to whom Harry had
made a loan—nevertheless this revelation did not darken Harry's
face at all; time after time he would lead those of little faith to the
two apples, to prove his words and to show quite clearly the size of
his apples and "don't say that Harry fooled you!"

These two apples lay rolling around Harry's cupboard until they
grew rotten and moldy and nobody could abide their smell. One
Sabbath eve the apples infuriated Hannah, Harry's wife, a stout,
pot-bellied woman whose face, nose, and eyes were always aglow—
because of her fondness for "mother's ruin"[2]—and to avoid her husband's wrath by impugning his apples' dignity, she approached him
cautiously as though seeking advice on the matter: "What do you
think, Harry? It seems as though the apples have gone off a little,
and they are beginning to stink. . . . I'm worried about them. Harry!

---

[2]Gin.

Harry, why are you silent?"—"Do they stink? If so stew them into a *tsimes*"—Harry answered her briefly. Hannah set to and stewed them—and that was the end of the apples!

Both his strength and his wealth, the two qualities of which he was most proud, Harry tried to exaggerate and maximize in front of people with imagined anecdotes and tall stories, all of which followed the same pattern. On one occasion three thieves who had cast their eyes on his chestnut and were planning to acquire it for nothing broke into his stable at night. And he, Harry, happened to go outside by sheer chance, or to the privy, clad in nothing but his underpants and a shirt. He looked and listened, stole up quietly, and ambushed them, grabbing two at once by their forelocks and cracking their heads together, while he felled the third to the ground with a deft kick, and he tied them up, put them in his cart, and brought them to the police station. Or something like this: there was an incident with five drunken yokels who challenged him to a fight, and he grabbed one by the legs and waved him like a stick, beating the others with him until they passed out. His stories about his wealth would start with a count or a general who had borrowed five thousand or twenty thousand rubles from him. And sometimes Harry would combine his strength and his money together: beginning with "a count who borrowed and didn't pay" and ending with an "episode": on one occasion he came to the count's house to demand his "bundles," and there was no one in the house except the count; Harry took him by the throat and said to him: "If you give me my money—good! And if not—you are a dead man!"

Harry used to relate stories of this kind in the company of the workers in the timber yards and the council of the hired cart-drivers, with their ramshackle carts and scabby horses in the wood merchants' street, who were available to fetch and carry timber for anyone who required it. They would congregate near Harry to listen to his pleasant anecdotes. If following his stories and his verbal evidence, there might still remain some skeptic—Harry would remove all doubt with irrefutable proof: he would stretch out two fingers, the thumb and the index finger like a pair of tongs, take hold of the skeptic's neck, and shake it until it wobbled to and fro like a reed, and while doing so he would say: "So answer me, go on, answer me, you little son of a flea, who is the greatest? You or me?"

"Mr. Harry! Mr. Harry!"—the youth admits unwillingly, struggling to get out of the vise that is squeezing him.

"Who's the strongest, who's the mightiest?"—Harry repeats and continues squeezing the neck of his partially conceding victim, writhing in his grip like a fish, with face turned crimson.

"Mr. Harry! Mr. Harry!" the skeptic groans aloud, subdued by the sharpness of the pain. "In that case run along, run along to your hole, dog, and don't raise your voice in front of your betters"—Mr. Harry would end his reproach and let him go.

"And where are you off to?"—Harry turns again on another cart-driver, who is backing away. "Just come here and let me touch you, my son. Don't be afraid, you big fool! Don't worry, I'm only going to put you on one nail and crush you with the other—like that—and you're a goner! . . . " And Harry clearly demonstrates with two fingernails the fate of a flea condemned to death by squashing, which reduces all the wagon-drivers to laughter.

And of course all this is only done good-humoredly and in jest. Both wagoner and Harry are merely intent on the amusement of the whole company. To those who doubt his wealth, Harry gives a short answer: he would rise up and outline the mound in his trouser pocket, pat it, and say, "Here's the bundles!"—and they were silenced immediately.

Pouring out intestines, breaking limbs, nipping off the head, smashing the skull, and ripping up the belly—these were the salt and pepper with which Harry spiced his conversations, as though he were lecturing on surgery. When a quarrel among the cart-drivers was brought to him, as happened ten times a day, he would advise one of them to pour out the small intestines of the other, and the second—to nip off the leprous head of the first or tear out his measly gullet—and everything would end peacefully. And for that reason the wagon-drivers respected him and made him their regular judge and referee to resolve all their many quarrels.

4

Truth to tell, Harry only spoke about these things "for embellishment"; and indeed he was not prone to use his strength; whether because the hot blood of youth had already calmed down, or because at fifty years old, it was beneath his dignity—in any case, few people were privileged to see him strike, spill intestines, or tear out people's bellies. Such activity was mainly left to his sons.

In his youth, however, Harry had schooled himself and become practiced in all these arts in the "*katsaps*' quarter." Even in childhood certain tendencies had sprouted that were no credit to a Jewish boy. As an infant he had fled the ḥeder; a foolish child, coarse and dull-witted, disinclined to listen to the Bible lesson; a wild unruly youth, kicking his teachers, and a young man straying along wicked paths— to the *katsaps*' quarter, to become a crony of their young men and be like one of them. From his early days the *katsaps*' children attracted him with their special character, their powerful faces, and their strong necks, and even their clothing and their gait appealed to him, and, needless to say, their flowing forelocks, and their caps pushed back on their heads and a little to one side—were not all these the marks of "regular guys"? And from the moment he noticed such things, he tried to be like them in all their habits: he grew his forelock and tilted his cap like them, adopted their stance, which was at once bold and relaxed, cracked seeds like them nonchalantly and without effort, whistled softly between his teeth like them and at the same time twitching one leg, and also assuming a certain hauteur, an hauteur that announced to everyone, "Anyone who gets too close has had it!" . . . Nor was Harry satisfied until he had managed to acquire a black coat narrow at the top and wide at the bottom, in the fashion favored by the *katsaps*' sons. And from that time, he was accepted as a welcome guest among the "regular guys" and took part in all their youthful pranks, imitating all their ways and customs and becoming their crony. At night he slept with them in the meadow near the grazing horses, and by day he practiced galloping on horseback and learned how to "spill intestines." As time went by, Harry grew up and took a wife, "his Hannah," but he still consorted with the *katsaps*, who had also grown into adulthood. He knew their activity and their repose, their comings and goings, did business with them, mainly shady business. That was when the night journeys began . . . taking horses from place to place . . . mottled horses went out, and piebald horses came back. . . . But all that happened long ago, and from the time that Harry acquired his "bundles" and had sons and daughters—he settled down and gave all that up; and of the deeds of his youth all that remained were the memories of the past, on which he built whole volumes of tall stories and exaggerations, and an abstract, platonic love for horses and everything connected with them: for horse-dealers and horse-breeders, for cart-drivers and gypsies, and for talk about horses. Ten times a week Harry would exchange his horse, which never left his stable for another horse: today a mottled for a piebald, and tomorrow a piebald for a chestnut, and so on. And all this not for any profit or gain, but for love of horses, and simply to take part in his favorite pastime. But all this was only a remnant of the days of his youth, whereas all the rest he had given over to his sons, who had also become adults.

Harry had acquired his "bundles," not, as you might think, by means of those shady dealings, horse transports, and night journeys from the early days—Not at all! Harry had become rich by means of . . . a handshake from the *Tsaddik* of K. It was Harry's wife who had brought it about. He had suddenly gone off her and was planning to divorce her after some fifteen years of domestic peace; but she had refused a divorce and had gone to enlist the help of the Rebbe. And the Rebbe, for the sake of peace, promised Harry to put a blessing on his house for his wife's sake; but Harry, a "simple man," interrupted his words and asked improperly: "Rebbe! How can I know that the Rebbe's word will come about? Will the Rebbe shake hands on it?" And the Rebbe—listen and learn—agreed and gave him a handshake! Or so the more credulous inhabitants of Wood Street relate. And Harry, who is anxious that his luck shall not deteriorate and that the evil eye will not have power over him, refrains from announcing it openly, lest any rash utterance undermine the power of the handshake. . . . But secretly he is delighted with this story, which is current among people, most of whom regard him with hostility; so that "all those lepers" may know that Harry has someone to rely on, and may their gall burst. In order to strengthen this belief, Harry shrewdly hints about it at times, and when he is openly announcing that he acquired all his power and riches only by his "ten fingers," he immediately adds: and "by virtue of the Rebbe." Not so Hannah, his wife, on account of whom the handshake came about and for which reason she became endeared to her husband—she mentions this virtue ten times a day, and on each occasion she raises her bloodshot oval eyes toward heaven, rubs her hand on the wall, and says, "May God be blessed first, and afterwards the Rebbe." . . .

5

Once Harry had acquired his "bundles," he didn't put on airs or seek the honor of "the big shots" or the self-importance of "the upper-class Jews"—and he remained the same Harry as before. The same companions, the same conversations and coarse remarks, the same behavior at home and in the street as before, except that he assumed a garb more in keeping and suitable for his years. He was the same Harry, a "regular guy," a disciple of the "quarter"—but an old "regular guy." The trappings of his house, the food on his table, and the manner of his clothing had not changed in any noticeable way. Not like those big shots, whose wealth endows them with other virtues and perfections, and since they have acquired wealth, they also suddenly become refined, learned, sages, sweet-voiced, and arbiters of taste; and even the sole of their foot suddenly shrinks and is easily shod in a small light shoe, whereas previously, in their days of obscurity, it could only be squeezed with great difficulty into a big coarse shoe. Harry could not find within himself the talent, the desire, the need, or the ability to escape from the confines of his commonness into the realm of the upper-class Jews. And so he entrenched himself within his limitations and was satisfied with the name "Big Man." This name fulfilled all his need and desire for honor, and he willingly renounced the name of "big shot," with its connotation both of importance and standing. Indeed, had he been asked, he would now have chosen the name "moneybags," which exactly projected the concept he preferred "Harry Moneybags"— What a lovely name! It was enough for him that "all those lepers" were aware of the many bundles lying in his bag, and as for everything else—sheer vanity. And of course Harry feels no obligation to behave "à la big shot" and to be punctilious with respect to "airs and graces" and the manners about which the upper-class Jews were scrupulous. He leaves all of that to them, the upper-class Jews, to indulge in at their house of study, and he gives it all a wide berth. In the first place, because it all "costs money." The importance and honor attached to the name "big shot" are not acquired for nothing. And second, all those "airs and graces" are foreign to his nature and detract from his joy of life. He does not want to put his thick neck in such a heavy yoke.

Ever since Harry gave up all hope of leaving his domain and joining the "top stratum," he conceived a great hostility to everything bearing the stamp of being spoiled, pampered, aristocratic, or spiritual. Not only the thin face of the slight, dried-up teacher, the "cylinders" (this is what Harry calls the side-locks curled like hollow tubes) of the portly ritual slaughterer, and the oval eyes of the weepy cantor—roused his wrath to the point of frenzy, but all kinds of important people and upper-class Jews were anathema to him and his natural enemies, because they were unlike him . . . and he, Harry, had no regrets and was not at all afraid of the scorn of the proud and the mockery of the big shots; that resulted only from their envy of his wealth. For his wealth was solid and durable, proper wealth based on holdings and estates, whereas their wealth—was all imagined and fly-by-night, "pi-pu-pa," which could disappear as quickly as it came.

In his conversations with the carters, he allowed no householder, whether respectable or not, to escape the lash of his tongue, but pointed out his shortcomings for mockery and scorn. Harry attached a nickname to each one in accordance with "his weakness" and any failing. In particular he displayed this art when he reached the name of any man who, at some time or other, had had financial dealings with him. "Reb Aaron Wild Ox"—he is "unspeakable"; "Hayyim Hirsh Leviathan—a bad lot; Jacob Nissan Intestine—a leech who lays four pairs of tefillin; Berish Cock—dyed in the same wool; Itzi Gizzard—a thief and as cunning as a bastard." In this way Harry would recount the praises of all the upper-class Jews in his neighborhood. And we must admit, to his credit, that he was endowed with a keen understanding and an insight that enabled him to pounce upon the slightest weakness in his adversaries and to use it for amusing conversation spiced with popular adages and coarse expressions to the delight of the servants and carters, who thirstily drank his words and endeavored to "loosen his tongue" with their questions.

"And what do you think, Mr. Harry, about Reb Baruch Panther?" asks a clever and jaunty carter who is on good terms with the "Big Man." "Reb Baruch Bar-Bar-Is!"—Harry repeats the name in derogatory fashion, drawing it out in a tone of surprise—"Reb Baruch Bar-Bar-Baris?!!"—and at once he quietly continues— "Gentlemen, don't do business with Reb Baruch Panther. He really is an upper-class Jew. He is not a simple thief, but he thieves by "bookkeeping." . . . If you don't know—let me tell you. Do you remember the forest that I had in partnership with him? The "bundles" for its purchase and development I supplied, and when we came to dividing the profit—I see one Thursday at dusk a cart standing in front of my house and Reb Baruch climbs off it. I thought that he was bringing me the "bundles," and I said to myself, "You Godsend!" And then I see Reb Baruch unloading from the cart—not bundles but—account books! One account book, a second, a third—fifteen "pieces"! All of them as thick and heavy as pigs. "Reb Baruch!" I ask, "where are you taking these? What is all this for?"—"I'm carrying the bookkeeping!"—"Very good! Bring the bookkeeping." The bookkeeping is placed on the table, and I still don't get the main idea. "And where are the bundles?" I ask— "Here!" Reb Baruch points his finger to the thickest of the account books. I open it, examine it, and still I see nothing. "I see nothing, Reb Baruch, I see nothing!"—"Look there!" Reb Baruch replies and turns over the page. I look and I look and I can't see anything, there is nothing except square letters and ruled lines with "fly droppings"—"There's nothing here, Reb Baruch!" I say—"Look here!" Reb Baruch answers and turns a few pages back. Come, let me see what is lying there between the square letters—"Hannah! Give me my spectacles!" I put on my spectacles and say to Reb Baruch: "Read!" and Reb Baruch takes it and reads: "Fodder—seventeen rubles and thirty-seven and a half kopeks." Good! What's written further on? "Oats—thirty-seven rubles, seventeen kopeks and a quarter."—Very good! Further!—"Horse—so and so; cart—such and such"; and so on: "horse—fodder—fodder—horse" to the end. That was the bookkeeping; and bundles—nothing to this day!"

"And Reb Mendel, how do you regard him?" the carter asks further. "I won't say a word against Reb Mendel. Reb Mendel stays on at the study house after prayers and chews *hok*,[3] and when in the course of study he utters a syllable—his voice comes out of his yellow beard and sounds like my red cow mooing. Do you know what the *hok* is, Berele?"—Harry suddenly asks the nearest carter as an aside—"You don't know, donkey? Then ask me and I will tell you. The *hok*—is a sort of book that is found in the bag containing the prayer shawl and tefillin of upper-class Jews, and they study it after the "Aleinu" prayer—a sort of "prayer dessert." . . . Now Reb Mendel is an upper-class Jew only since yesterday or the day before. And this happened from the day he took the possessions of a wretched widow and her little orphaned children and left them destitute; and since the day he went bankrupt in Leipzig . . . he has also attached a silver crown to the top of his prayer shawl, the dog!"

---

[3]An anthology of pious writings by the sixteenth-century Kabbalist, Isaac Lurie.

"Oh, fools, fools!"—Harry used to conclude his scorn and mockery. "Do you not know that we are all flesh and not God, and that man is motivated only by the "kopek" ... and what will be there ... there in the upper world—only our Father in heaven knows. And what are we?" Harry used to hold forth with mocking sermons of this kind after the midday meal, while sitting on the stone bench in front of the gate of his yard, surrounded by carters and humble and impoverished wood merchants, among whom he would walk and converse as friend and brother, without any self-aggrandizement or snobbish ways—just like one of the gang. And they too approved of his modesty, intent on penetrating his meaning, and assuming an air of naive belief in all his tall stories about horses and *katsaps*, counts, and generals awaiting his loans, and about the robbers upon whom he inflicted broken limbs five at a time. They listened with awe and affection to his speculations about what "will be there" at the conclusion of his conversations. And once Harry had reached the theme of death, he immediately changed his tone and lightheartedness, as though contrition had entered his heart from the sin he had committed with his lips ... and with his particular humility and modesty, he proceeded to expound his views about that whole topic. In his own fashion he began to denigrate all the life of this world, which was not worth even a "rotten egg." "Death is the final end and the last game, you big fool!"— Harry would humbly conclude. "Yesterday—him, today—you, and tomorrow—me. Everyone goes to the one place and they will uncover the bottom of our shirts, naked to the neck. . . . Lie down, important sir, and don't turn on your side!" And the carters would sigh and fall silent for some considerable time.

6

Humility in general was one of Harry's qualities. He was always the first to say, "Good morning," even to a gentile in the marketplace; he was not ashamed to thrust his hand into the dirty pocket of some carter or peasant and bring out a handful of squashed tobacco leaves for a smoke; nor was he ashamed, when the opportunity arose, to engage in a trial of "strength" with one of the peasants in the marketplace and wrestle with him in front of everyone, and afterwards to repair with the vanquished to the nearby inn to drink at the bar a "victory glass" paid for by the peasant. In short, Harry is extremely modest and humble. But apart from that overall modesty, he also displays another kind of modesty, found particularly in people like him, one whose essence springs from fear and crude superstition and from nervousness about his wealth. That is what causes him, for all his trust in his strength and riches, to have the name of heaven constantly on his lips, and to make the mercy of the Holy One a partner in the work of his hands—whenever the matter touches on his money. And it is that which leads him to believe in all kinds of superstitions: wizards, Rebbes, charms, and remedies; to slaughter an owl with a gold coin and bury it under the threshold— for good luck; to watch over the polecat that lives in the basement of his house like the apple of his eye, because it preserves his luck; to whisper three times in the morning when he opens the gates of his yard his usual mantra. And it is that which causes him to open his bundles, more precious than his body, to the Rebbe of K-bi, and to slip away at the moment when they convey a "corpse" in front of him and the charity boxes start rattling. . . . Some kind of base fear and great terror comes over him, when he sees Satan dancing nearby and God's judgment stretched out at his side. Then Harry suddenly undergoes a great change, so that no one would recognize him. Harry Goat, like other men of low birth snatched by fate from the gutter and raised by good luck above their station, is sometimes terrified by the threat of some cruel and powerful force that is easily angered and could topple him suddenly from his perch and return him to the gutter from whence he came. And like a donkey climbing a ladder, he would stand and tremble, lest the rung break beneath him—and his limbs get broken. . . . And even though he had something to rely on—the well-known handshake—for all that, there was reason to be anxious . . . for even a fly can do damage and don't "haggle with God," as people say. And for that reason it was best that you should try, first and foremost, to distance yourself well out of sight of that mysterious power, so that he might not pay attention to you, and pass you by and not harm your affairs. What then? Was he likely to forget you completely?—But even then the harm would not be so great as long as there were bundles in your hand and you were in possession. . . . This device cost nothing and it was Harry's favorite. And what a sight it was to see how this great body curled up and contracted like a hedgehog whenever it happened to be in the vicinity of someone who was dangerously ill, a dying person, or

an important "corpse." Where, then, did all that solid flesh go?
Where then did "Big Man Harry" go, the hero, the self-assured, the
mocker, the swank, and the fantasist? How humble and wretched,
how soft and smooth were Harry's sayings and utterances, then,
when he was interpreting the day's events to the group of wagoners!
Harry would then speak solemnly and in low and muted tones
about all the vanity of life, which was not worth even a rotten egg;
that men were no better than animals; and of the folly of anyone
who imagines that "he is different and the verse doesn't apply to
him"; and that wealth and money are sheer vanity and even less
than sheer vanity! But while speaking he lets fall a drop of comfort
to the despairing and brokenhearted wagoners, that God, so to
speak, does not come upon His creatures with ill intent, and He, our
Father in heaven, is merciful and compassionate. And whence does
this fellow derive such words and such a style? Just as though he
were reading from the *Shevet Musar!*[4] And while he is still speaking,
the funeral passes by. The "corpse" is carried on a bier of planks
and poles fastened together for the occasion, as is fitting for an important "corpse"; the people follow after him, mourning with bent
heads; the officials shake their boxes—kish, kish—charity safe-
guards against death!—and Harry who just now had been denigrat-
ing silver and gold as the dust of the earth begins to curl up and
shrink still further, shrinking and shrinking until he—vanishes altogether . . . and at the moment when the beadle with the box passes
in front of the group of carters, who hasten to put worn-out coppers
into its slot, Harry is already lying in his cellar, or shut up in his
house, bending his ear to the sound of clinking as it recedes and di-
minishes . . . and why all this? Only to distract God's judgment
when it came near to him, as though to say: "Am I so important in
your eyes, that you should visit me and take me into account? Look,
I am nothing, O Lord of the universe, and I slink away from it all."

Since, however, negative stratagems alone are not sufficient for
rescue and protection, for there are times when Satan can find you
even in the cellar and no amount of evasions and hiding places can
avail; some positive strategy is therefore necessary and a "counter-
force," like an offering, a prayer, or an argument against that fierce
and hidden power. Apart from the charms and incantations men-

---

[4]A popular eighteenth-century treatise on ethics.

tioned above, Harry Goat realized the need to employ for all emergencies (may it never come to that!) some advocate or constant intermediary between him and the hidden power, to mollify it when angry, to appease and bribe it in times of need: in short, a reliable intermediary to undertake for him all the "business" between him and heaven so that the burden could be taken from his neck completely. And for this purpose Harry found no one better than the Rebbe of K-bi, the son of that same *Tsaddik* who had given him the handshake. No sooner did he scent the slightest whiff of danger—he would immediately harness his wagon and rush to the Rebbe, to anticipate the blow. Harry maintained an absolute and utter faith in the power of the *Tsaddikim,* without differentiating between one *Tsaddik* and the next. And it was not because of spiritual reasons or Hasidic lore, but because the *Tsaddikim* in his opinion were "craftsmen" who are always necessary, like wizards, pardon the comparison, and "if a thief is needed, take him down from the gallows," as people say. But just as you have a "craftsman" who is skilled and expert, so there is an ordinary *Tsaddik* and a master *Tsaddik.* The latter does not perform his task dishonestly; his promises are fulfilled. But in everything apart from their craft, *Tsaddikim* can be simple folk just like everyone else, and they too keep an eye cocked on "the pennies."

Harry chose the Rebbe of K-bi because of the help that he had received through the Rebbe's father's handshake, and he cherished the kindness. Apart from that the Rebbe, too, was regarded as a respectable "craftsman," not, of course, like his father, but in time of need, "when there are no fish, even a crab can be called a fish," and he would do. And even the Rebbe of K-bi's full beard must be worth something! None of the *Tsaddikim* in the region had such a beard. His beard alone was enough for him to be considered a *Tsaddik.* ... And truth to tell, Harry never stinted in rewarding the Rebbe's heavenly intervention. And the Rebbe, too, knew the nature of his beast and on each occasion exacted for himself a respectable agent's fee at whatever level he decided. In times of crisis, he would send his collectors who did the rounds of the little towns to exact from him something on account in advance. With respect to the visits of these collectors, which were always too frequent for him, Harry would boast in public and grieve and groan in secret. "Leeches!" Harry ground his teeth in mute rage whenever he saw one of the holy "messengers" approaching his house for a gift on account. And when speaking he tried to publicize the event, saying, "Let the Jews hear that the Rebbe sends to me and needs me"—and the collector was brought into the house with pomp and circumstance until the whole street was aware that "the Rebbe has sent to Harry." In this way Harry would groan and give, and the Rebbe would intervene and take. But did Harry have any option? Was he not compelled to pay the Rebbe "a proper fee," for a physician who heals for nothing is worth nothing. It was sufficient that the Rebbe saved him from any confusion over the heavenly domain, including the commandment to give charity to "leeches" (the name he gave to all beggars and persons asking for charity), and the fact that he discharged his duty with gifts to the Rebbe—that too was worth money! Moreover, "Wasn't the Rebbe also a person, and how would he live if we didn't support him?"

These latter aspects of his gifts to the Rebbe, Harry would only disclose in front of others, even though everyone knew that Harry was a "goy" in whom there was not "a single Jewish sinew," a Noahide[5] who would rather be killed than spend so much as a penny, completely devoted to his pocket, without worrying at all how other folk might live. The beggars knocking on doors on the eve of the new moon, a charity collector, and the "officiants" of the synagogue—the cantor and the beadle—would avoid his threshold with a stream of curses. And any "emissary" who trod on his porch by mistake would praise God and thank Him sincerely for allowing him to leave in one piece. And for a whole day thereafter, his ears would tingle and his face would turn crimson at the memory of those imprecations with which Harry Goat had greeted him: "O, my little Reb Tsaddik!"— Harry would greet the "emissary" at the door. "Out! Out! I have no money, I have none! It's not my custom . . . Get out, my friend!"

In dire straits, when Harry could not wriggle out of giving anything, he would send the "leeches" to his wife, Hannah, from whom the cantor and beadle would sometimes benefit, for example, on the two memorial days for her parents, about which Hannah was very punctilious, and for whom the beadle was enjoined to recall their memory and light candles, and the cantor—to study Mishnah, and recite Kaddish—for which both received five kopeks as a reward.

---

[5]A gentile.

Needless to say, Harry never advanced a noninterest loan as an act of charity. And it is no surprise, therefore, that people would complain to heaven and grumble about the ways of the Almighty, saying, "It would appear that He doesn't know what to do with His money, and that He has found no better place to invest His wealth than here: a gold ring in a pig's ear."

Harry was mortally hated by the humble, impoverished wood merchants, who flattered him to his face and cursed him heartily behind his back. "Have you seen this son of Esau, may his name and memory be blotted out, how he and his 'bastards' snatch the crust of bread from our mouths?" The less successful merchants would always complain about him. The latter nickname was appended to Harry's sons. These three sons, who help their father in the wood business by standing at the gate of his property to attract buyers, or go out to the market to purchase timber from the farmers—are worse than wild beasts! Woe to anyone who stumbles on them, and even worse for anyone they stumble on. They snatch the plums from a person's very hands, jumping in and adding two coins for the price of the farmer's merchandise after some poor Jew has labored and struggled to fix the right price—and get away scot-free; while others who have tried to interfere with them in any way that might be regarded as the slightest trespass—or even to protect their own rights—are threatened with death. Harry and his sons know of no punishment lighter than death: "If you don't get out of here, you putrid drop—you're a dead man!" "If you don't clear off, you abomination—your innards will be spilt!" Such were the threats of Harry and his sons. And if the father's strength is confined to words—the sons are of the kind that put their words into practice. And by sheer strength they go and conquer the whole market and the best of the produce, to the great vexation of the other merchants who reluctantly have to content themselves with the leftovers. And how very fortunate Harry is! All the farmers are attached to him and are like wax in his hands. Nearly all the farmers who bring timber are his good companions and on close terms with him. Even more than they respect his great strength and his powerful hand, even more than they love him for his choice opinions, for his ready tongue with all its turns of speech, and the fluent and pleasing conversation that amuses them and appeals to them in their own particular way—even more was Harry regarded, God knows why, as an upright and honest man who would not defraud or deceive anyone, although all the virtues outlined above served him, in the words of his rivals, only as a stratagem and a means "to extract the farmer's soul with a kiss."

On market day the sun is shining over the earth. All the other wood merchants have risen before dawn and sallied out to the day's work like lions. Even before daybreak, they have girded their loins and walked out of town a distance of four miles to the old inn and beyond to anticipate the tardy farmers who had delayed coming to the wood market the previous night. Perhaps God would have mercy and provide a bargain for them, favoring them with a good deal in honor of the Sabbath. But, alas, even the farmer in this generation has become smart, because of our many sins, and under no circumstances is he willing to listen and make a bargain on the high road. His heart is drawn to the market. "Mr. Harry is there," a farmer recalls and hurries along without paying heed to the capers of this "Mendel" or "Yankel" leaping up and down before him. "Wait, wait just one minute, Ivan!" Yankel shouts at Ivan's cart as it proceeds forward, grabbing hold of it and dancing in front of it like a dog, clinking coins in front of him and thrusting them toward his bosom as the farmer draws near the inn, which is redolent with the odor of spirits to whet his appetite. . . . "You astound me, Ivan! You're a clever one, Ivan! Don't you recognize me, Ivan? Do it for our old friendship, Ivan! Remember your Creator, Ivan. . . . "—In vain! In vain!—Ivan turns his face and shoulder coldly to Yankel, communes with himself for a while, as though wishing to say something, but regretting it at once, angrily waves his whip over his weary horses and shouts, "Gee-up!"

At that very hour Harry Goat is making his way round the area of the big wood market, pushing himself between the tight carts and wagons all loaded with timber, inquiring as a close friend about the health of the old farmers next to their wagons, good-heartedly playing and joking with their young ones, scratching the ear of one and flicking the nose of another, or amusing them with some coarse jest, and meanwhile feeling the sack lying on one cart and the basket on another, patting the belly of one horse and examining the teeth of another—as though timber and forest produce were the furthest things from his mind, and he had only come to ask about their health and chat with them a little for their amusement. Meanwhile a group of peasants gathers round him, and there are more inquiries about health, and detailed questions about whether Petra's cow has calved yet and whether Mitra's mare has had a foal (Harry was an expert in the overall affairs of many farmers), conversations about the snows of yesteryear and about the coming fair, and meanwhile he puts his hand into the dirty pouch of some farmer and takes out fragments of tobacco and a piece of paper, rolls them into a cigarette, applies a light, and smokes them; not that Harry enjoys any such smoking: but in order to endear himself to them further by his modesty and bring their minds into accord with his own about the deep affection with which he regards them. . . . And meanwhile the fountain of Harry's conversation keeps increasing, and his tongue wags more and more. His torrent of words has already reached the stage of anecdotes concerning Jewish customs, which he loves to expound and use for the amusement and satisfaction of the farmers in the market. As usual, he describes and demonstrates for them in detail all the customs of the Passover, the order of service for the Day of Atonement, and the customs of the other festivals—whatever serves to astonish the farmers and arouse their laughter. In particular he emphasizes all the customs that involve a Jew in expense, going into great detail about the preparations for the Passover, putting money in the charity boxes on the evening of the Day of Atonement, and the like, to let them know how difficult life and its traditions are for a Jew, who is burdened with additional expenses and a great variety of needs. "That's how it is, that's it, kind sirs," Harry used to conclude these conversations. "Our situation is not like yours. We are overwhelmed by commandments; our needs are greater than yours." With conversations of such kind Harry entices the farmers' hearts, entices and entices—until he entices them, their wagons, and their loads of wood into his yard. The actual purchase is always concluded with one remark. He always targets the right moment in the conversation, which revolves from one topic to the next—and some ten wagons piled high with forest produce suddenly disappear from the street with the sound of creaks and groans to be unloaded in Mr. Harry's yard under the strict supervision of one of his sons.

7

Since there is no rule without exception, fortune did not always allow Harry to leave the street in peace. There were times when the

street caused him great trouble and sorrow and left him with worry
and stress for many a day. A particularly unsavory example of the
sort occurred when he happened to be bargaining against Alter
Cockerel. . . . But here I must pause to inform you about the character of this Alter Cockerel.

In standing, Alter was a middle-ranking "householder" among
the middle-ranking wood merchants. Physically he was a small man,
thin and wizened (for that reason he was called "Cockerel"), with a
scowling face, a pointed nose, and bleary eyes flecked with numerous blue veins. By temperament—he was an angry man, despised
and without respect, both choleric and melancholic at once, hating
everyone and being equally hated by everyone. Even when he was
silent, his entire little "being" was like a bottle of boiling filth, boiling and boiling away . . . and when he opened his mouth—it was
only to curse and malign the whole world; while doing so he would
raise his little fist in great anger and foam at the mouth—once again
against all the world. . . . This little creature was the husband of an
Amazonian woman, strong and tall, a valiant woman famous for
her heavy fist descending on her husband's skull, and for her pickled
cucumbers of wide renown. In winter days, she would go out wearing coarse yellow gum boots, which served only to increase her
stature and masculinity. The splendid pair served as father and
mother to five large sons, strong as cedars, who had inherited from
their little father his anger and bad blood, and from their big
mother their stature, sheer size, and strong hands. Confident in the
offspring of his loins and his marriage partner "Baba" (such was her
name), the little flea Alter Cockerel was in no way prepared to stand
in awe of Big Harry, Harry Goat. The encounter of two such creatures was impressive, and here is a small instance of such a meeting:

Harry sees Alter standing in the market bargaining over wood beside the cart of a farmer who was one of Harry's closest cronies.
This impertinence was not to Harry's taste. "What's this? The
farmer—was his, and the farmer's wood—was certainly his!—and
all of a sudden this Cockerel dances into the middle and separates
them. . . . Time to shoo him away." . . . "Kish—kish—kish!" Harry
hisses at Alter from behind, as though shooing away a cockerel,
with the intention of riling him by alluding to his nickname.

The blue veins flecking Alter's face and nose begin to tremble; the
poison in them boils, quivers, dissolves, and ascends into his bleary
eyes, turning them red. . . . Nevertheless, he hesitates a little at boil-

ing point, inclining his little head toward Harry and shaking it from side to side, looking him up and down from head to foot with an angry glance and a mean expression. "Good morning, Mitra!" Harry turns to the farmer, as though unaware of Alter's presence and not admitting his existence at all. "What's happened to you, Mitra? Have you brought grain for the market without telling me? I'm surprised! Don't you know that cockerels peck and scratch on the rubbish heaps in my yard, too, thank heaven, and they need grain, those cockerels. But what do I see here? My eye has deceived me! Not grain—but planks in your cart and what have cockerels got to do with planks? Kish—kish—kish!!"

That was the last straw. The point of Alter's nose grows longer and sharper, his eyelids narrow, as though to suck the depths of his anger and to concentrate his wrathful villainous eyes on one focus, to hurl poison at Harry and burn him up on the spot. . . . "Goat! The devil take your father's father!"—The Cockerel wanted to screech bitterly—except that he suddenly felt chastened, remembering the danger bound up with such a cry with not one of his offspring in the vicinity to stand in front of the Goat at the right moment. . . . This bitter thought descended like a stream of cold water onto his boiling anger to quiet it. But so as not to stand with folded arms in the presence of his enemy, Alter suddenly cries out bitterly, "Harry! Harry!! Harry!!!"

In this triple cry torn from the bottom of his raging and fearful heart and uttered through clenched teeth, Alter combined the thousands of curses and myriads of insults that crowded on the tip of his tongue and struggled for expression—until they were crushed between his grinding teeth. But Harry went on stirring him up, continuing in his previous style: "I tell you plainly, Mitra, it was foolish of you to bring logs instead of millet to a place where cockerels are to be found, but since you have brought logs—take them to Harry's yard, and you can be sure that he will pay you a proper price; after all, I think you have known Harry not just since yesterday, is that not so, Mitra? What are you waiting for? Come along!—and leave the matter of cockerels to me—I will attend to them." . . .

Alter lifted up his eyes—from whence cometh help? He sees his sons far, far away. There at the other end, they're dancing round other peasants and their carts. The situation is very grave!—Help is far away, and danger close at hand.

For his part, the farmer is in no rush or hurry to move his cart. He is well versed in such miracles and foresees the end from the beginning. Every cart that is lucky enough to become a bone of contention between two merchants will in the end receive twice the price. In such a case, there is no reward for the overly hasty; and therefore he very calmly puts his hand into his trouser pocket, takes out a wad of tobacco and a pipe, and begins to prepare himself for a smoke.

But Alter regards this delay as a good augury and comforts himself that the farmer would not dare to cross him after he had labored so hard on this deal; and so he, too, takes money from his pocket to meet the price they had finally agreed upon before the Goat butted in, pushing the money in front of the farmer, who is ostentatiously busy with his pipe, and saying, "Here you are Mitra, as you wish, even though the merchandise is not worth it—only so that I may witness my enemy's discomfort—and my effort is not in vain." "And how much are you giving there, Mr. Alter?" the farmer asks all innocently, while lighting his pipe. "How much? Twelve rubles and three guilders? But did I not say, fifteen and a half?" "That was at the beginning, Mitra, that was at the beginning. . . . But afterwards you agreed to twelve and three." Alter tries to stir Mitra's memory, which has suddenly succumbed to forgetfulness, and raised the price by three rubles. "No! Mr. Alter, that wasn't it, but such and such." . . . And the farmer is about to return to the starting point and begin it all anew. But Harry, who had grown impatient with their chatter, jumps forward, takes the whip from Mitra with his left hand, and seizes the horses' reins with his right, and says: "Do I have to stand all day listening to your crowing?—Gee-up!" And with that he whistles and pulls the horses' reins, and the horses dig their hooves into the ground and get ready to move. . . . "No!" Alter cries, clutching the horses' reins to stop them. "You won't move from here, Goat!" "I will move, Cockerel, I will move. . . . Gee-up!" "Stop!" "Kish—kish—kish, Cockerel!" "May the charity boxes rattle kish—kish over your bier! May the cockerels pick over your grave, may the . . . " "Move away, if you don't want yourself killed! Here's my Shefil coming. Gee-up!" "Goat! Goat! Goat!"—Alter shrieks with all his might, holding back the horses—"Esau, Ham, Bastard! Let me also earn a crust of bread!"

But at that moment a mighty blow descends on Alter's little head. This blow came from the fist of Shefil, who had hurried along at the

cry of "Goat," thrusting his way between the carts and jumping behind Alter. . . . Immediately after that, he sprang on the farmer's
cart, took the reins from his father's hand, pulling and shouting:
"Gee-up, gee-up!"

Alter, however, whose mind was reeling from the force of the
blow, did not let go of the horses' reins but was dragged after them,
shouting with all his might: "Goat, Goat, help! Save me!" And a
few moments later all his five sons, who had come running in response to his cry, stood by him—and the wagon was stopped for a
second time.

The next moment Harry's two remaining sons came to his aid to
strengthen his hands in battle. The battle lines were drawn, and they
stood like two groups of goats, with one side pulling the horses forward, and the other holding them back.

A few moments more—and warfare broke out; and very soon, it
reached a climax. The four staves, stuck into the four corners of the
cart—to secure the planks—were pulled out, to be used by the as-
sailants as truncheons, and the planks fell out and were scattered all
over the ground.

The tactics were very simple. The fighters divided into three
groups. The first—the sons—concentrated on cracking skulls with
their truncheons; the second—the fathers—limited their activity to
beard pulling and face smacking; while the third group—the two
mothers, Hanna and Baba, who had come running to the fray with
their infants—expended their energies on trivialities and nonsense in
the manner of women, such as snatching ornaments, pulling hair,
scratching faces, and trifles of such sorts.

And round all this strife and confusion the little boys and girls
from both sides stood watching in a circle, howling, wailing, and
wringing their hands.

Meanwhile Mitra, unmoved, unharnessed his horses for the time
being and hung a basket of fodder on the cart's peg, coolly and
calmly intending to return to the matter of his pipe, with which he
had begun, and watching the struggling Jews at the same time; but
because the pipe had gone out in the meantime and the stem was
jammed, he took it from his mouth and turned it upside down to
empty the ash into the palm of his hand, preparing himself to fill it a
second time and await the outcome patiently.

But at that moment a policeman came hurrying along. . . . The
sight of a new face inflamed passions again, and warfare resumed in

a completely different manner. All the contestants suddenly joined in one solid mass, like a cluster of worms twisting and struggling together. There was no clear sound, but confusion and panic, from which emerged heads shamelessly uncovered, scarlet faces streaked with blood, matted hair standing on end, forelocks grasped in hands, fists rising and falling, a large disheveled woman swaying this way and that—and the whole moving, writhing, struggling, and jostling together. . . . The policeman was so confused at the sight of this complex and intertwined dance—that he produced his whistle and proceeded to blow it with all his might . . .

The battle raged on that occasion. Finally an officer and policemen and two physicians arrived to bandage the wounds of the victims, and statements were written down and witnesses produced. And the battle concluded in proper fashion—but the people did not disperse to their tents. They remained to celebrate the victory with great splendor. And the victory was—Harry's! The disputed planks, which were loaded on the wagon a second time, after having been scattered—were finally sold to Harry Goat at twice the price; and to the accompaniment of a crowd of carters and shouts of hurray, the wagon was brought to the gates of his yard—to the chagrin of Alter Cockerel and his sons. Harry felt extremely honored on that occasion! Such moments were the most precious in his life.

The victory also lent luster to the spoils that had been rescued with such jeopardy to life. Almost all the carters undertook the unloading and stacking of the planks with great enthusiasm, and Harry allocated an important and prominent place in his yard for them, instead of piling them on the other planks and beams stacked up in disorder throughout his yard.

8

Harry's wood yard, his pride and joy, was supervised by his three sons: Shefil, Zelig, and Moshe, in this order: Shefil, a powerful, silent young man with his father's frame, was Harry's right-hand man in conquering the market, and in time of need—his was the first fist to strike. Zelig, who combined something of his mother's earthiness and Harry's humility, calm and withdrawn by nature—looked after the internal affairs of the wood yard, the unloading and stacking of planks; and last but not least—Moshe, who imitated in every respect the young aristocrat Lampidretzky, who had taken a loan from Harry. He was entrusted with the task of talking to the "squires" who came to Harry's yard to buy on credit. These were Harry's favorite customers because they were not inclined to be penny-pinching or to drive a hard bargain. What did it matter to them? After all, they were buying on credit. Moreover—there was always the hint of a loan; for the present the squire would give a promissory note, and buying on credit could be regarded as a loan. One squire taking a loan was far better than ten "*katsaps*." The fate of these squires was placed in the lap of Moshe, the youngest son. It was not for nothing that he had learned to speak Polish and play the flute well. His nose supported blue spectacles, and his mustache was shaped in the form of two leeches raising their tails and facing each other—exactly like the son of the noble Lampidretzky. All these accomplishments, according to Harry, bespoke a great future, for which reason he called him "Candidate." "My Candidate"—Harry would say when speaking of Moshe—"had an interview yesterday with the Governor and said to him . . ." or: "My Candidate reproved the Chief of Police last night in the "treater"[6] for not paying attention"; . . . "My Candidate is invited this evening to General Timofeioff's party." . . . And that was Harry's term. But Hannah did not agree with the title "Candidate" that Harry used, but preferred another title to define Moshe's nobility. "My Moshe," Hannah would say, "is fashioned from quite different material and does not resemble any of us in any way. My Moshe is like the son of a perfect 'aristocrat' and all the ladies are enthralled by him" . . . "My Moshe is an *Agent!!*"

Agent—in her opinion this was the highest possible level of nobility. "Is so-and-so an Agent?" she would scornfully remark, whenever she saw anyone preening in clothes that she did not consider to be suitable, or sporting blue spectacles—when his nose was not properly shaped for them. With regard to her two sons, Zelig and Shefil, she was not overlavish with her praise and defined their quality briefly, "Shefil—he is Harry down to a 't'; and Zelig—he is a decent soul, just like his mother."

And between these three the work of the wood yard was divided to the last detail.

Apart from the task of "talking to the squires," which was left solely to the "Candidate," or the "Agent," Harry entrusted another

---

[6]Mispronunciation of theater.

elevated task to his son: namely, the craft of writing. Moshe was the sole exponent of this great art in all his father's household. Whenever the Almighty burdened Harry with the task of signing any letter or document—the matter was entrusted to Moshe, and he fulfilled his father's requests in perfect fashion under the control and supervision of his father.

"Come here please, come here, my Candidate!" Harry would call to Moshe while fixing his spectacles on his nose, and spreading the document that was waiting for signature on the table. "Come here please and show me your great skill. Please sit here and sign for me, as I tell you."

Moshe sits at the table, takes the pen, begins to flourish it rapidly as a skilled scribe, and awaits Harry's command.

"Now write carefully, as I tell you. Stop! I will dictate it to you." And Harry dictates. "First of all, put down a capital *H!*"—And the "*H*" safely finds its place. "Now write an *a.*"—And an "*a*" is added. Harry always pronounces the "*r*" emphatically and properly rolled, and he likes the writing to reflect the dictation—and the trilled "*rr*" is safely installed.

"Now dip your pen a second time, and throw in a little *y!*"—and the "*y*" is thrown in. "Now read me what you have written!" Harry commands. The name is read out loud and clear: "Harry!"

Beyond this the Candidate's skill was not put to use: the art of writing was only created for signature. Harry readily admits the benefit of signature. Signature is something for which there is always a need, for without signature—there is no loan document and no lender, no interest and no "*katsap*s," and no "squires," and the whole world reverts to chaos—and then where would Harry be? . . . Indeed, is not signature a wonderful invention? "Take, for example, Lampidretzky! That gentleman is a man of substance, tall and sturdy, with a belly and a mustache! Moreover, he is very well connected, the scion of a long line of aristocrats, and obviously he has plenty of "honor"—and yet, great gentleman as he is, when he comes to me to take a single loan, I take a little piece of paper on top of which is written one short line: 'Loan agreement for one thousand rubles: R 1,000,' and say to him: 'My noble sir! Please put your great dignity and honor to the trouble of signing, with all respect, here below, at the edge of this piece of paper lying in front of you!' And the honorable and awesome gentleman—comes and signs! And from that moment he is completely mine and in my hand. . . . I take the piece of paper on which Squire Lampidretzky's name lies, and I fold it and double it up, and crease it and screw it into my hand like one squeezes soft wax. . . . These hard, intimidating gentlemen—once they have put their signatures on the paper, become soft and pliable as wax. . . . Even the 'honor' changes completely—you can press and squeeze it as much as you like . . . and afterwards I lower this fine gentleman Lampidretzky into my trouser pocket to rest in one bundle with others of his ilk—and there rest in peace! . . . From that time on, Squire Lampidretzky lies in the chest all folded and doubled up like a baby in its mother's womb—from that moment the top line of the piece of paper begins to grow and grow, while Mr. Lampidretzky on the bottom line shrinks and shrinks . . . and what is the cause of all this?—'The signature!'"—Thus Harry would muse to himself with much pleasure and satisfaction, imagining the great Lampidretzky caught in the palm of his hand like a bird, while he toys with him. . . .

As for Harry's wood yard—the business has no need for writing. Harry doesn't believe in account books. What can't be seen—won't be discovered in account books. The best kind of bookkeeping—is in his pocket. Indeed, it is remarkable why people in this world should waste their time keeping accounts, since Harry's wood yard is run in the best possible way without account books, and nothing is lacking, thank heaven.

9

Truth to tell, there were things to be seen in Harry's yard that could not be found in other yards. Harry, who derived a good livelihood from his other properties and his loans—was not a wood merchant for mere pennies, but a trader by natural inclination, trade for its own sake. After horses, his main love was dealing in timber, in which he was very skilled and in which he found particular pleasure, like a "lover of antiques," for example, who understands the value of an old master or any other unusual work of art. Thus Harry was especially fond of all kinds of timbers whose use was uncommon, which were needed only by specialists. Harry made every effort to enrich his yard with such items until he raised it to the level of a veritable museum of the arts and crafts of timber. Even in its external appearance and in its disorder, the yard resembled antique shops in the Jewish quarter. Long thick beams of more than twenty feet, which had once been the pride of the forest, were piled up and stacked on top of each other in strange confusion, pressing beneath them old oaks that had already turned black from the heat and rain of many seasons of summer and winter. And these old oaks pressed and squeezed in their turn strange planks and ancient beams for which there was never any need, which could serve only as ships' masts. Below them . . . but what was below them nobody could know, because everything below was already pressed and squeezed into the ground from the weight of the load on top of them. Even Harry himself had forgotten what had been lying there originally and been swallowed into the ground. Near these great giants was the place of the "frenchies"—that was Harry's name for the long thin planks with wispy ends, which he did not much like—and on top of them broad planks of more than a foot in width had taken up position, and on top of them all were scattered roof tiles made in the old fashion, which had already lost all hope of ever being used on a roof. . . . Next to them lay heaps upon heaps of all kinds of thin timbers, cuttings, ribs, small boards, pieces of carts, and wheels . . . all piled up in complete disorder, no two bits alike, new and old, black and white, short and long, thick and thin mixed up together, pushed and squeezed to the last inch. All these kinds of merchandise, although they were no longer of any use to carpenters or builders— nevertheless went on deteriorating of their own accord, even without customers. . . . The earth swallowed up a third of them, a third of them were stolen by neighbors for firewood, and a third were plundered by the peasants unloading timber in his yard and filling up the diminished loads so that they would always be full. . . . This plunder was taken with the excuse that they needed it to repair their wagons, which had broken down on the way, and Harry did not refuse them. Harry despised such pettiness. One "squire"—could repay him sevenfold, and he would pay for what was stolen, swallowed, and plundered four or five times over. For the most part Harry's reckoning was not wrong. Anyone who needed uncommon timber, after visiting all the yards without success, was finally compelled to fall into Harry's hands. He sensed what was required and what kind of bird his "Father in heaven" had sent his way—and he would ensnare his quarry skillfully.

But just as the proverb says, "All cobblers go barefoot"—Harry saw no need in the early years of his prosperity to change his old dwelling, a lowly, miserable ruin that he had purchased some years ago together with some land for almost nothing, and build himself a pleasant dwelling and acquire good furniture, as people do. This old hovel had two dark narrow rooms and a very big kitchen. But Hannah, in whom Harry had already recognized signs of a kind of desire for importance and the name of "Lady," who could see no merit in this ruin with its roof sagging in the middle like a horse's back, had already tried more than once to drop hints to her husband about the need to have a proper house like everyone else, and to rid her of the rickety ruin of which she was sick and tired—but Harry paid no heed to this strange desire; not, God forbid, because of miserliness or ill will; but because it was extremely difficult for him to discard his attitudes and change his status. He was very, very careful about his luck. Deep down he nursed the illusion that he must remain the same Harry that he was when he struck it lucky. That Harry would succeed, and any other Harry would not succeed; any slight change would cause harm and a change of luck. In vain Hannah argued that the Holy One, Blessed be He, would not bring misfortune on her account, since good luck had favored him only because of her; and since she was advocating this, it must certainly be good advice, and the Holy One, Blessed be He, would agree with her—but Harry was like flint and would not change his mind! Hannah had almost despaired of any hope of ever reaching the standing of a "Lady," and she was already beginning to complain about her bad luck: "Oh! what good was all this wealth—if she was still regarded as a servant girl in the street and in the women's gallery in the Synagogue. Oh! how fed up she was with her lowly position among the ladies! And what shame and degradation she felt whenever a pair of ladies collecting charity came to her "tomb" (namely her dwelling). Alas! better for her to be swallowed in the ground than that two such ladies should behold her wretchedness. A dark, narrow grave, poor rickety furniture—just like a pauper. While Harry—two hundred and fifty plagues in his belly, Lord of the Universe!—would sit there with the carters without a care in the world." . . . Thus Hannah grieved in bitterness and refused to be comforted. These complaints had become ever more bitter since she began to receive furtive visits from certain women with whom Hannah would whisper in a corner secretly and cautiously. These women were traders who brought under their aprons "real bargains"—jewelry and remnants of cloth—to women who were on bad terms with their husbands and had stashed away

their own moneys. Hannah, too, did business with them. She had already accumulated in the recesses of her wardrobe many precious
jewels stored in two slippers together with her hidden moneys; and
only the lack of a new house and nice furniture prevented her from
being a Lady to the Manor born. But on occasion, time will succeed
where common sense fails, and what Hannah was unable to achieve
by persuasion was granted her by a single chance event—and this is
the way it happened:

A magician once came Harry's way: a circus owner or tightrope
walker, a climber of poles fifty feet high—in short, one of those
"birds" that Harry used to wait for. . . . This circus artist needed an
unusually tall pole for his tricks and stunts, and such a pole could
only be found in Harry's wood yard, and the man bought it at the
asking price. Now since this pole lay peacefully among the lower
strata, half buried in the earth beneath a multitude of piles of other
poles—Harry was forced to hire workers to clear away the top
strata and descend into the depths to dig the pole out. And while
they were digging—whole treasuries of forest produce were discovered in the earth—a complete "wood yard" buried in the ground
nine feet deep! This "Pompeii," which Harry found in the depths so
suddenly and unexpectedly, presented him with a quandary: where
could he possibly put all this wood? And here an idea occurred to
him. Perhaps it might be well to accept Hannah's advice, with which
she had been tempting him so long, and build a new house in place
of the old one, which was gradually collapsing, and show all those
"lepers" that Harry, too, thank God, possessed a pleasant, spacious
dwelling. In truth he had refrained thus far from building a new
house not out of meanness or stinginess but because of his fear of
changing his situation, lest his luck might change; now this sudden
discovery, which the Holy One, Blessed be He, had afforded him,
must certainly be a sign from heaven that this would be permitted
him without harming his luck, God forbid.

So Harry ordered all the sunken, swallowed-up graves to be
opened, and to wake the ancient, encrusted sleepers from their rest,
and request them, with all due respect to their antiquity, to return to
the light of day. Whoever has never seen giant beams and mighty
joists rising from the belly of the earth has never really witnessed
broken pride, a slighted lineage, and the glory of old age trodden
underfoot. . . . Great carcasses lay on the ground stretched out,
heavy, moist, and blackened, with gaping hollows where ants and

worms had nested and decay had consumed them from within. The smell of the grave wafted afar. . . . Yet in their day they had been the pride of the forest! . . .

These giants, stripped of their glorious lineage beneath the ax, were sawn into planks and boards of all sizes and brought to rest in peace within the walls of the house that Harry had decided to build. Watching the dismemberment and stripping of these giants, Harry remembered the good old days and all the delights of former times before the earth began to swarm with these new "little creatures," who amounted to no more than "pe-pu-pa." He remembered with nostalgia and related to the young carters the deeds of their fathers in the previous generation, how they, and only they, really understood the art of eating: how to eat, how much to eat, and what to eat. Only they properly "understood how to get the best out of dishes." Harry recalled "the great cheese pancakes that were brought in deep earthenware bowls onto the tables of our fathers, each pancake as big as a loaf; and these gigantic pancakes were encrusted in pockets of pastry filled with cheese, half a liter of cheese to each pancake; and they were brought to the table floating in piping hot butter and croaking like frogs. And the pies that were called *trembla* in Russian and were shaped like three-cornered bags, filled with cracklings and onions? And the roast geese? And the gizzards? And the strong brandy, 'five star,' which warms you from head to foot? And the pickled cucumbers?—Oh, Oh! Those were the days! This generation has never tasted real food and drink." Whereas he, Harry, is still alive by virtue of the food he had eaten in those days . . .

Not long afterwards . . . And "all those lepers" both great and small looked longingly at what Harry took delight in showing: one corner of a long house jauntily jutting toward the street and standing proudly at an angle in a fenced courtyard, a sight for sore eyes, with a little porch over its entrance.

Needless to say, the house could not be erected without the help of the Rebbe. Before the building was finished, Harry went to the Rebbe to get his blessing and his amulets. Nor did the Rebbe withhold his favor from him, but presented them to him generously: four old worn-out coins to bury in the earth at the four corners of the house, 138[7] iron needles to be placed beneath the lintels, and

---

[7]Corresponding to the Kabbalistic notion of 138 "doors of wisdom."

charms and amulets to be fixed over the beams of the entrances and
in the corners of the house. Laden with all these valuables, Harry returned home in excellent spirits and decided to have a "housewarming" and invite all the neighbors . . . including the dignitaries and
the big shots; all this at the insistence of Hannah, his wife.

10

On that same Sabbath of the housewarming, Harry and his wife
welcomed into their new home all the residents of the neighborhood, who did not spurn his invitation and came together with their
wives and children and infants cluttering round their feet—with the
sole object of eating him out of house and home!

Harry felt greatly honored on that Sabbath! Simply everyone witnessed his great wealth and the might of his bundles. First he explained to his guests that his house was not built of "frenchies" and
thin rods like the houses, for example, of those dignitaries, which
perch miraculously "on chickens' feet"—but of firm solid oak,
which would last a long time. "Harry—you all know Harry—
doesn't go in for toys." Next he led them through all the rooms and
showed them his new furniture, praising it in passing: "Have you
ever seen chairs like these? There are a dozen less one. They used to
stand in the drawing room of Count Petinkewicz. One day a large,
fat general came to his home and sat on one of them and it broke
under him. Since he could not find a carpenter or joiner who knew
how to turn out a chair in the same pattern to make up the set, the
Count proceeded to sell them to me for next to nothing—130
rubles." In similar style he lavished praise on all the other furniture.
He was particularly proud of two large antique mirrors in gilt
frames dating back to Methuselah, which he claimed had hung sixty
years ago in the cabinet room of a minister, or a kind of minister,
and had ended up in the town almost miraculously. The guests tried
looking into the mirrors to determine their quality and suddenly
found that their shapes in the mirrors had undergone a strange dis-
tortion, as though they were seized by convulsions. . . . Similarly,
praises were lavished upon a thronelike chair and a worn-out
couch, neither of which was sound of limb, and Harry had placed
them prominently because of their importance and pedigree. And
after he had finished praising all these possessions, Harry returned

in good spirits—like a man who has performed his duty—to the dining room, and besought the guests to enjoy all the good things laid out for them on the table.

Nor did the good guests refuse on this occasion. They fell upon the "feast" laid out before them, grabbing, chewing, grinding, and eating hungrily, as well as putting something in the pockets of the children with them; and all to fulfill the commandment to consume the last crumb. Harry, meanwhile, affected not to see or understand; indeed, he became so confused at the sight of all those chewing mouths, rotating tongues, and grinding and cracking teeth, and was so bewildered by the shouts of *"Le-ḥayim"* surrounding him on every side, that when Reb Aaron, the oldest and most senior of the big shots, took his hand to congratulate him—Harry suddenly took hold of his beard, with the intention of kissing him as he would the carters, and Reb Aaron escaped only with great difficulty.

As for Hannah—if you missed seeing Hannah in her finery on that Sabbath, you never in your life saw a real lady. All the precious jewels and finery that had lain in darkness for so long, hoarded and stored away in a stocking in the depths of her wardrobe, now earned the right to rise from the depths to be hung on Hannah's body and gleam to the delight of every eye. She towered incongruously over the invited male and female guests, striving to display her adorned limbs to everyone, as if to say: "Come and have a good look, important ladies! Here are my ears on which two glittering earrings hang like two large peas . . . but do you think that is all? Have another look and get an eyeful! Here's a big thick gold chain, clinking and flashing from my neck to my bosom; gold bracelets on my hands and rings on my fingers—and here are my two hands, spread out in front of you. Come and examine them"—thus proclaimed Hannah's very being. All this, indeed, did appear a little strange and surprising, and she too appeared in her own eyes strange and unfamiliar, like an unschooled lady. But no matter— here she was completely covered with gold, shining and glittering . . . and even her face and eyes were unusually silvery and golden, and her bovine expression was hidden for a moment beneath this semblance of importance. Her double chin was rounded and swollen like half an apple, and her cheeks were fiery red like a sliced watermelon, or as if they had just suffered a couple of slaps from Harry's hand. . . . Even the high wig, plaited like a Purim loaf, encircling her head, added a measure of charm—all of her declaring that henceforth she was a lady! And she almost succeeded in attracting the glances of a few ladies, glances full of stinging fury, envy, and scorn, which were quickly transformed into winks and malicious whispers from one woman to the next; but the demands of hospitality and the preparations sent her to the kitchen from time to time and brought her from one room to another.

Then came the turn of the pastries to appear on the table. Hannah had made use of all her culinary skills (she was a butcher's daughter) to provide the "spread" for the housewarming with the best of Sabbath delicacies. To this end she had prepared three kinds of pastries, of which the finest was the "stomach pie," which most women never learned to make properly, because it can go badly wrong . . . but Harry had encouraged her to do it on the Sabbath eve, saying: "Let them eat—and may their gall burst." . . . But the angel appointed over the Sabbath cholent betrayed them on this occasion in a mean and ugly way and quite uncharacteristically: the important pie, the queen of pies, because of insufficient heat in the oven, did not settle properly, and no sweet savor accompanied it when it was put on the table. . . . Some of the guests who had come to settle old scores found an excellent pretext here, and they suddenly began fidgeting and screwing up their noses as a hint to the wise. . . . But the more sophisticated among them turned their eyes to the senior dignitary who was sitting in the place of honor, to see the reaction of his nose.

The senior dignitary lowered his nose right down to the pie; he turned his nose to one side—and sniffed with his right nostril, and then he turned it to the other side—and sniffed with his left nostril, and without further ado he returned the piece with the fork stuck in it to its place, closed his eyes, quietly whispered the final grace and rose from the table in order to take leave of his host and return to his house with the full dignity and status of "a big shot." But because he saw Hannah preparing herself to implore him to taste the pie, on which she had labored only for "his sake"—he hastened to shake Harry's hand peremptorily as he mumbled the usual congratulations, and while so doing, escaped from the house. All the remaining important guests took their cue from him and left in haste, as though fleeing from a revolution—to the embarrassment of the stomach pie, the queen of pies, which was left standing on the table like a wretched orphan, causing great distress to Hannah and secret satisfaction to Harry.

As for the carters—Hannah had allocated a section and a table just for them, and laid before them their own "spread": a flask of watered-down brandy, little honey cakes, and three salt-herrings prepared in oil and vinegar. Of the other delicacies and dainties that came to the main table, she gave them nothing. This angered them to the point of fury, and they cursed her through clenched teeth. And in order to avenge their besmirched honor—carters very easily take umbrage when they are invited to a festivity—they vented their wrath on the brandy, finishing off the flask entirely, and went home in high dudgeon with suppressed hatred in their hearts, without taking leave. . . .

"Thank God that's over!" Harry said, sitting at the table after the flight of the important guests. "Did you see, Hannah, how those gluttons and drunkards fell like locusts on everything put in front of them, and polished it off without leaving a crumb? They even stuffed their pockets! It's a miracle that the stomach pie managed to escape!" And Harry put into his mouth some remnants of the radish and onion mix. "I am sorry about it," Hannah replied. "But did you notice, Harry, that Sprinza herself spoke to me in a friendly fashion and also . . . ?" "Tut! Women's business," Harry interrupted her. "But why do you say that you are sorry? What is there to be sorry about!—Bring me the liver and onions!" Hannah served Harry with chopped liver and onions.

"For my part," Harry continued, as he filled his mouth, "I would rather have the carters than these fine fellows: they at least are grateful for the honor that you do them, while these fine folk are only clowns who come to see what's lacking in the house and afterwards to make a song about it. Today they stuff their bellies with dainties, and tomorrow they make you into a laughingstock. I hope I am mistaken—Hannah, give me the egg and onion!" . . . In this fashion Harry and his wife exchanged views during the Sabbath midday meal. And it was clear that both were well satisfied, and that all they were saying was only good-natured banter after their fashion, the sort of conversation that takes place at the Sabbath meal over a full glass and a well-cooked cholent consumed heartily and with satisfaction.

11

And it was evening and it was morning—Sunday. And the world went on as usual. Hannah's hope that by virtue of the housewarm-

ing and her pies, she might rise a little from her lowly status in the
eyes of the ladies was not realized, nor was Harry's wish that the
galls of all his enemies should burst from envy. And by the following
day, not a single gall had burst, and apart from two or three stom-
achs that required castor oil, no unfortunate event occurred, God
forbid, because of Harry's Kiddush. Instead, his prophecy about
mockery that he had voiced at the Sabbath meal came true. From
first thing on Sunday morning, Harry's Kiddush and his pies became
material for exposition. And when the big shots gathered for morning prayer at the Synagogue, the previous day's Kiddush was immediately put on the agenda, and all the upper-class wags (and which
of the upper class in that street did not attempt to be a wag?) tried
to direct arrows of scorn and witticism, and heap mountains of
mockery on every single aspect of the Kiddush. And of course the
poor old stomach pie was given a complete chapter and attracted its
own particular mockery, with the majority of the sharpest and most
pointed witticisms falling to its lot. And the old gentleman expounded in detail and with great importance how the "pig"—
Harry—actually dared to lower his snout right opposite his own
face, to kiss him, and how he had managed to evade him. And the
middling rich, grubbing round the big shot, added each in turn a
spicy anecdote from their own personal observations, and the
ridicule rolled forth as sharp and pointed as need be to the satisfaction of the big shot and the amusement of all the middling ones.

As that was the case—Harry no longer had any need for many
rooms without any particular purpose—at noon on Sunday, the day
after the housewarming, he closed up most of the rooms of his
house and confined his dwelling to four. The closed-up rooms were
only opened on special occasions: when the Rebbe of K-bi came, or
when any prospective in-law arrived, to consider one of Harry's
sons as a possible bridegroom.

And as that was the case—there was clearly no need for Hannah
to put to use all the silverware she had bought to adorn the table
and the household, for all these things do not serve everyday needs,
but are only for show and ornament—at noon on Sunday, following
the Sabbath, Hannah hid away in a chest all the silver knives, forks,
and spoons, which she had rattled so loudly on the previous day in
front of the guests. These precious items would remain in a cupboard until the wedding of one of her sons, when their turn would
come to be revealed a second time and be jingled loudly.

All that Sunday, Harry was not in a cheerful mood. He sat on the step of his new porch in front of his new house, vexed and moody, without looking at the old bench in front of the gate, where he had always sat for some fifteen years. The previous day Hannah had implored and entreated him to take pity on her and not to spin his yarns in the company of the carters. This no longer suited him; even the carters themselves would look down on him. She even threatened him severely that if he didn't listen to her—she would simply uproot the seat, smash it, destroy it, and finish it off without mercy, and moreover she would pour a pot of boiling water on the carters, and scald those scurvy dogs, and stop them congregating by the gates of her yard to her reproach and shame. "How did my old fool come to be so proud?" Harry wondered. All the same Harry was not afraid of her. He was not henpecked, nor was he under her thumb—except that he looked from afar and saw that the carters were also keeping their distance and were nursing a grudge against him: they had not forgotten yesterday's insult, and they turned away from him and passed him with lowered eyes and angry faces. Moreover, he was himself aware that even if the carters did congregate around him now, his conversation would not go well, as though the inspiration had departed and some sort of barrier now separated him from his former world.

Suddenly his ears rang with the noise of loud laughter coming from the group of carters who had gathered together on one of the empty carts in the middle of the street. Harry looked at the group sideways and saw Yankel, the oldest of the carters, sitting on a bag of fodder on his low cart, with his pipe between his rotten, yellow teeth, smoking, spitting, and talking all at once—an accomplishment peculiar to veteran carters—in the company of younger carters hanging and perched miraculously on every bit of the cart that gave them a fingerhold or a bit of a seat; and they were guffawing and baring their teeth in wild laughter and looking sideways toward Harry. It was clear that they were talking about him and mocking yesterday's Kiddush, and it seemed to him that the word "pie" could also be heard from the group . . .

"They are mocking me," Harry muttered, sinking even deeper into his thoughts. "Serves me right, old fool that I am! Didn't I know in advance that it would all end in mockery and ridicule? I dwelt in peace for fifteen years and kept clear of all the stuff and nonsense of those big shots, and suddenly I went and invited 'all those lepers,' a plague upon them, to a housewarming! As though I would feel honored by them or as though I needed their self-importance!—And all for what?—Because my old fool has not yet given up the idea of becoming 'an important Lady.'"

And Harry recalled all the events of the previous day's Kiddush—and felt hot all over. He remembered all the fine guests with their important faces radiating arrogance, complacency, self-satisfaction, and endless, limitless self-importance. . . . He remembered their pompous entrance, their arrogant gait and cautious manner of sitting down, as though they were endowing the seat with honor by merely sitting on it. He remembered the ridicule and scornful laughter that accompanied them from their arrival to their departure, their expressions spoken in *loshen truvki* (as Harry called the Holy Tongue, for which he had no use) as they sat down to eat, which certainly included mocking references to Harry and his household. He recalled how all that self-importance had suddenly melted away and vanished as soon as the delicacies and tasty items arrived on the table; how they had fallen on every morsel like starvelings and simple gluttons, and eaten, chewed away, ground, and destroyed the last remnant. Did not he, Harry, understand all the scorn and contempt they showed him with such gluttony? Would the guests have behaved thus, when sitting at the table of "an important big shot"? All they would get there would be "a big headache on a little plate," and yet they would eat with good manners, scarcely touching a thing, and leaving more than was given to them—but here—no! "They did not come to enjoy my hospitality—but to eat me up alive! They didn't come to honor me—but to despoil me, to shame me, to tread me into the dust! And why? Because I don't know the craft of how to be a big shot; because I don't know how to mouth *truvki* or read the small print like them; because I don't put on four pairs of tefillin and I don't hang on to the big shot's *kapote*. Now, Alter Adder also doesn't know how to mouth *truvki* and read the small print—nevertheless he understands the art and craft of self-importance and has achieved the title 'big shot,' even though when it comes to 'bundles,' he doesn't reach my ankles. . . . For all his shortcomings, his skill in hanging onto the old big shot makes up for it all." . . .

Wrapped in these thoughts, Harry remembered how in his confused state of mind he had bent down to kiss the old big shot, and how the latter had escaped with the help of Alter Adder. And similarly he recalled the entrance of the "stomach pie," Hannah's beaming countenance at that moment, the sniffing noses, how the old big shot had stood up, the flight of the guests, and in all this confusion Hannah prancing like an untamed heifer, running hither and thither, shaking her great earrings, entreating, despairing, looking after the guests, pleading with them—and then the poor abandoned pie ... and suddenly a thought flashed across his mind like an arrow: the pie had been abandoned out of malice and deliberately; the guests had fled maliciously, to turn him into a laughingstock and trample his reputation in the dust. With this idea in mind, Harry suddenly sprang from his place and ran to Hannah, who was standing at that moment in the kitchen, and shouted in a terrifying voice: "Silly cow! Stupid beast! Butcher's daughter! You are to blame for all this; it is your fault that I am humiliated! All you want is to be an important Lady—but I am going to spit in the important faces of all the big shots! Do you hear, stupid? I will spit at all their self-importance and all the shame they pour on me. Your husband has no desire to be a fancy fellow! Harry can never be an important big shot. Harry was not born for that, and Harry will go back to being what he was. Importance cannot be bought with 'bundles.' ... Importance—is a kind of gift, a kind of art, it's a something—that Harry doesn't need and doesn't want. Harry as an upper-class Jew, Harry as an Elder in the Synagogue, Harry dispensing favors, Harry mouthing *truvki*—ha-ha-ha!—Stupid woman, an upper-class Jew has to mouth *truvki*, to read the small print, and put on four pairs of tefillin! And Harry has no skill in all that. Harry has bundles—and that's good enough for him!"

12

That very evening, a summer evening when the moon was shining, the stars glittering, and frogs croaking in the distance ... when the windows of the houses in the street were open, and strange violin melodies penetrated the street to the delight of the "important householders" (the fathers of the fiddlers), who were sitting on the steps of their porches, or slowly pacing up and down the length of the verandah at the side of the houses, dressed in light, thin coats, with light, silk skullcaps and light sandals ... about the time when the windows of Harry's new house were open and emitting, just for spite, the squeaking sounds of flutes (Harry's sons were playing), at that pleasant hour, Harry was again sitting on the old bench in front of his gate, the favorite bench, which had served him faithfully and borne his weight so patiently for fifteen years; looking in the moonlight at the important big shots and listening to the squawking of the discordant violins competing noisily with the squeaks of his sons' flutes—Harry's thoughts were of this kind: "Those self-important people strolling about slowly, confidently, and self-satisfied—one cannot deny—are important from their very beginning. And God be with them! Let them keep what they have! For why should I lie? I and they are two opposites. But my own personal opinion is that this importance, which up to a few years ago was very salable, is no longer worth even a single kopek. It is true that I, Harry, am a boor, an ignoramus, and a kind of 'bastard' in the congregation of Israel; and even the 'bundles' do not refine me and have enabled me only to climb up to the status of a coarse man of substance—*baal guf*[8] and no more. And I have always been kept at a distance and remained an outsider as far as the community is concerned—but the future, the future, belongs to my *Candidate,* who is now playing the flute, and not to the sons of the big shots, who are playing on their violins. There is a different kind of importance on the market now! Quite different from the empty importance of that lot. Who goes walking with the district official's daughter? My *Candidate!* Who plays cards with the police chief? My *Candidate!* Who has talks with the governor?—My *Candidate!* And who is invited to General Timofeioff's party?—Again, my *Candidate!* The day will come when this *Candidate* of mine will have influence with the governor, and then—get your noses ready, you big shots! All of them, all of them will be in his hand!"—And Harry pats his pocket full of bundles.

And the notes of the fiddles gradually die away. Only two or three still wearily scrape out their sounds. But the sound of the flute grows ever stronger, ever louder, spreading far and wide in the silence of the night. . . . Which shall triumph? The refined violin or the coarse flute?

The song of the nightingale was also heard ascending in the distance, and Harry opened his mouth and yawned widely. Suddenly he cried: "Shefil! Have you watered the chestnut?"

---

[8]A coarse nouveau-riche. The Hebrew title of this novella is *Aryeh* [Harry] *Baal Guf.*

Shefil poked his head out of the window, flute in hand, and answered: "I have, Father!" "If so, go to sleep! Quick, it's time already. You have to rise early tomorrow for the market!"

And Harry raised his heavy limbs from the bench, turned, and walked first to the wood yard to put his marks on the piles of wood for fear of theft, and to check the doors of the cowshed and the stable—and then went off to bed.

4

The Shamed Trumpet

❖ ❖ ❖

Composed in 1915, *The Shamed Trumpet* describes the tragic
uprooting of a Jewish family from a Volhynian village on the
eve of Passover as a result of the promulgation of the notorious
"Temporary May Laws" in 1882. These laws banned Jews
from further settling in the villages of the so-called Jewish Pale.
Their impact, coming after the even more infamous pogroms of
1881–1882, was traumatic. According to Simon Dubnow, the
prominent historian:

> With this [act] a large part of the area that hitherto had been open
> to Jewish settlement was closed to them. Millions of people were
> imprisoned within the crowded confines of the cities and towns of
> Western Russia.
>
> The situation was aggravated by a provision that empowered
> the local rural councils to expel any "undesirable settlers" (i.e.,
> Jews) from their midst.[1]

The literary device employed by Bialik is the frame story. The
narrator is other than the implied author, and he tells the story
of the expulsion of his family about thirty-three years previously (i.e., in 1882) in the first person. He is a Jewish soldier of
about forty, the youngest son of the exiled family, who is a

---

[1]Dubnow, Simon. *Divrei Yemai Am Olam (History of the Eternal People)* (Vol.
10). Tel Aviv: Dvir, 1965. P. 79 [with deletions].

guest at another Passover Seder during World War I. He was nine years old when the tragedy occurred. The account thus is told by an adult recalling a crucial incident in his childhood.

The story opens with a portrayal of the idyllic, if uncertain, situation of two Jewish families living in a village. The setting echoes Bialik's quasi-autobiographical reminiscences of his childhood in a similar village (see *Random Harvest*). It suggests the Garden of Eden before the Fall.

Despite the non-Jewish environment in which the two families reside, they scrupulously adhere to their Jewish way of life. The soldier's family had settled in the village one day after the anti-Jewish decree went into effect. However, the father managed to delay their expulsion for some time by bribing and cajoling local and provincial officials. In the end, pressure from a "higher authority" compelled the local officials to enforce the new law and order the family to abandon their property and leave the area. They are served the evacuation order on the eve of Passover, shortly before their eldest son, serving as a bugler in the Russian army, arrives home on a holiday leave.

Passover and the son's trumpet are the two key motifs of the story. Passover commemorates the freeing of the Jews from Egyptian bondage, their triumphal exodus from Egypt, and their march to the Promised Land. In Jewish tradition it symbolizes the redemption of the Children of Israel and of all humankind.

To the naive family, who viewed the decree of expulsion as originating from mysterious "authorities on high," the news that their soldier son would be joining them for Passover was taken to be an act of divine mercy—an omen of good tidings. The nine-year-old was enthralled by the prospect of seeing his brother's glistening trumpet, more so than even the brother himself. For him and his parents, the trumpet had become the instrument heralding salvation.

In an ironic twist, fate changes the hoped-for redemption to enslavement. The exodus is not a march to a Promised Land but an exile from a childhood paradise to a crowded and dismal Jewish town offering little prospect of a decent living. A new slavery is imposed upon the family by a modern Pharaoh.

At the close of this monologue, one of the children at the Seder innocently asks the soldier: "And the trumpet?" Despite the grim story he had just heard, the child still believes in the saving promise of redemption, the recapturing of a lost Eden. The soldier replies that after his leave had ended, his older brother returned to his barracks. "I never had the privilege of hearing its [the trumpet's] sound again. All those days it remained in its case under one of the beds at the inn, where it was deposited with the rest of our things. It never dared to come out and sound its call. The trumpet was ashamed."

But the child's hope is not totally unfulfilled. Bialik hints that as bleak as the tragedy had been and as irrational as the human dream of redemption seems to be, it is sustained by faith. Two passages illustrate the tenacity of faith. Shortly before the exiles' wagons reach town, the mother orders a halt. It had turned dark and it was both Sabbath eve and the first night of Passover. She did not forget to light the candles.

> The carts and their peasant drivers stood respectfully to attention. A moment later, two little golden flames shone on the hilltop. The blind woods suddenly regained their sight, as if two living eyes were placed in them. The trees silently wondered at the Jewess wrapped in a shawl who stood among them at that time spreading the palms of her hands over the candles and quietly weeping. However strange and sad that entire gathering appeared at the time, it seemed to me nevertheless that at the very instant when the two little flames flickered among the trees, holiness had descended upon the woods. In one of its dark corners, in a sanctuary hidden deep within it, a small gate of mercy had opened and a good angel had poked his head out of the gate. The two flames were like two golden dots, marking the end of a verse on the rim of the sky, and indicating that up to those points was the realm of the secular and beyond them began the Sabbath and the holiday.

Equally poignant is the passage that appears near the end of the story:

> I lifted my eyes to the heavens. Tonight they, too, had wrapped themselves in blue, displaying all their jewelry, big stars, and small and tiny. Here and there silver chains of light were linked to them in veils of clouds, which, in pure lightness appeared as a splendid adjunct to the glorious blue of the holiday. Now a hid-

den hand raised the "silver bowl" of the moon, carefully removing its white coverlet, the veil of the flimsy cloud, and displayed it
in full glory.

The sky had turned into a Passover Seder plate. The sky was
celebrating the holiday. The hope of redemption survives the
tragedy of exile.

❖   ❖   ❖

1

The following story was told to me by a fellow guest at a Passover Seder. He was an army reservist, about forty years old, who had been called up to serve in the war. I recount his tale in his own words without embellishment.

"This is only the second time in my life," so he began, "that I am celebrating a Seder at a stranger's table. The first was about thirty years ago when I was a small boy of nine, but on that occasion my entire family celebrated the Passover away from home: father, mother, brothers, sisters—even Styupe, our servant. 'How come?' you ask. Well it was like this:

"My father and our entire family had come to live in a small village near a little town just one day after the government had decreed that Jews could no longer reside in the villages.[2] Had he got there only one day earlier, matters would have been different. But he was one day late and was classified as an illegal. Not that he was a deliberate criminal. He was compelled to act as he did because he had just been given a post in one of the neighboring forests. And when it is a question of a living, you ignore the law and its dire consequences. At first, the district police appeared to be strict, but in the main, they enjoyed their role very much. After all, one Jew residing illegally is better than ten who are legal. The former is a fruit-bearing tree, the latter, fruitless. Indeed within a few days 'normal relations' were established between my 'criminal' father and the law-enforcing police. He and his family lived in the village and the police, each according to his rank, received a monthly 'payoff,' in addition to such sporadic gifts as holiday bonuses and petty cash loans, which need never be repaid, as well as other presents and goodies on their religious holidays or on

---

[2]In May 1882, as part of its anti-Jewish policy, the Russian government issued a decree prohibiting Jews from settling in the villages of most of the provinces of the Jewish Pale of Settlement.

the birthdays of the captain, his wife, and all his children. Such folks, as you well know, do not turn up their noses at any gift, be it a pair of stuffed geese, a keg of wine, a bottle of vodka, a hundred eggs, a cone of sugar in its blue wrapper, a liter of tea, a plug of tobacco, a packet of soft cheese, hamantaschen—they take it all. And they are so correct! The captain, for example, would never demand anything; he only made a request—'Yose,' he would say to Father, placing his heavy hand on his shoulder: 'Please ask them to bring me a cord of wood for the fireplace; winter's about to come,' or 'Please don't forget, dear fellow, to send me about a thousand wooden tiles. You can see that my roof needs repairing.'

"The cross-eyed sergeant used another technique. He would shower praise upon any object that caught his crossed eye. 'Itah,' he would say to my mother, as he cast his eyes on a fat hen pecking at the garbage pile in our yard, 'Where did you find such a first-rate hen?' Rest assured, following such a compliment, that beautiful hen would find itself lying tethered in the sergeant's blue wagon. He would time his visits to our home on Sabbaths and holidays and precisely at mealtimes. The family had only to sit around the table and through the window we would spy his tawny mare and blue wagon and, of course, the sergeant himself. What could we do? We would welcome the guest and invite him to dine. The Sabbath hymns were dispensed with, and the book that Father perused between dishes was discarded. The drunken stench his mouth exuded and his banal chatter would mar the holiness of the occasion. Moreover, you were obliged to respond with hearty laughter to his compliments and stale jokes despite the fact that you were sitting on pins and needles, your fist growing taut as you wished you could grab him by the scruff of his neck and throw him out.

"Indeed as time went by, the family got used to him and no longer feared him. Sometimes, after he had emptied a full bottle of vodka down his gullet and got soused, he would join us in humming the tunes of the Sabbath hymns, of course, in his own way, mouth aslant and lips limp and his besotted eyes blinking away, smiling at the lady of the house and, at the same time, pawing Parasha, our fat, pock-marked shiksah. Only our tutor, imported from town, was not able to feel comfortable with him, or with the dog chained in our yard. Both remained strange and frightening to him, even though Father paid the extra poll tax for the tutor.

"So five years passed. During that time, my father had built himself a house with lumber from his forest. He invited all the village peasants to the housewarming and spread a special table for them. Behind the house, Mother had planted a large vegetable garden, which stretched to the foot of the hill. There were three milk cows in the barn and two horses in the stable. Chickens pecked away and geese and goslings cackled in the yard. In the pond in front of our yard, two ducks swished and spluttered, and a calf and pony grazed in the nearby field. Everything in country style: the living was scant, life impoverished, but things were calm and peaceful.

"Father spent all the weekdays in the forest. He would return home on Fridays or the day before each holiday on his wagon and spend a day or two with the family. The children would await his arrival anxiously at the edge of the forest, trembling with joy. When they heard the faint tinkling of his horses' bells approaching from the outskirts of the forest, which ended just before the village, they would take off like birds and run toward the wagon, shouting gleefully: 'Daddy! Daddy!' In a flash, they would climb and tumble into the wagon and hug their father, resting on his knees, hanging on to his neck, or fingering his pockets to discover what presents he had brought. Even Styupe, the wagoner, who also served as watchman, an overgrown, broad-shouldered lad, would join in the fun. Flashing his firm, white teeth in delight, he would crack his whip fiercely at the horses to please the children, and the horses would break into a brisk trot toward our home.

"I've not yet told you that in that very same village there lived a Jew by the name of Zelig, who was a legal resident. His house stood on top of a hill at the edge of the village, while ours was in the valley below. These two Jewish houses, standing somewhat apart from the houses of the village and differing from them in height and in the shape of their roofs, formed a separate quarter, so to speak. Soon a thin pathway was cut through the grass, linking the two yards permanently, like a white parting in one's hair. There was a single tutor for the children of both families and neighborly sharing was the rule. Each mother knew what was cooking in the other's pot and each would send her neighbor delicacies or cakes baked in her oven. Each would lend a pot, a sieve, or a spatula to her friend. They would both share a bunch of greens, a basket of eggs, or a pair of chickens. On winter nights or during long summer days, they would visit each other's homes or porches for a chat, shell peas, put up jam, pluck feathers, or darn socks in each other's company.

"Only a little time elapsed before relationships began to cement. Neighbors became in-laws.[3] Father had a veritable bevy of children, male and female. Samuel, the eldest, had already reached twenty and had a draft exemption. Zelig, too, had many children. His eldest daughter, Zelda, was of marriageable age. They drew up a marriage contract and set the wedding day. But the bridegroom's military exemption was canceled and he was drafted. To the distress of both families, the wedding had to be postponed indefinitely, that is, until the bridegroom had completed his military service.

"One thing upset Father very much: the village lacked a regular minyan. 'Sabbaths and Holy Days without public worship,' he would say, 'lose half their charm.' All of the males fit to be counted for the minyan added up to only seven: four from our home, Father, my two brothers, and the tutor; and three from Zelig's. When my brother left for the army, the number was reduced to six. Consequently, Father took special delight whenever God sent him guests for the Sabbath, whether they were lumber merchants who came to the forest, colleagues who were forest clerks, or Jewish itinerants such as peddlers or glaziers. On such occasions, Father would send word to Pesach-Itzi, the dairyman, a simple, childless Jew, who lived with his barren wife and his milk cows on his isolated farm in a nearby valley within walking range of the Sabbath limit of the village.[4] Zelig would rise early and walk to our home on a Sabbath morning, cutting through gardens and fields, wearing a white *talit* under his Sabbath caftan, so that he might make up the ten. Not that he was so circumspect about the prohibition against carrying on the Sabbath—most country folk are not so strictly observant. However, if one is to fulfill the mitzvah of public worship on the Sabbath, one should do so properly. Sometimes, when there was no way out, they would count a minor versed in *Humash* as a member of a minyan. When minyanim became more frequent, Father

---

[3]The closest equivalent to *mehutanim*, a term designating the relationship between the two sets of parents of a married couple. The term was used not only for actual *mehutanim* but also for potential ones, who had approved arrangements for a prospective marriage.

[4]The furthest point outside a village or a town's borders beyond which an observant Jew may not walk on the Sabbath without violating the prohibition against laboring on the Sabbath.

brought a Torah scroll home from town, which he hid behind a curtain in a small ark set up in a special corner of the schoolroom. The Torah, with its hidden holiness, would then cast a mysterious fear upon the children. The chanting of the Torah by our tutor with the proper cantillation before the tiny rural congregation wrapped in *talitot* and outfitted with *Humashim* and eyeglasses would suffuse the Sabbath morning with a unique sanctity, which was also sensed, so it would appear, even by the copper pots glistening in the cupboard opposite us and smiling their soft, gentle Sabbath smile. In the adjoining room behind the wall, Mother, clad in her clean Sabbath dress and her silk kerchief and holding her heavy shawl in her hand, would be standing, her lips whispering and her eyes full of joyous tears, as if to say: 'True we are cast away in this village among the Gentiles, but the gracious, merciful, and loving God does not abandon His people. In His great compassion, He grants us this Sabbath day and places His pure and holy Torah in my home.' In honor of such a Sabbath with a minyan for Torah reading, Mother would add an extra dessert to the menu and following the service would treat the worshippers to brandy and honey cakes for Kiddush and feed them other Sabbath delicacies. The Jews, as was their custom, would drink small gulps of brandy and toast Mother and Father: '*Le-ḥayim*, Yose, may God grant salvation and consolation to Israel, and *le-ḥayim*, Itah, may God soon return your son safely to your home.' And Mother would sigh and respond: 'Amen, by Your will, O Lord of the Universe.'

"At times, our home was the scene of a friendly meal and a small celebration. After the close of a winter Sabbath's day, when a calf or a goose was to be slaughtered and its fat fried, the *shoḥet* of the adjacent village, a clever Jew who was always well dressed and a good conversationalist, would come to our house wrapped in his winter coat and carrying his case of ritual knives. He would bring with him a whiff of urban Jewry and a touch of elation. In honor of the night's event, the minyan members would gather in our home immediately after Havdalah: Reb Zelig, our in-law, his wife, and children; Pesach-Itzi, with his barren spouse; and two or three of the forest clerks, whom Father had invited before the Sabbath. They would huddle about the boiling samovar, which stood on the table, drink tea, and perspire. Father and Zelig would play 'Goats and Wolf'[5] as

---

[5]A popular home game.

the tutor stood over them, swaying as if studying Talmud and giving advice to each of the players. The forest clerks—most of whom had a good sense of humor, would amuse the ladies with their jokes. Pesach-Itzi, the dairyman, never took his pipe out of his mouth, and he would fill the house with smoke and the stench of cheap tobacco. My elder brother, who was something of a musician, would play Hasidic or Wallachian tunes and strum upon his fiddle.

"As soon as the *shohet* was escorted into the room, he would be greeted with 'Welcome, have a good week,' and a place would be cleared for him at the head of the table. After hastily downing two or three glasses of tea to warm him up, he would go out to 'the slaughterhouse,' that is, to the barn, looking like a bandit, with hitched-up coattails, rolled-up sleeves, and a glistening slaughtering knife, to do what must be done to the calf and the tethered geese. The yard dogs would hear the screeching of the geese and the bellowing of the calf and would stand guard at the barn, awaiting, as they growled impatiently, their share of the prey to be thrown upon the garbage pile. After the slaughtering and inspection were completed, the *shohet* would return to the house and take his place at the head of the table, his appearance restored: a *shohet* of respectable mien, wearing a wide girdle, and a good talker. 'Goats and Wolf' would be abandoned and all faces turned toward him. Reb Gadi—that was the *shohet's* name—would sit, wearing his clean velvet yarmulke above his broad white shining forehead, and he would tell his stories about Elijah, remembered for his goodness, or the Baal Shem Tov[6] of blessed memory, and another tale about the Grandpa of Shpola,[7] may his merit protect us, or about one of the thirty-six righteous men.[8] Everyone was silent and all ears. The tutor would sit, eyes closed, holding his scant beard in his hand, swaying as if he were studying Talmud and listening intently, emitting a pious sigh from time to time. Pesach-Itzi would wrap himself in a cloud of pipe smoke, his hat tipped toward the back of his neck. The frivolous forest clerks would suddenly turn serious, and one of the modest ladies would quickly tuck an elusive braid under her ker-

---

[6]"Master of the Good Name," the title of Rabbi Israel Baal Shem Tov, the alleged founder of Hasidism.

[7]A leading Hasidic holy man.

[8]Hasidim believed that in every generation thirty-six holy men, whose identity is concealed, sustain the entire world.

chief. Now the samovar would lower its voice to a low hum. Hush. The *shohet's* talk, sweet, modulated, but clearly enunciated, would flow gently, pouring out drop after sweet drop, which entered the heart as an elixir of life. The world, then, is still not lost. The Guardian of Israel, then, neither slumbers nor sleeps.

"After that: the *melaveh malkah*[9] meal, which started with brandy, was followed by stewed fruit, chicken cracklings, and chopped duck's liver. More brandy as an intermezzo was followed by steaming, boiling borscht and kreplach. As its finale, brandy again and then hymn singing, fiddle playing by my eldest brother, and fervent dancing until dawn. On such an evening the usually taciturn Pesach-Itzi would sometimes let himself go and attain the highest degree of ecstasy, dancing and singing like a madman. As he danced, he would throw off his caftan. Face lit up like a torch, eyes closed, and the palms of his hands stretched out in a prayerful gesture, he would dance and roar, 'Israel, O sacred people, I'd give my life for just one of your fingernails.' Or, in tears: 'Merciful Jews, let me be martyred, have pity on me, sacrifice me, and drag me to the stake. Oh my heart is on fire with the love of Israel!' And so he would dance, roar, and weep until he collapsed on a bench in a dead faint. Early next morning, after he sobered up, he would slip away like a thief, return to his home, his cows, and his pipe and resume his silent ways.

"We would pass most holidays in serene and unostentatious joy, which was mixed with quiet sadness. The enforced separation from the Jewish community was felt acutely among the villagers at these times. The heart would become full with longing. The commandment that 'the holidays be holy unto you' would be observed to the letter: eating, drinking, sleeping, and leisure; but the close of the verse 'and unto the Lord' could not be properly kept: there was no house of prayer, no Jewish community, nothing. At times, there would be no minyan, because the tutor would be away visiting his home and there was no itinerant available. For what Jewish pauper would go out on the road during a holiday? And even if a minyan was scraped together—what flavor did things have when, because of our many sins, we could parade only a single Torah scroll and shake only a single lulav. The schedule of holiday visits was likewise not

---

9"Accompanying the Queen" (i.e., the Sabbath). The late-afternoon Sabbath meal marking the approaching end of the Sabbath.

very extensive and hardly satisfying. Zelig and Pesach-Itzi's family would visit our home, Pesach-Itzi and my father's families would visit Zelig, and our family and Zelig's would visit Pesach-Itzi, and with that the cycle was completed. During the visit, we would sit in the neighbor's house, split hazelnuts and pumpkin seeds, and tell old news, strumming on the table and yawning until our temples ached.

"When my eldest brother went off to the army, a new bitter drop was added to Mother's silent cup of sorrow. Its effect was most noticeable on Sabbaths and Holy Days. The 'gang' at home was small: my brother's fiddle would hang on the wall silent and lonely day after day. The eldest son's seat at the table would be empty, and to my mother it always appeared like the gap left by a missing front tooth or a severed finger. Whenever she would pass a plate of food to us, she would cast her sad eyes upon that vacant seat and suppress a sigh so as not to violate the spirit of the Sabbath or the holiday.

"My father got along peacefully with the village's peasants. Since his arrival to cut the timber, there were more jobs. Some worked in the forest, others transported the trees to the nearby train stop. Moreover, building timber was now available at a reduced price and on installments. As a result, better-looking structures began to rise: new homes, new silos, new barns, and new pens, in place of the rickety ruins and the mud huts. Two or three straw roofs were replaced with wooden tiles, and the many breaches in the fences were repaired. There were, of course, occasions when lumber was 'lifted' by one of the peasants. It would be impossible for such a thing not to happen in a village bordering upon a forest. Father would usually not resort to the full force of the law when this occurred and, on occasion, would ignore the incident completely. After all, he was living among them, and illegally at that. Goodwill is best for a Jew. The peasants showed him great respect because of his behavior, and they would frequently bring their quarrels and their litigations before him for adjudication. Father knew how to talk their language and understood their customs. He would calm one man and reprimand the other, and all sides would depart contented. With their dignitaries, he would exchange Purim gifts: we would send them hamantaschen and rolls, and they would reciprocate with a live hen, eggs, or a bag of poppy seeds. Vasili, a clever peasant and an old friend of Father's, even sent his little son to our tutor's class for him to be taught how to write with the other children. The village had forty homes but no school, church, or priest. Pyetka—that was the little fellow's name—almost turned Jewish. He knew many parts of the liturgy by heart and most of the Bible stories, which he either heard from his Jewish friends or picked up unwittingly. He would write Russian in Hebrew characters and from left to right. On Christmas Eve, the village children would gather and sing their carols under our windows. Yavdoha, our old nurse, would hand them slices of white ḥallah, dough cakes filled with peas and beans, and small change. In the spring, my eldest brother, Samuel, would set up a swing between two trees in the nearby woods on which all the village children, Jews and gentiles alike, would swing. In the winter, he would fix sleds for them and the children would glide from the top of Zelig's hill to its bottom. On summer evenings, the village youngsters—boys and girls—would gather round our home, and Samuel would stand inside the window playing his fiddle as they danced outside. By the way, old Yavdoha had nursed three of our children, and she loved them and our family deeply. She would care for the children loyally, feed them, give them drink, put them to bed, and waken them. She would, like a Jewess, remind them to wear their little *talit,* cover their heads, recite the morning prayer, study Torah, and be pious. She would caution them against mixing meat dishes with dairy dishes, and when any of them was sick, she would secretly bring a bottle of 'holy water' and sprinkle them so that they be cured."

2

"A 'Satan' arrived in the sixth year of our stay in the village. A changing of the guard occurred in the district capital. One governor left or died and was replaced by another. Suddenly, laws were being strictly enforced, decrees and expulsions occurred with great frequency. Day after day bad rumors spread from the surrounding villages, causing worry and panic among the isolated Jewish homesteads in the area. Life was threatened, and jealousy and meanness increased. Everyone feared for his bread and suspected his neighbor. Father would return home from the forest unexpectedly, his face worn with worry. He would carry on long, whispered conversations with Mother and his in-law and then travel in haste to the county seat or to the district capital in order to 'sweeten' the law. The very thought of leaving the village was enough to freeze one's blood.

Father's home had become rooted in the village, and shortly before the laws began to be enforced severely, he had begun building a tar refinery, a project in which he had invested most of his limited capital. Nevertheless, Father's efforts in the 'proper places' were, it seems, to no avail, since he always returned from his trips more upset than before. The officials in the 'proper places' had again become very severe. The 'tax' rate rose sevenfold and even then nothing was sure. The sergeant started visiting our home frequently, as though on guard, but now he timed his visits at night like a thief. His right eye, which seemed to be even more crossed than before, had suddenly turned strange and cold, almost angry, its whiteness having increased, as if it no longer recognized us. The village's peasants had also changed. A kind of surliness that had not previously existed now showed itself. Worse, there was not a single night in which lumber was not stolen. There were even peasants who did not try to hide this pilfering, knowing that it was best for Father to be silent and overlook the matter. Things reached such a pass that one of the peasants, Sashke the Wolf, a well-known pilferer, was apprehended with his two sons by our night watchman, Styupe. They beat him severely and took the lumber to their home. On this occasion Father could not remain silent and he had them arrested. From then on, Father endured numerous enemies because of the thieves and their relatives. One of them, the village notary, famous for his drunkenness, began writing hate letters against Father week after week, using the well-known format: 'Be informed that the Jew X, son of Y, dwelling in our village illegally, in clear violation of the law, corrupts the spirit of our community and does harm to the State.' The thieving peasant would carry the letter to 'the proper places.'

"The 'proper places' would summon Father for an interview. When he returned, he looked as pale as a corpse. Once when he came home from wherever he had gone, he arrived with only one of his horses. The other, the better horse, had been left with an official of the 'proper places' as a 'payoff.' The salvaged horse, since Father had not been able as yet to find him a partner, returned home alone with his master, as if punished, with the hitching pole attached to the middle of the wagon, dragging unnaturally alongside it. Father's face was flushed with the shame of it all. It was as if they had shaved off half his beard and cut away half his caftan. Styupe, the driver, was almost weeping from distress. When he unhitched the single horse from the wagon and put him in the stable, he cursed him severely, gritting his teeth and beating the horse on the mouth with his fist, venting his anger upon it. The missing horse was, indeed, replaced later. Father traded his single, good horse for two poor ones, an act that pained and shamed Styupe. Peace of mind and confidence were never again restored. Not knowing what the next day might bring, Father completely abandoned the project for the tar refinery; the building was left only half completed. Father said that the boards for the pens and the barns that were left among the trees in the copse would come to him at night in his dreams and weep.

"In the meantime, the strictures of the law grew in severity. At first they would serve notice and only then would they expel, later they expelled without warning. Bribes had no effect. Family homesteads built by years of labor were destroyed by sudden decree or on short notice. On the dirt roads stretching between the villages and the town, peasant carts laden with the household goods of expelled Jews crawled day after day. On the morrow, the very same peasants would return to their villages laughing at the distress of the remaining Jews, who had not yet been touched by the law. A dark terror fell upon our home; hearts prophesied evil.

"Once on a gentile holiday, when Father was at home, Styupe suddenly rushed in and told him that the village's peasants were at the local tavern, mostly drunk, and they were preparing some sort of a 'paper' against Father. The chief inciters were Sashke the Wolf and his relative, the notary. The arguments of Father's supporters were drowned out by the bottles of vodka with which the plotters had treated the crowd. The text of 'the paper,' it was rumored, contained a petition by the community to the 'proper places' to remove Yosi, the *Zhid,* from the village—first, because he lives there illegally and, second, because he is 'harmful.' There seemed to have been some basis to the rumor that a Jew was involved in the matter. About that time, a Jew had purchased a tract of forest alongside of Father's forest, and as was to be expected, there was competition between the two forests, which frequently led to quarreling.

"Father did not waste a minute and went to the tavern himself. He thought that 'they wouldn't dare do it in his presence.' And so it was. Father's sudden appearance in the tavern left the plotters abashed. Two or three of them slipped away, and the rest lowered their eyes. One of them reached for the abandoned 'paper' and tried to hide it. A pious old man who respected my father beat him to the punch, grabbed 'the paper,' and, after first crossing himself, tore it to shreds. As he did, he said to Father: 'Praise God, Yosi, you've been saved from trouble and we, from sin. Order drinks for the people.' Father gave the order. At once the people reversed themselves and their mood changed. A sense of justice arose and the defense was victorious. Some of the penitents had so repented that after a few drinks they bore witness against themselves under oath that they were dogs and sons of dogs going back ten generations. One of them wailed like a beaver, begged Father's forgiveness, and threw himself on the floor and cried, 'Trample upon me, Yosi, trample upon me.' Another beat his breast and shouted that he would defend Yosi to the last drop of his blood, and that he would kill the Wolf, kill him for sure. As Father returned, he heard screams rising from the tavern. As an act of repentance, plotters and defenders had come to blows; one peasant grabbed the hair lock of the other—as was the custom.

"The 'paper' was torn up this time, but the danger did not disappear entirely. The village people were now divided into two hostile camps. There was no end to quarrels and battles. Letters of accusation reached 'the proper places' from both groups. The captain would invite one side and then the other to his office, stomp his feet at both of them, and roar like a lion: 'To Siberia, in iron chains.'

"On one of the days of Hanukah, the captain summoned my father to come to him. Father put a pair of fat geese in his sled as a gift for the captain's wife and rushed to respond to the summons. The lady of the house accepted the gift graciously, and her husband ushered my father into his secluded room and said to him: 'Yosi, for heaven's sake, I can no longer hide you. Enemies are plotting against you, and the district office has become a stickler for the law: severe action, warnings! A Jew in the village, God forbid, should neither be found nor seen. They are as tough as nails.'

"'Is it possible, only because of a single day?' Father argued. 'Because of a single day.' 'What should I do?' Father asked. 'Perhaps, there is after all some way out.'

"The captain stretched out his palms and puckered his lips, as if to say: 'Do whatever you can. I—I'm unable to help.'

"Father did not return home but hurried off in his wagon to the county seat. From there he dashed to the distant capital. And so he ran from pillar to post until he returned home after some time, exhausted and depressed, having gotten almost nowhere. He did, indeed, find some people who advised him, but one man's advice contradicted that of the other. There were also lobbyists who made him promises, but these were slim. One of them who had, he said, contacts in 'the proper places' took it upon himself, for a decent fee, of course, to ask one of them to 'legalize' Father's status, that is, to antedate his arrival date at the village by one day, to before the prohibition was promulgated, but most people said that the man's words were worthless, that he was a well-known liar. Despite it all Father gave him an advance. Who knows, perhaps?

"By dint of this 'perhaps,' the lobbyist 'milked' Father for about three months, and the matter never got beyond the 'maybe' stage. Every week one discovered new parties who required 'appeasing' and Father kept 'appeasing.' One day the lobbyist informed Father that it was impossible to avoid the decree. It was sealed, signed, and on someone's desk. What then was possible? Postpone its application, and this would cost so much. But a few days later he was again informed, after all the postponements, the paper was again on its way and required further postponement. So Father again made another payoff. Thus the matter dragged on and on. The lobbyist stood guard, postponing with both hands, but the 'paper' was on its way again, crawling slowly, step by step, invisibly, like a thief in a tunnel, but on its way. Every move or delay cost Father dearly. Above all, it cost him untold agony and loss of dignity. Going over and over again to the courts, receiving requests to come back tomorrow, bribing, cajoling, lying, and the flattering of cruel, drunken high officials, and arrogant and dissolute younger ones. There were also secret meetings in filthy taverns and unsavory negotiations. From such trips, Father would return bloodied and take to his bed for several days. When he recovered, he would confine himself to his room, pacing back and forth for hours on end. Once, at twilight, I found him standing in the corner before the Holy Ark, weeping silently.

"Those difficult days added many gray hairs to his head and wrinkles to his forehead. When Father realized that salvation would not be coming by earthly means, he pinned his hopes on the mercy of heaven. He never ceased trying. Scripture says, 'I shall bless you in all that you endeavor,' but he no longer believed in total salvation. He prayed silently that the catastrophe would not, at any rate, come too quickly. In the meantime, who knows, perhaps . . . perhaps a miracle might occur, some kind of riot or a war or some other political disaster, which would make them forget the existence of Yosi of the village of Koziovka.

"In the meantime, April had arrived and we suddenly received a letter from my brother Samuel, who was serving as a trumpeter in the army band. The letter contained two items of good news: first, that because of his special talents, he had earned a stripe and, second, that he was granted a two-weeks' leave and would be arriving on the day before Passover with his trumpet. Father read the letter aloud before the entire family—and we all rejoiced. The children broke into a dance: 'Samuel's coming, bringing his trumpet.' Mother's face beamed for a moment and her eyes glistened with tears.

"'Hey woman, why are you crying?' said Father, as he wiped a hidden tear from his eye as well. 'This is a good omen, now you will see God's salvation! May it be so, O Lord, may He grant it for the children's sake.'

"Alas, neither prayer was heard. We were not ready at all for the catastrophe, which fell upon us earlier than we had anticipated: on the day before Passover.

3

The guest paused for a moment and then resumed his story. "That particular day was the eve of Passover, which fell on a Friday, and every detail of that day is engraved on my memory. The sun shone from first dawn all day long. The houses of the two in-laws, the one on the hill and the one below it, smiled and sparkled at one another, each newly painted white and sporting a blue belt of paint beneath the windows, in honor of the holiday. Behind our house arose the singing of the farmers' wives, the first to waken, who had gone out to turn the soil of the vegetable garden, adding a new, black, moist vegetable bed every hour. Following the rain, Zelig's hill was covered by a thin, green fuzz of soft, silken grass. The strip of path that ran down the hill through the silk had suddenly turned a new yellow. The entire strip was strewn with damp, golden sand. No one saw who had strewn the sand, but everyone knew that it had been done secretly by Samuel's bride, early in the morning, in honor of her bridegroom, who was expected that day. I was worried that I might spoil the decorous belt with my footsteps before the bridegroom's foot could tread upon it.

"There was much activity and noise in both yards. All the utensils were scraped, rinsed, and purified. Benches and tables were scalded with boiling water and red-hot stones and scrubbed by the thin, veined hands of wrinkly old Yavdoha, the judaized gentile, who was more circumspect about the laws of *kashrut* than any Jewess, and by the coarse fat hand of Parasha, the pock-marked shiksah. The two mothers-in-law worked piously and bravely, worked and put others to work, as if competing with each other. For this was no small matter: Samuel, the bridegroom, was coming today, after two years of military service.

"You must understand that from the very day my brother's letter arrived the two in-laws had been quarreling with each other. My mother argued: Samuel was her guest. Parents have precedence over in-laws. But the in-law shouted in reply: 'Not so! Samuel is a bridegroom. Have you ever seen a bridegroom who has not spent a single Passover at his in-laws' home?' Both men intervened and came up with a compromise: fifty-fifty, the first Seder at the parents' home, the second at the in-laws'.

"A similar conflict erupted among the children. Each of them wanted to join Styupe in his wagon as he rode out to the nearby train station to meet the guest, who was expected on the afternoon train. Finally, I was given the honor. I stood waiting impatiently for the wagon, which had been hitched and was all decked out, and stood at the gate of the yard for almost an hour without moving an inch. It was delayed by Styupe, who was still sitting in the yard on a carpenter's 'mule,' carving and sharpening white poles with his ax: new Passover handles for rakes and spades. I very much wanted to help him and put an end to the waiting, but Mother dragged me off for a shampoo and a change of linen. She was concerned that I might be held up on the way and begin the holiday with an unclean body.

"To save time, I surrendered my head to the tub of hot water and the partly toothless comb, and my flesh to the starched shirt, whose white coldness irritated me. At an opportune moment, I tried to urge my mother to dress me immediately (not for my own sake but in honor of my brother) in the rest of my new clothes: my hat, coat, and trousers and above all my shining new shoes. I wanted to appear before Samuel in full glory. But Mother rejected my appeal with a mother's argument, that my clothes would get soiled on the trip and it was best for me and for all concerned to put them on after my return. Against my will, I agreed to a minimum and emerged victorious, half renovated and improved, with the starched shirt rubbing my neck, and feeling half the pleasure of the holiday coursing through my skin and bones.

"In the hall, I ran into my sister, who was sitting on a stool crushing matzah with a mortar and pestle twice her size. My other sister, little more than a baby, was shaking the crushed matzah through a little sieve onto a white tablecloth, an act that lent her a special Passover charm.

"On a round wicker mat serving as the salting-board lay torn pieces of fowl surrounding a disjointed goose, with their bluish gizzards and strips of yolk dripping reddish juice. My middle brother was hacking the horseradish with a chopper, contorting his face and sneezing. Parasha stood at the kitchen doorway in a clean dress and white apron and shawl, like a bride in full array, totally kosher for Passover, her pock-marked face all shining; she was scaling a fat and quivering fish with a dull knife, preparing it for the copper pot beside it. From the kitchen itself could be heard the sweet sounds of spices and condiments being ground and the hissing of the flaming fire in the refurbished stove, while the new pots stood gleaming. Father was preparing the haroset. Mother was dipping a long string of polished forks and spoons into a well in the yard. Wooden vessels, benches, shelves, a barrel, and a white bucket were already in their allotted places, washed, rinsed, and ready for action. In a second hollow the small flame of burning *hametz* still flickered, with its light cloud of smoke trembling in the air. Passover eve was already wafting its smells and noises everywhere. But Passover itself was still locked inside the parlor, in the special room that Mother forbade anyone to enter. There it sat behind the curtain, hidden like a king in his chamber, amid the glory of white pillows and glittering glassware, engaging the prophet Elijah in whispered conversation. Only when Mother opened the door for a moment, as the need arose, did the Passover spirit throw us children a good-natured glance, as if hinting: 'I'm here, children!'

"About half an hour after the burning of the *hametz*, the wagon finally moved off, with me in it. Now I knew that I was on my way and that in two hours' time I would, God willing, be seeing my brother, both him and his trumpet.

"As the wagon turned onto the road leading to the station, the singing of the peasant women working in the vegetable garden caught up with me. I turned my head back toward our quarter; the two white houses stood girded with their blue belts and looked at me, as if warning: 'Don't tarry on the road, it is Passover eve!'

"The road between the village and the station, although somewhat softened by the night's rain and beset with patches of soggy mud, was not too bad. The horses trotted at their usual cautious gait. The distance between the village and the station was about a two and a half hours' ride by wagon each way. If nothing delayed us, we would be back with the guest between two and three o'clock, that is, when the entire household would already be ready for the Passover. I imagined how great the joy would be when the wagon returned with Samuel. Both households would gather together and go out to welcome him, including the bride.

"The horses ran through the fields with their bells tinkling. A light breeze fluttered over my face, and I was very, very happy. The charm of Passover eve rested on the entire world. The small clouds in the sky were separated by great spaces forming paths of new blue, Passover blue. In the clear air, waves of sweet warmth and refreshing coolness vied with each other, lightly playing on my face and neck in turn. Pools of water lay in the fields like glass mirrors, some of them smooth, reflecting the pure blue sky, and others shivering from the cold and shimmering with gold and silver, like the crystal and glassware of Passover. Even the dirty remnants of small piles of snow, which sometimes emerged as we passed a ditch, did not spoil the view. To my eye, they seemed to be the residue of hardened *hametz* that had hidden in the dirt ditches because it was ashamed.

"The wagon dashed on. We went in and out of woods and fields and fields and woods. Meanwhile, my mind was full of Passover thoughts. Our house will indeed experience great joy this Passover, day after day. On the first day, the in-laws will come to us: wine, honey cakes, dumplings, nuts, and nut games. On the second day, we will go to our in-laws' home, and again wine, honey, cakes, dumplings, nuts, and nut games. On the eve of the second day once again we will all gather in their home. The in-laws will come, the bride, Pesach-Itzi and his wife—everybody, everybody. Samuel will play his trumpet, the children will dance. And again wine and honey cakes, dumplings, and nuts.

"I must confess my joy at the expected arrival of my brother was further enhanced by the thought of the trumpet that he was bringing with him. It was this thought that had induced me to go to the station. I had never seen a real trumpet. I knew it only from a photo that Samuel had sent us shortly before he joined the band and that now hung on the wall next to his fiddle. He was pictured there in uniform holding the trumpet in his hand. Indeed the trumpet was a beautiful and lovely thing. In less than an hour, I would have the privilege of seeing it and perhaps blowing on it. That 'perhaps' filled my heart with boundless glee. I was unable to restrain myself from talking about it immediately with Styupe, who was sitting in front of me with his back toward me.

"'Tell me, Styupe,' I said to the driver, 'have you ever in all your life seen a trumpet?' 'So what,' he turned a startled face toward me. 'Don't you know, Samuel is bringing a trumpet back with him, a real trumpet, made of copper!' . . .

"This good news did not affect him, it would seem, at all, because he turned back toward the horses without a word and calmly kept on driving. I dismissed him from my mind, 'What does he understand, a stupid goy.' I immediately joined my fists in the shape of a tube and began to blow and toot into the air, bouncing myself to the rhythm of the music. Opposite us drove several wagons of peasants who were returning from the station, and a coach, with tinkling bells bearing two kinds of uniformed officials. I continued trumpeting, unconcerned. Only Styupe turned back his head several times and stared unhappily at the officials, as if his heart told him that they were up to no good.

"When we reached the station, we found Samuel there, standing in uniform on the platform, waiting for our wagon. How coarsened he looked, and where was his beard? I jumped from the wagon and ran toward him. Hellos, kisses. Styupe watered the horses and transferred my brother's luggage to the wagon. I searched for the trumpet with my eyes, but I saw only one crude, heavy chest and a smaller and prettier piece, a kind of case. I immediately understood that this case contained the treasure. Nevertheless, to resolve my doubts, I asked my brother: 'What's it for?' 'That's the instrument's case,' he replied. My hand that had fondled the case retreated out of respect. The instrument! I wanted to ask my brother to show me the instrument itself immediately but dared not. I raised my eyes toward him pleading. My brother understood me and said, 'We have to hurry home now, it's Passover eve.'

"He was right. We had to hurry home now; it's Passover eve. The three of us mounted the wagon swiftly. The horses began to canter gleefully along the road, bells tinkling the good news: Samuel is coming; Samuel is coming. Samuel involved himself in endless talk with Styupe about the affairs of the village. One asked and the other responded. And as for me, my thoughts were only on the case and its contents. I almost lost hope of ever actually seeing the trumpet. It was doubly locked in its case, like the Passover in our parlor. But the good Lord, it would seem, did not wish to deny me a reward for my trip. With still some distance to go before reaching our village, He put a good thought into my brother's mind, namely, to announce his impending arrival from afar with a trumpet call. No sooner said than done. The case was opened; in an instant, the trumpet suddenly flashed in my brother's hand. It was the epitome of shining brass, with an array of stops, whose glare almost blinded me. A moment later, from beneath my brother's fingers pure lilting sounds began to pour forth and resonate. The instrument cooed like a baby, then all of a sudden its brass throat thundered with all its might across the wide fields, and a powerful and wonderful march exploded into the thin air.

"Styupe cracked the whip. The horses took wing and raced along. The bells on their necks seemed to be overwhelmed for a moment by the force of the march, and their song went off key, but soon they recovered and their gleeful, rhythmic tinkling announced with renewed vigor: Samuel is coming, Samuel is coming. The trees on the roadside danced before us and gave way. The pools smiled. Everything shouted and proclaimed: Samuel is coming, Samuel is coming.

"And while the wagon was racing along, the coach with its two officials again came toward us. The same coach and the same officials we had met on the way to the station. This double encounter I viewed as an evil omen, which boded no good. The trumpet trembled in Samuel's hand, as if its brilliance had suddenly been tarnished. Samuel hurriedly lowered it into the wagon, covering it with his coat. Coach and wagon passed each other rapidly. The passengers of each vehicle, as if by a single intuition, looked back and eyed each other suspiciously for some time.

"In the meantime, with a short, stifled clatter our wagon thundered across the little bridge spanning a narrow ravine and entered the village area. We had hoped that our people would come out to meet us at this spot, as was agreed before we left. However, much to our surprise, no one was there and we began to feel anxious. My brother blew one last feeble blast on his trumpet and returned the instrument to its case. Styupe suddenly stood up and whipped the horses with all his might, sending them full speed ahead. One after another the isolated peasant huts at the approaches to the village rushed by: they and their fallen fences, and their barefoot and grimy children splashing in the puddles, roused by the whip, the bells, and the sight of the soldier on the wagon

"Now the two houses, one on the hill and the other below, sparkled before our eyes. A group of men and women stood in front of our yard. They must be some of the company gathered in honor of the guest. But why does nobody move toward us? The whole thing is a puzzle.

"And Styupe was still standing erect, legs spread out and lashing with a heavy hand. The crack of his whip resounded like bursting bubbles as the wagon approached noisily and rapidly. I could already make out each one of the group. The in-laws' family, big and small, Pesach-Itzi and his wife, and others. The clothes were mixed: a combination of holiday and weekday garments. New hats, shawls, and shoes and the bride all in white was also there. So too was the village elder with his garlic-colored beard and his red girdle. He stood there to one side, carrying his silver-headed cane. What's he doing here at such an hour, and why don't we see any of our family?

"A moment later, when the wagon halted before the gate and we were able to see the faces of the assembled folk, everything became clear. Without words, without speech, everything became clear.

4

The guest lowered his voice a little and continued: "The solution was most cruel, too cruel for a small boy, such as I was then, to contemplate. It all happened so suddenly! Who could have ever imagined that by the time my brother and I returned home from the station, we would find nothing there! Who could have foreseen that within four or five hours, while we were on the road, people would enter the family home, load furnishings and inhabitants into carts, and tell them to go wherever they could. And when? On that very day!

"The decree had crept along for several months, crept like a silent python, and now, when no one was expecting it, suddenly it emerged from its hiding place and struck—and how savage and poisonous was its bite!

"The faces of the hatted and shawled assembly of men and women who greeted us silently told us immediately what had happened to our father's home. Their depressed and gloomy faces streaming with tears made them look like a band of mourners rather than a welcoming crowd.

"When my brother Samuel descended from the wagon and I after him, a piercing cry suddenly erupted, rising like an arrow—a lone cry of anguish, which was immediately cut off as if by a sharp knife leaving a deep gash in the air and in the heart. It was the future mother-in-law who had screamed in this fashion, and this short cry was like the last gasp of a dying man. The children sobbed loudly, and the men turned their faces away and their lips and eyelids trembled.

"My whole world turned dim. I recall the events that subsequently occurred, as if seen through a soiled and broken mirror: many fragments smashed in halves, thirds, and quarters.

"Samuel and I were standing in the courtyard. I did not know why we had entered it. Hats and new shoes without bodies between them were silently walking behind us, as if floating on air. Someone near me was speaking. I heard each individual word but did not see the speaker or understand what he was saying or why. From the bolted barn, whose door I could only see, rose the bitter and mind-piercing cry of a bleating calf. Why was the calf crying? Another hat floated toward us from the house, beneath it a beard and two sleeved hands. The hands weeping like a baby's, as if to say: 'Look Samuel, what they've done to us—Father?—Is he then still here?'

"And there is Yavdoha. Looking at Samuel's face from afar, shaking her little head like a gizzard, and sobbing quietly; the darling, the favorite . . .

"We stood inside the house: a ruin, a desolation. The Passover table, the walls, the windows—were all laid bare. The beds were stripped. Two or three chairs lay upside down—destruction and ruination.

"Only the little Holy Ark remained hidden in its corner, standing with its face covered with clean, white curtains, so as not to see the house in its disgrace.

"Old Yavdoha wandered about within the chaos, clapping her hands in despair and silently whimpering.

"The wicked men came. They came, loaded the wagons, and sent Mother and children away.

"Does one have to relate the details of the expulsion? They are very short and simple.

"Two officials sent especially from the district capital—it was they whom we had encountered on the road—arrived suddenly at noon with three wagons from the village. Heeding no pleas or arguments, they gave orders that people and furnishings be loaded and transported to one of the neighboring Jewish townlets. Mother and the children were forcibly seated in the wagons with the pillows, the bolsters, a bundle of matzahs and the paraphernalia of exile. Even the fish pan and the roasting kettle were removed from the oven while still cooking and were dispatched with their owners away from the village.

"With the exiles went the best of our three cows, which the children needed for milk, the mother of the abandoned calf. Only after much difficulty was Father permitted to stay behind until his two remaining sons, Samuel and myself, and the wagon returned from the station, on condition that he and his sons would then leave the village immediately on that very day and on that very wagon. The village elder was ordered in the most stringent terms not to leave the place until the law was fully implemented. And so it was.

"Father handed over the Torah scroll and its small ark to Zelig, his in-law, and his bunch of keys to old Yavdoha, who remained there to watch over the house. He quickly urged me and Samuel to get on the wagon so that we could catch up with Mother and the children.

"The time for our final departure had now arrived. The old nurse clasped my head to her heart and sobbed loudly. The womenfolk started wailing again. The future mother-in-law fainted, and the bride hid her face in her hands and her shoulders trembled.

"The wagon moved out. The two grown men, the father-in-law and Pesach-Itzi, escorted us silently to the edge of the village where the woods began and then returned home. Not one of the village's farmers came to say good-bye. Those who saw us in the distance hurriedly hid themselves in their homes. A moment later, the entire wagon disappeared completely into the woods—and everything was left behind us: the two white houses, the hill, the escorts, the village elder with his staff and copper badge, and Yavdoha. Thus ended the village!

"Through the slender trees and their foliage, to the left of the road, a round clearing appeared, with an unfinished building standing at its center. This was the tar refinery that had been abandoned in the middle of its construction. The courses of brick stared at us in desolation through the tree trunks. To me it seemed that they had awakened from deep slumber, a slumber of despair, and appeared to be complaining silently, 'Yosi, Yosi, why have you forsaken us?'

"Father turned his head away so as not to look at them. Suddenly one heard a sob and a furtive groan. . . . Father was crying.

"Styupe angrily lashed the horses, as if intending to drown out Father's cries and groans in the noise of trotting and the ringing of bells, but the horses were tired. The road to the village was poor, and the wagon labored along. Once again it passed woods and fields. The bells again sounded their thin, weak tinkling—but this time the sound was so sad.

"As evening fell, we finally saw the three carts in the distance, wending their way through the woods with their cargo of people and furnishings. The cow straggled along tied to the last cart. From time to time she turned back her head and bellowed to the sky. My ears again heard the bleating of the calf that had been locked in the barn.

"A moment later our wagon reached the caravan of carts. Shall I tell you how Mother met her son on the road? That is beyond me. I would do better to skip over it. After the encounter, Mother reclined, as if dead, for more than an hour, sunken into the bundles of bedding. At her side, my little sister lay folded up; she had fallen asleep crying, the tears still on her cheek. My other sister and my middle brother sat in the other two carts—their faces also streaked with tears.

"At sunset, the caravan reached woods standing about a half-hour's journey from the town. Mother suddenly stirred, straightened the kerchief on her head, removed a small package from one of the bundles, gave the order to halt the carts, and decamped. 'Where are you going?' Father asked when he saw her turning toward a hillock in the woods. He, too, stopped his wagon. 'To light candles,' Mother replied.

"No one was surprised. The day was both a Sabbath and Passover, and she had never in all her life missed blessing the candles. No one thought that even in the mad confusion of exile, she would have forgotten to bring along the candles, lest darkness fall while she was still en route.

"My brother Samuel immediately rushed to assist her. The carts and their peasant drivers stood respectfully to attention. A moment later, two little golden flames shone on the hilltop. The blind woods suddenly regained their sight, as if two living eyes were placed in them. The trees silently wondered at the Jewess wrapped in a shawl, who stood among them at that time, spreading the palms of her hands over the candles and quietly weeping.

"However strange and sad that entire gathering appeared at the time, it seemed to me nevertheless that at the very instant when the two little flames flickered among the trees, holiness had descended upon the woods. In one of its dark corners, in a sanctuary hidden deep within it, a small gate of mercy had opened and a good angel had poked his head out of the gate. The two flames were like two golden dots, marking the end of a verse on the rim of the sky, and indicating that up to those points was the realm of the secular and beyond them began the Sabbath and the holiday. The sadness that had seized us at that hour appeared to soften. It, too, became holy. Even the peasants seemed to sense this, and after the lighting of the candles, as they and their animals began to move away, I imagined that their exit from the forest in the twilight darkness was more deliberate and mysterious than their arrival. And the 'giddy-ups' with which they urged on their tired animals were uttered in a lower key and compassionately, as if the grief of the moment had overcome them and suddenly affected their hearts and voices.

"Mother was not willing to return to the cart again after the blessing of the candles but walked alongside the road, with Samuel and Father walking silently on either side of her. The children in the wagons were moved, at Father's suggestion, to our cart. Styupe was ordered to hurry them to the nearby city before the wagons could get there. Soon the wagons and the woods were left behind us. Once again I turned my eyes toward the hillock in the woods. The two flames sparkled at me for a little while and then suddenly disappeared. 'They've burnt out,' I said with concern, and my heart was very sad that the woods had become blind once again and reverted to darkness. The gate of mercy had opened for a moment and was closed again. The good angel withdrew his head, and everything around us sank into silence.

"The town rapidly drew closer and closer. It winked at us through the darkness with many sparks of light—holiday sparks. These signaled the splendor of homes—rooms that were all brightness and purity, white tablecloths, laden with all sorts of goodly foods and blessings, glistening pillows, wine turning precious glass goblets red, shining forks and spoons, handsome clothes and jewelry, and generosity and beaming faces.

"It was quite possible that we were the only Jews in the whole world who were on the road at this hour.

"I lifted my eyes to the heavens. Tonight they, too, had wrapped themselves in blue, displaying all their jewelry, big stars and small and tiny ones. Here and there silver chains of light were linked to them in veils of clouds, which in pure lightness appeared as a splendid adjunct to the glorious blue of the holiday. Now a hidden hand raised the 'silver bowl' of the moon, carefully removing its white coverlet, the veil of the flimsy cloud, and displayed it in full glory.

"A silent grief poured down with the moonlight and filled our hearts with sorrow. Our throats choked and our eyes brimmed with tears. Suddenly we were aware of everything that had befallen us, and the tears flowed.

"When we came to the town, the moon had already reached the middle of the sky. At our brother Moses's suggestion, the wagon went ahead while we descended and walked along the sides of the road, through dark alleys, trying to hide ourselves, moving furtively through the shadows cast by fences and houses, to avoid being seen too much. This caution was actually unnecessary because the streets were empty at that time. People had not yet left the synagogues, and all the way, as far as the only inn in town, to which we went on Father's instructions, we encountered nobody.

"After a quarter of an hour, the carts and passengers arrived at the tavern. . . . Just then the people dressed in holiday finery coming out of the Synagogue saw, to their amazement, three carts laden with furnishings parked in front of Moses Aaron's inn and from one of them matzah crumbs falling to the ground in the moonlight. . . .

"That night," the narrator concluded, "for the first time, I celebrated the Passover Seder, together with my entire family, at a stranger's table, the table of Reb Moses Aaron, the innkeeper, whom

I remember for his kindness. This good man kept us all together and did not allow us to be separated. Moreover, wishing to please my father and mother, he honored me, their youngest son, by inviting me to recite the 'Four Questions.'[10]

"And the trumpet?" a little blushing boy, a guest at the Seder but previously unnoticed by anyone, suddenly asked. The guest chuckled and replied:

"The trumpet. After two weeks, when his furlough had ended, my brother returned to his unit, and I never had the privilege of hearing its sound again. All those days it remained in its case under one of the beds at the inn, where it was deposited with the rest of our things. It never dared to come out and sound its call. The trumpet was ashamed."

---

[10]Near the beginning of the Passover Seder, tradition requires that the youngest child ask four questions about the meaning of the ritual and its symbols.

5

Short Friday

❖ ❖ ❖

Short Friday is a tragicomic story about a pious provincial Rabbi who, because he succumbs to the temptations of good food, drink, and bonhomie, overstays his visit at a circumcision party and as a result is forced to violate the Sabbath.

European literature and folklore are replete with anecdotes about "straying" clergymen. Many of these are acerbic satirical attacks upon *prêtres rusés* (deceitful priests) or naive and ignorant clerics. These attacks appeared with greatest frequency during the Enlightenment. Other depictions of errant priests simply reflect the good-humored reaction of believers and skeptics to the all-too-human foibles of country priests and Rabbis.

As a budding poet, Bialik composed several light verses mocking the naive adulation of Hasidic holy men by their followers. In contrast, *Short Friday* has been characterized as a post-*Haskalah* (Jewish enlightenment) story, devoid of any polemical intent. Its tone is tongue-in-cheek, modulated by a good-natured empathy with the pietistic concern of a simple Rabbi who stumbled unwittingly. The narrator lives at a time that is beyond the era of militant antireligious polemics. He is able to be objective.

In a postscript to this story, Bialik notes that its contents and "its course but not its manner of presentation were given to me by Mr. Eliyahu Levin." He apparently had read Eliyahu Levin's Yiddish story by the same name, published in 1899, about ten years before Bialik's story appeared. Levin was a minor Yiddish and Hebrew essayist who rarely wrote fiction and who published his version of a popular Jewish folk story as a feuilleton.

Short Friday is the common term used by observant Jews to designate the shortest Friday of the year—that is, the Friday that falls on or nearest to the winter solstice. Orthodox Jewish law prohibits most forms of labor on the Sabbath, including traveling in vehicles, writing, cooking, and sewing. Only those tasks that are necessary to preserve life are excluded from this rigorous restriction.

The Jewish Sabbath begins on Friday evening at sunset and concludes on Saturday night. The Rabbi meticulously observed all the numerous regulations prescribed for the preparation of the Sabbath. His routine is disrupted by a tempting invitation to act as godfather at the circumcision of the grandson of an ignorant but affluent tax collector who lived in a neighboring village. At the festivities following the rite, the Rabbi and his gentile driver overeat and overdrink. Finally well fed and intoxicated, they leave the party almost too late to arrive home before sunset. En route, disaster strikes. They both fall asleep and their horse goes astray. When they awake it is dark— Sabbath!

A comedy of errors ensues. Tired and half frozen, they arrive at an inn late at night, after the Jewish innkeeper and his family had gone to bed. Weary and conscience-stricken, the Rabbi falls asleep. In the morning, the innkeeper is shocked at the sight of the Rabbi still sleeping. Assuming that no Rabbi would travel on the Sabbath, the innkeeper concludes that he had miscalculated the date and quickly removes all signs of the Sabbath on the assumption that it was actually Friday. When the Rabbi awakes and sees that signs of the Sabbath are removed, he assumes that he had slept through the entire Sabbath and that it is now Sunday. He hastily dresses and departs for home, only to arrive there as his congregants are emerging from the Synagogue dressed in their Sabbath best.

Using the raw material of Levin's version, Bialik recasts the anecdote into a delightful comic vignette. The reader will note the skillful interplay of sacred and profane themes: the Rabbi leaves his home to attend the ceremony "splendidly arrayed in clothes that are a mix of the sacred and the profane." The Rabbi's attempt to enjoy the best of two worlds is doomed to failure. Bialik's description of the postcircumcision feast also reminds us of the feast at the housewarming party thrown by Big Harry and its dismal end, as well as the more modest but hilarious post-Sabbath party celebrated in *The Shamed Trumpet*.

Short Friday presents a rich portrait of Jewish life in a Volhynian town and its array of types: the country Rabbi, the tax farmer, the butcher, the innkeeper, and the gentile peasants employed by them. To infer, as do several commentators, that the story also has a serious message—namely, that any attempt to mix Jewish religiosity with the pleasures of the senses is bound to fail—can hardly be taken seriously.

❖   ❖   ❖

1

If on an ordinary Friday there is not a moment to lose, how much more so on Short Friday. On Short Friday you dare not be slack. Slackness of any sort may cause you to desecrate the Sabbath, God forbid. Satan is particularly out to snare you at such a perilous time.

No wonder, then, if the Rabbi, Reb Lippa, long may he live (a frail and timid Jew), would try from first light to steal a march on Short Friday. He was very severe with himself, very fearful about being thrown off schedule even by an hour and disrupting his routine for the day.

And do not make light of Reb Lippa's routine. Figure it out for yourself: the midnight *Tikkun*s, including *Tikkun Rachel* and *Tikkun Leah,* Psalms, and *Maamadot,* recitations and supplementary prayers before and after the morning service, the service itself, studying selected chapters from the Mishnah, a lesson of Talmud, two or three sections of the *Shulḥan Arukh,* and closing with the assigned weekly Torah reading in both the original Hebrew and its Aramaic translation. All this for the sake of heaven, and now come the duties toward oneself, namely food and refreshment. What can one do? We are, after all, flesh and blood and have to eat. Then in the afternoon there is a whole order of other things to do: taking a ritual bath, clipping one's nails, grinding snuff for the Sabbath, and so on. There still remained the adjudication of religious law and, sometimes, a litigation. People do tend to quarrel on Fridays. Before you realize it, the day is over! Before you turn right or left, sunset arrives!

No wonder, then, that Rabbi Lippa girded himself like a lion and rose with first light on Short Friday. Immediately after the ritual washing of his hands, he hastened to begin his chores. May he succeed in accomplishing all he has set out to do! He is very meticulous about not wasting a single moment. From time to time, he casts a glance at the antique clock hanging on the wall opposite him, deeply concerned that he might fail to fulfill one of the requirements of the daily routine and find himself entering the Sabbath befuddled, God forbid.

But as our sages said long ago, "Everything depends on luck." And against bad luck, intelligence, good counsel, and diligence are clearly of no avail. Now listen to this hair-raising tale.

2

After Rabbi Lippa had finished all his preliminary prayers at dawn and had begun preparing his soul for the morning service, his door suddenly creaked open, and a cloud of vapor entered his house, accompanied by a gentile.

"What brings him to my door so early?" the Rabbi wondered, somewhat taken aback and shrinking as a blast of cold air entered his home.

The gentile leaned his whip against the doorpost, removed his gloves, reached into his pouch, and drew out a folded, crushed, and soiled letter, which he handed to the Rabbi. The Rabbi finished reading the letter and shrugged his shoulders.

"The devil's doing . . ." he pondered. Reb Getzi, the wealthy tax farmer living in the neighboring village, had invited him to a circumcision: "Since he" . . . so the letter stated . . . "since he, Reb Getzi, is about to enter his first grandson, his eldest daughter's first-born, into the covenant of Father Abraham, he therefore, wishes to honor him (i.e., the Rabbi, long life to him) to act as the child's godfather. His reverence must take the trouble to come down to the village—immediately. The sleigh sent for him is waiting for him."

Reb Getzi's handwriting was not, begging your pardon, very elegant. A reader must decipher it slowly. On this occasion, however, he was clever enough to append three adequate explanatory "footnotes" to the letter. The first: a new three-ruble banknote, enclosed in an envelope ("money talks"), which was passed immediately from hand to hand—that is, from the gentile's hand to the Rabbi's (pardon the comparison). The second: a sack full of large potatoes, alongside of which was tied a gobbling, fattened gander. This handsome pair was taken off the sleigh by the maid and put in the kitchen. And the third, to make things clearer: a warm, ample fur coat and a pair of felt boots, taken from Reb Getzi's own winter wardrobe, so that the Rabbi, long may he live, might wrap up snugly in them and keep warm en route.

These three explanatory "footnotes" immediately appealed to the Rabbi, and with his quick wit he at once grasped the importance of the proposal.

"What, what to do?" sighed the Rabbi. "Certainly this was God's will, a circumcision, such an important pious occasion." . . . Nevertheless, better consult the Rebbitzin.

Rabbi Lippa went into the Rebbitzin's room, did what he had to do, tarrying there as long as he had to, and then emerged dressed in a white Sabbath caftan and a Sabbath robe, ready for the road. Here, in the first room, he wrapped himself in the overcoat Reb Getzi had sent him, pulled the yellow felt boots over his black shoes, donned his Sabbath headgear over his yarmulke, tied the messenger's red belt around his hips—and dressed elegantly in these clothes, an odd mixture of sacred and profane, Rabbi Lippa rose, kissed the mezuzah, and left his home.

The sleigh standing before the house was large and heavily padded with hay. Rabbi Lippa mounted it and sat down comfortably, as if he owned the sleigh. The gentile covered the Rabbi's legs with straw; he too mounted the sleigh and seated himself. One whistle, and the sleigh was gliding over the snow.

3

The road was good and smooth. The mare was swift. It was as if the journey was miraculously shortened. . . . An hour later, before the sun had risen, the Rabbi had arrived at the village and reached the home of the celebrants.

The guests had already assembled. After a glass of hot tea, everybody rose, and forming a quorum, recited morning prayers. A butcher who had come to the village by chance to purchase a few calves turned out to have a good voice and was invited to lead the service. His Hebrew was a little imperfect. He confused the prayer referring to winter with the one referring to summer, but this was no serious matter. Finally the worshipers concluded with the Aleinu, ending their prayers peacefully. The rite of circumcision began in good spirits.

The infant, wrapped in his diapers, was brought in and passed from hand to hand: the mother's uncle passed him to the father's uncle, he to the cousin, who passed him to the paternal grandfather, and he to the maternal grandfather, and so forth, until he reached the lap of the godfather. They performed what had to be done . . . and afterwards the crimson little body, whose arms and legs where tightly bound and who was bawling and writhing all over, was lifted and passed from hand to hand until he was returned to his mother's breast. Then his crying abated somewhat.

And now we come to the main event: the festival meal.

Reb Getzi was indeed a genial and gracious host, even under ordinary circumstances. Now that God had kept him alive and granted him the good fortune to see a grandchild, his eldest daughter's first boy, he was even more so. Quite naturally this was a royal feast! Fish, as Scripture says, sea monsters! Meat—an entire calf! A dozen geese and three stuffed turkeys. Needless to say, there were all kinds of side dishes, such as stuffed gullet, fried breasts, tongues, gizzards, and their like, all sorts of tidbits, and turnips, those famous pickled turnips!

We shall now stop talking about the dishes and focus upon the various beverages. Reb Getzi, you should know, is an unassuming Jew, without any pretentions. When you say "brandy," you mean brandy, plain and simple, not less than 95 percent proof and, of course, aged, that is to say, brandy that had been stored in his cellar for years. Do you follow me? The brandy had been stored from the beginning in honor of the first grandson, who was destined to arrive at some future date. "Come now, Rabbi, you must drink one more glass, this tiny jigger-full." Getzi thrust a tall gill-sized glass into the Rabbi's hand: "Come on, drink up, Rabbi, don't be afraid! Do you think this is brandy, not at all, it is pure olive oil! It pours into the glass soundlessly. It's really olive oil, as my name is Getzi. Come now. *Le-ḥayim*, Rabbi, *le-ḥayim*."

Getzi was high. His fat, hairy jowls were aflame and glistened like the burnished samovar; his eyes were steeped in fat. From time to time, he would thump on his heart with one of his fingers and mutter to himself thick-tonguedly: "You know, Getzi, from now on you're an old man . . . you're a grandpa, you hear. Ha, ha, ha, you've become a grandpa. And what's your wife?—she's a grandma. Where are you, grandmama? Come here. Grandpa wants to drink a *le-ḥayim* with you. Come, come. Don't be embarrassed, the Rabbi will say, 'Amen,' won't you, Ra-Rabbi?"

At this point Reb Getzi grabbed the Rabbi by his arm, grasped his shoulder tightly, shaking it like a bag of potatoes, then suddenly threw himself on his neck and began to kiss him passionately. Overcome with both joy and pleasure, he laughed and cried simultaneously, delighted at the honor. "Heh, heh, heh, the honor that Rabbi Lippa, long may he live, had done him, to him, to Getzi; by God, the honor. Were it not for the Rabbi, long may he live, my, my, my! Nu, nu, enough, *le-ḥayim.*" Rabbi Lippa soothed the weeping Getzi and cautiously took a gulp from the glass: "*Le-ḥayim!* Why all this crying? There's no need to cry, no need."

Reb Getzi is consoled and wipes a tear off his cheek with his sleeve. "The Rabbi is right, as my name is Getzi. There's no need to cry, no need, only *le-ḥayim* and *le-ḥayim* once again! Indeed *le-ḥayim,* that's to say a real *le-ḥayim, le-ḥayim!* Here's to a decent living." At this point, Getzi began to cry again profusely: "Oy oy, a decent living."

Rabbi Lippa, who was by nature a weak and timorous man, could not abide the suffering of his host and, therefore, as an act of sincere sympathy, ate another morsel and another.

In the meantime, the sun began to set; it was a short Friday. Rabbi Lippa, who was also slightly in his cups, had indeed bestirred himself once or twice, trying to rise from the table and stand on his unsteady legs: "Eh, eh, eh," he argued, stretching his arms and muttering, "Sabbath Eve, the shortest day . . ." But Reb Getzi would not hear of it. He grabbed him with both hands and refused to let him go.

At the same time, Ivan, the wagon driver, sat serenely in the kitchen and also enjoyed eating a festive meal. He took pleasure in the fact that the proper rituals were performed over the tender baby. In joyful celebration, he downed one shot after another; one, two, three. . . .

Just then the grandfather clock struck three. Rabbi Lippa in great haste tore himself away from the table and rose. But the legs were not at all in a hurry. He stood up, wrapped himself doubly in the bear coat and the sheepskin, put on the red girdle, and inserted two feet in the felt boots. Once again his legs did not respond at all. Instead of dislodging himself, the heavily clad Rabbi Lippa suddenly bumped against a bench, and he found himself sprawled in the middle of the house. Rabbi Lippa tried to move his body. "Eh, eh, eh," but in vain. He was unable to budge.

The "oil," which had entered his bones, performed its function. But Rabbi Lippa was not at all distressed. On the contrary, he was in jolly good spirits, and whenever his body tried to force him to move by stretching his hand and wiggling his fingers, his mouth would chuckle in a thin chirping voice, chuckling and muttering, "Ha, ha, ha, Reb Getzi, the feet . . . " "Ha, ha," laughed all the guests as well, "the Rabbi . . . "

Finally, with the aid of Him who giveth strength to the weary and a few of the guests, the heavily clad body was dislodged, and the two handsome creatures, Rabbi Lippa, long may he live, and his escort, Ivan, pardon the comparison, seized an opportune moment. Each assisting and supporting the other, they climbed up and mounted the sleigh unharmed.

Once again our Rabbi sat comfortably inside the wagon, his body wrapped and his legs covered. And once again, Ivan sat in the driver's seat. A loud, jolly whistle, and the mare lifted her legs. . . .

And now we reach the main part of our story.

4

As the sleigh took off, the Rabbi snuggled deeply into his fur coat and was suddenly swept by a warm, pleasant feeling, sweet as honey, which spread through all his limbs. His eyelids were heavy with sleep, and his head began to nod. "Ha, ha, ha, the oil," the Rabbi smiled inwardly, feeling as if there were grains of sand in his eyes. "Pure olive oil . . ." And as soon as the wagon crossed the little bridge outside the village, he fell into a deep sleep.

Ivan, the gentile, was still sitting at this time in the driver's seat, having a friendly conversation with his mare. He promised her any number of goodies later on if only she would follow a straight path and not deviate. While still talking to her in this fashion, both his whip and reins slipped from his hands and his sheepskin hat slid to his coat. In a moment, he, too, was snorting like a pig.

The mare, sensing that she was now free, immediately forgot her master's admonitions and sweet promises for the future. When she reached a crossroads, she hesitated for a moment, as if considering which way to turn: here or there. Suddenly she pulled the sleigh with all her strength and turned, as a compromise, neither here nor there, but took a middle road leading to the fields.

The day meanwhile clouded and darkened. Wet snow fell in abundance, confusing the world and blurring the roads. The mare started, it would seem, to wonder whether she had acted impulsively

and began to repent, but as she could not see very well, she tried to
correct her error by abandoning herself to heaven. She continued
walking in the dark, sadly, her ears aslope, pacing slowly, as if with
closed eyes, on pile upon pile of snow and tangles of thorns, dragging the sleigh and its contents behind her. . . . Who knows where
the mare would have gone had she not stumbled? The sleigh capsized. Our two travelers awoke in great fright, lying on a pile of
snow, and found themselves surrounded by utter darkness.

"What happened?" the Rabbi wondered as he wriggled out of the
snow. Suddenly he remembered everything that had occurred. It was
as if a heavy ax had struck his head: "How could it be? Sabbath!"

The Rabbi wanted to utter a loud and bitter cry—but was unable
to. His entire being had collapsed and frozen into a frightful
thought formed by that single word, "Sabbath!"

When his power of speech was partially restored—a roar rose of itself. "Ivan! Oh, woe!" This roar burst from the depths of his heart,
expressed in the only three words our Rabbi knew of the language of
the uncircumcised; they were accompanied by a bitter shout, a plea
for mercy, a fear of God, a resignation to His judgment, a regret and
complaint, and many other feelings that words could not express.

While all this was happening, Ivan stood cursing as he tended to
the capsized sleigh and its tangled reins. From time to time, he
kicked the belly of the scraggy mare, reminding her of the sins of her
fathers and mothers through a thousand generations. Upon finishing the repairs, he invited the "Rabin" to mount. The Rabbi lifted
his eyes to the night. From whence cometh help? None came.

For a moment it occurred to him that he should not move from
this spot. Come what may, he must spend the night in the field and
observe the Sabbath right here. Better to perish than to transgress
the commandment. Were there not many "tales" about pious and
righteous men who found themselves on the road when the holy
Sabbath had arrived? The story about Ariel is proof enough. "Did
not God appoint a lion to guard that pious man in the desert until
Havdalah?" But when Rabbi Lippa looked once again at the darkness of the night, his eyes discerned something looking like a real
forest, full of loud noises and the wail of storms. As we all know too
well, any forest is considered to be fraught with danger, full of bandits and wild beasts.

To the left stretched a desolate field entirely covered with white
shrouds. Out of the snow rose all sorts of golems and threatening

objects, a mixture of black and white. They looked like gravestones. Only God knows who they were: demons, beasts, ghosts, or just tangles of brambles . . . from every corner and every side, packs of panthers and dens of vipers all about, all ready to attack him out of the dark.

"No," mused Rabbi Lippa, having changed his mind. "Saving a life supersedes the laws of the Sabbath. 'He shall live by them,' and not die by them.[1] One must never rely on miracles. And who knows whether I am deserving of miracles?"

Rabbi Lippa imagined a huge and terrible panther confronting him, with eyes shooting sparks at him and with crooked, snarling teeth. Rabbi Lippa's skin crept and his eyes froze.

"No, no, no!" the Rabbi decided, seized by a deathly fear and chattering teeth. He remounted the sleigh. "In truth, and by the profoundest understanding of the law, I am not at all obligated to sacrifice my life in this situation. On the contrary, traveling on the Sabbath is only a later Rabbinic prohibition, not derived from Scripture."

Rabbi Lippa in the meantime found himself sitting in the wagon, but sighing and groaning, he tried to sit in an abnormal position— so that traveling in this fashion would at least belong to the *category of change*.[2]

The sleigh wended its way through the dark and slippery snow. Depressed and contrite, Rabbi Lippa whispered the prayers greeting the Sabbath, but his heart was broken and depressed. . . .

May you, wayfarer, never experience such a fate. The winter filtered through Rabbi Lippa's eyes like a stream. The poor mare was so exhausted that she was barely able to walk. The sleigh bounced along upon the rutted road, causing Rabbi Lippa's broken body to bounce with it. His bones were almost scattered along the way. Wide-branched and laden with heavy snow, the ancient oak trees passed before his eyes. They were angry and condemned him silently. The tangled oak bushes, the smaller minions of the forest, whose pointed tops were capped with snow, stared at him amazed. "Who is this Rabbi Lippa, the town's chief religious leader, who

---

[1]*Scriptural basis*, which permitted the violation of the law in case of possible loss of life. Leviticus 18:5.

[2]*Category of change*, since the act is not a normal act, under Talmudic law it might not be considered a form of traveling.

dares to ride on the Sabbath?" Thorns and thistles lowered their heads in shame; the wind was sobbing: "Oy, oy"—at this profanation of the Sabbath, "oy, oy," at this shaming of the Torah.

5

At midnight, the sleigh finally arrived at a wayside inn covered in snow up to its windows. The dead-tired mare exuded vapor and frost. The travelers were battered and exhausted. The Rabbi's beard, earlocks, mustache, and overcoat collar had frozen into a single icy mass. No one could proceed beyond this point. An old gentile, the inn's attendant, came out toward them. The Rabbi descended and entered the inn, while the wagon disappeared inside the courtyard gate.

The room he entered was cold and desolate and lit by the dim light of a small and sooty storm-lamp. From the adjacent room came the snoring of the innkeeper. Two copper candlesticks stood on the table, holding stumps of burned-out candles. The thick, hand-woven tablecloth was covered with crumbs and bones, the remains of the Sabbath meal. Rabbi Lippa turned his face away so as not to look at the table. Stiff with cold and weighed down by his heavy clothes, he threw himself on a bare, hard bench before his strength gave out, and buried his head inside the collar of his overcoat.

"So, he, the Rabbi has violated the Sabbath, what a terrible profanation of God's name! How could he show his face tomorrow? How could he face judgment day? The shame of it!" Tears flowed from the Rabbi's eyes. His earlocks, beard, and mustache also dripped water. The Rabbi's head and limbs weighed heavily upon him. He tried to move but was unable to do so. "Was it possible that the hour of death had arrived?" The Rabbi was seized by a mortal terror and his teeth chattered. "Yes, this was death. The time had come to say confession. . . .

"His lips began to whisper the confession on their own: "Oy, oy, Merciful and gracious God, long suffering and full of loving kindness. Please, please God, have mercy upon me. O Master of the World, forgive and pardon a man who is but flesh and blood, a maggot, a worm . . . ! I have indeed sinned, erred, and transgressed . . . but these lambs of mine, my wife and my children, what sin have they performed?"

The unfortunate man had not slept for more than a day. His whole body was drenched in cold sweat, and his bones felt as if they were on fire. His mind wandered feverishly. He recited strange biblical verses in a whisper, combining them with random excerpts from the Mishnah, verses from the Pentateuch, quotations of the Rabbis, prayers, and petitions—it was a sort of a "*Tikkun* for Shavuot." Thoughts about Heaven, reward and punishment, Hell and Paradise, the torments of the grave, and the angel of death raced through his distraught brain and were mixed with his domestic concerns: a widow, orphans, a daughter of marriageable age, the loss of his Rabbi's hereditary rights, the yeast tax. . . .

These worries tortured the poor Rabbi, as he sighed and groaned until dawn. At sunrise he fell into the deep but confused sleep of a tortured soul—breathing heavily in short gasps.

6

At the very hour that Rabbi Lippa was stretched out on the desolate inn's bench, wrapped in his overcoat, entirely bathed in sweat and wet from the melting snow that once had covered his beard and earlocks, and wracked by bad dreams and asleep—the good Lord was sitting in Heaven, busy with his own tasks: causing the roosters to crow and rolling away the darkness before the light. As soon as the cock crowed and a pale, angry, and freezing winter dawn's light penetrated the house through its frost-covered window, Feibke the innkeeper sneezed, belched, and awoke from his sleep. He leaped from his bed, laced on his heavy boots, flung his short overcoat over his shoulders, and entered the large room to see who had come to his inn at night. Upon entering, he looked and turned to stone. Before him stretched out on the bench lay the Rabbi, Rabbi Lippa, fully clad in his overcoat.

At first he thought this must be a piece of witchcraft, the devil's doing. He bent and took a second look, carefully examining what he saw. He glanced up and down and sideways—"As I live and breathe, the Rabbi! It's him! With his shofar-shaped nose and that gizzardlike face!"

Feibke started like a mad man. "What's this, it's the Sabbath and . . . the Rabbi . . . am I drunk or crazy?" All of a sudden he struck his head with his fist. "Oh Feibke, son of Ham, there must be some mistake, an ugly mistake. You've made a mistake in counting the days. Feibke, yes indeed, Feibke, you have been snared. Woe to you, and woe upon you. Living as you do with Esau, and because of your many sins, you've confused the calendar. My, my, a fine thing you have done, a fine affair, as I am a Jew. . . . Tomorrow the whole town will know about it. . . . Ugh."

Once Feibke understood his dilemma, he immediately hurried to erase all signs of the Sabbath from his home. First, he removed the copper candlesticks from the table, then the remnants of the Sabbath meal and the white tablecloth. He then dashed into the bedroom and hastily made his family get out of bed. "Hurry, hurry, you unclean corpses; oh, oh, there's going to be a plague here."

"Who's here, what's happened?" His wife woke up in panic.

"Go to hell, you dumb animal. Shut up. Get up at once and take the cholent out of the oven."

For a moment his wife did not know what her husband was talking about, but when he explained things clearly to her with a groan and a blow of his fist—she jumped out of bed, got dressed, and rushed to the oven.

"Everything, everything, take out everything, a plague on you," the husband cried. "The porridge, the pudding—pour the whole pot into the garbage can. Don't leave a single trace!"

In a moment, the whole scene was altered. Sabbath was over and replaced with a weekday atmosphere. A fire burned in the big stove. The fat samovar was loaded with burning coals and began to sizzle. The sounds of hammer and ax were heard in the house. Yokum, the servant, was chopping wood, fixing wedges, and hammering nails whether they were needed or not. Feibke himself was standing bent over the dough trough and was kneading dough with all his might. His daughter, a tall girl of marriageable age with a plump and sooty face, stood dazed in the middle of the house, not understanding what was going on. In the meantime, she had received two slaps in the face and a pinch from her father's dough-soiled hands. She rose and began peeling potatoes into a large pot full of water. "Peel them, peel, a plague on you"—Feibke cried, urging her on, while he himself kept kneading the dough furiously. He expected the Rabbi to wake up at any moment, but when he finished kneading and the Rabbi was not yet awakened, he hurried and put on his worn, creased yarmulke with bits of cotton pulp peering from it holes, bared his arm, began to put on his phylacteries, and chant the week-day morning service aloud.

The door kept opening and closing ceaselessly as farmers wearing heavy coats and holding whips entered and left. The house filled up with snow, frost, and the smell of cheap tobacco, the odor of coats, the stamping of feet, and chattering.

Feibke purposely passed the Rabbi's bench, reciting his prayers aloud, using the weekday melody: "Haleluyah, haleluyah." Simultaneously, he cast a sharp glance sideways at the Rabbi, the kind that said: "Sleep, sleep my Rabbi, enjoy, now I'm no longer worried about you. Now you may even wake up."

Indeed, at that very moment, the Rabbi moved his feeble body slightly. "Bravo, Feibke," the innkeeper said to himself. "See to it that you don't spoil things." Feibke disappeared into the cloud of cheap tobacco smoke, the motley crowd, and the pile of coats. From there he kept his eyes on the Rabbi as he chanted his prayers in the weekday style and in a triumphant tune, "Haleluyah, haleluyah."

7

Once our Rabbi awoke, all his pains awoke with him. "Oy, oy, oy, my whole head aches, and all my bones are broken." With great difficulty, he straightened half his body and opened his eyes. "What's going on? Where is he? At the bathhouse? No, at the inn. Where did the Sabbath disappear? There is no trace of the Sabbath. Farmer's weekday noises. Look, the samovar is boiling right opposite him!"

"If so," a terrible thought set all his bones atremble; his sallow face grew even sallower. "If so, I've slept through the entire Sabbath day as well as Saturday night. Here, on the bench, in sight of Feibke and the gentiles, I was lying asleep for an entire twenty-four-hour stretch! Without Kiddush, without prayers, without Havdalah. O God, what have you done to Lippa?"

A dark terror gripped the Rabbi—a terrible despair pierced his heart. He almost fainted. God had indeed embittered his lot, beyond all measure. . . . "Why," his heart cried out, "tell me, God, why?"

Out of the cloud of cheap tobacco smoke, Ivan emerged, whip in hand. "Time to go, Rabin, the wagon is ready."

The Rabbi rose groaning and turned his face to the door. He swayed like a drunkard and cut a path with difficulty through the crowd of peasants. At the door, Feibke's broad and gnarled palm suddenly grasped his hand: "Good-bye R-Rabbi." "Good-bye, good-bye," the Rabbi withdrew rapidly. "No time." "Good-bye, good-bye, R-Rabbi. Go in peace, R-Rabbi, may God protect you." His departure pleased both parties, and neither delayed the other. Feibke quickly slammed the door behind the fleeing Rabbi, as if to say—"God bless you." The Rabbi mounted the sleigh with alacrity. "Tally ho, Ivan, Ivan," the Rabbi urged Ivan on.

Why all the rush? to flee? where to? The Rabbi himself did not know how to answer these questions, but at that time Rabbi Lippa was not inclined to ask any questions or probe very much. Whatever he did seemed to be done automatically, unconsciously, and without reckoning. He asked for one thing, prayed for it with all his heart: "O God in heaven, perform a miracle on my behalf. Let the road extend for thousands and thousands of miles, let years pass, hundred of years—and just let me travel, travel, travel. And if I am unworthy of such a miracle, take my soul. O God in Heaven, pardon me everything—and take my soul." ...

However, Rabbi Lippa's prayer was unheeded. The sleigh carried him on eagle's wings. The polished and slippery road speeded his way.

Following the cloudy night, a winter sun rose. The white earth glistened gaily. Crows pecking along the road cleared a path for the flying sleigh, greeting it with their hoarse cries: "Caw, Caw, Caw."

Rabbi Lippa felt ashamed facing the crows, the brilliance of the sun, the whiteness of the snow. He buried his head again inside his coat collar and relapsed into thoughts of despair. From then on and beyond, he no longer saw, heard, or felt anything. He placed his soul in the hands of the God of all spirits and his shattered body in the hands of the racing sleigh! "Come what may!"

8

At midday, as the congregation of the townlet emerged from the Synagogue, walking calmly and in Sabbath majesty along the sides and in the middle of the road, while everyone wished his neighbor, "Shabbat Shalom" (a peaceful Sabbath), at that very moment a light, speeding sleigh emerged from the alleyway toward them, *and in it—what a dreadful sight—the Rabbi, Reb Lippa.*

6

The Legend of the Three and Four

❖   ❖   ❖

$\mathcal{T}$*he Legend of the Three and Four*[1] is the most important work written by Bialik after he left Russia in 1922. It belongs to the same genre as "The Scroll of Fire," a prose poem composed in 1905. Both works are based upon ancient Rabbinic legends. Their theme is akin to that of the medieval European legends about the quest for the holy grail—the symbol of salvation.

"The Scroll of Fire" utilizes and refines several Jewish legends about the heavenly fire once used on the altar of the Temple in Jerusalem, which was salvaged and hidden in a cave in a distant land. Once the Temple is rebuilt, so the legend goes, the fire will be returned to the altar. Bialik transfers the hiding place to a mountain crag and introduces a devout youth who sets off in a quest to recover the fire in order to hasten the promised restoration (i.e., salvation). He finally reaches the fire but cannot hold onto it. It tumbles into the abyss of perdition, and he is cast into eternal exile. *The Legend of the Three and Four* has its source in a Midrash[2] about King Solomon's daughter, who was enclosed by him in a high tower on a remote island to protect her from unsuitable lovers. She is rescued by a daring

---

[1]Second Version.

[2]"Introduction," *Midrash Tanḥuma*, ed. S. Buber, (New York: Sefer, 1946 [1885]), p. 136.

youth who comes from afar and with superhuman effort manages to scale the tower and conquer her heart.

Bialik first published a reworked version of this Midrash in 1917.[3] It was reissued several times and later reentitled *The Legend of the Three and Four—First Version.*" Although the second version is also based on the Tanhuma source, it is a separate work—a highly sophisticated, semiallegorical modern short story.

Bialik was an avid admirer of the Aggadah, the nonlegal portions of the Rabbinic literature consisting of a rich repository of legends, aphorisms, anecdotes, and so on. He coedited a brilliant compendium of the Aggadic material, which itself became a classic of Hebrew literature.[4] He also evinced a profound interest in medieval Jewish folklore and drew upon it for many of his charming children's stories. However, his was not an antiquarian obsession. He believed that this rich lode of legends should be mined, refined by an aesthetic sensibility, and recast to fit the needs of contemporary readers. He stressed that it should also serve as a source for symbols, plots, and literary models for modern Hebrew authors.

"There is an absolute need to secularize the Aggadah, to detach it from its (exclusively) sacred atmosphere, to expose it to the open air, and include it in our modern literature." He suggested that throughout Jewish history the Aggadah had been redesigned and revised to respond to the cultural needs of generation after generation: "Its interpreters often ignored the original context of these materials, not because they thought lightly of them, but used them as a compost from which to raise new plants, elevating their contents to a higher sphere."[5]

He deliberately chose to fashion a new Hebrew style for both "The Scroll of Fire" and *The Legend of the Three and Four,* rejecting a purely biblical style because he felt that it had been overused and had lost its vitality. Instead he forged a lyrical

---

[3]"The Princess and Her Mate," *Ha-Am,* July 7, 1917.

[4]The English translation of this work is *The Book of Legends,* trans. William L. Braude (New York: Schocken, 1992).

[5]Hayyim Naḥman Bialik, *Devarim Shebaal Peh,* Vol. II. Tel Aviv: Dvir, 1935. Pp. 69.

prose style "that was ... at least an octave higher. ... I do not recall similar phrasing in Hebrew (literature) ever being employed before."[6]

He claimed that he used

> the same rhythms and forms [found] in our archaic poetry and carefully avoided [the current] biblical style [and], at times, used Talmudic phrasing that was consistent with the tone and rhythms of this style. ... An option was created to write about very delicate and modern matters in a very ancient Hebrew. ... Perhaps this is the best instrument for writing about ... matters that could not be grasped by the standard linguistic instruments that had been hitherto used.

But for all of their similarity, the two works are decidedly different. "The Scroll of Fire" is steeped in despair; the young hero reaches the flame only to drop it into the swirling sea. On the other hand, Netanyah, the protagonist of *The Legend of the Three and Four,* after much anguish, penetrates the tower, wins the princess, and the two return triumphantly to celebrate their marriage in Jerusalem at King Solomon's court.

A major theme in both works involves the attempt to reconcile tradition with modernity, Judaism with European culture, Jew with gentile. In the prose poem the attempt is a tragic failure. In our story it is a success. Bialik replaced Solomon's daughter with a gentile princess. Ketziyah is the daughter of the King of Amon. Netanyah is a diaspora Jew. Their encounter in the land of Israel is a triumph.

The emerald carried by Netanyah as a gift to the Temple in Jerusalem was a gem that once belonged to his dead mother. It is sewn on the curtain of the Holy of Holies. The first emerald, which symbolizes tears, orphanhood, tragedy, and suffering, is placed alongside a second emerald, the wedding gift that King Solomon gave to Ketziyah, as a symbol of joy and integration.

The story can be read on several levels. It is a beautiful romance about two young people who overcome all obstacles and consummate their love. It can also be understood as an

---

[6]Ibid., Vol. I, p. 25.

Erziehungsroman (a novel of education). Young Netanyah ventures out of his home, breaking first with his father and then with his old mentor. Shipwrecked Netanyah is tossed into the stormy sea but survives the mishap, sailing on a raft. The raft (his mother's womb) is made of two wineskins that sustain him "like an infant between his mother's breasts." He is wrenched out of the sea by a white eagle (good fortune, ideals, hope) and cast upon a barren island. There he discovers the tower and the oak tree (masculinity) and finally the girl, with whom he immediately falls in love: "Am I not her redeemer?" While pondering how he can enter the tower, he falls asleep and dreams that he is again afloat, tied between the two wineskins. Suddenly he spies a woman rising from the sea, wearing a crown with a shining emerald. It is his mother. He cries out to her, but she cannot hear him. He tries to move, but his body and arms are bound to the wineskins. Suddenly the bonds loosen, but his mother disappears into the depths. At this point he discovers the snake, a recurrent symbol in Bialik's works, representing the libido, the animal instincts. The snake seizes and holds the "holy emerald" in "his disgusting mouth." Now his mother's image reappears to him "pure and lustrous as she had been before." But she was not alone, "accompanied by another figure . . . younger than she. On her head is a garland of white lilies." The emerald is no longer on his mother's forehead nor in the snake's mouth but adorns the young woman's forehead. The two women clasp each other's hands. The transference had occurred from his mother to his beloved. The snake, too, turns out to be the guide who will ultimately assist him to get to the tower and to his bride-to-be. The libido is not only a negative phenomenon; it can also lead one to mature love.

Ketziyah also matures, changes from the lonely, frightened little girl who tearfully longed for her father. She is no longer the woman-child who toys with the parrot. She is ripe for love and ready when Netanyah penetrates the tower.

A good part of *The Legend of the Three and Four* was written in Germany, where the Bialiks took the waters in 1929. Bialik was also making a statement against international hatred and the rising Nazi tide, perhaps even the ultranationalism of some Palestinian Jews. The whole tone of the story is a plea for reconciliation and rationality.

For Bialik, in accord with Jewish tradition, King Solomon represented moderation and wisdom. He ruled over Israel during a golden age and, in contrast to his father, King David, desisted from war, maintaining peaceful relations with his neighbors. He earned the privilege of being the builder of the Holy Temple.

Some Bialik scholars suggest that the cordial relationships between the aging king and Netanyah's father and the young couple also represented Bialik's own views about the so-called conflict of generations, which was raging at the time in Hebrew letters, focused as it was against Bialik's dominant role as elder statesman. Others believe that it was a veiled criticism of the ultranationalist Zionist parties who challenged Chaim Weizmann's leadership of the World Zionist Movement. Intergenerational conflicts, the story seems to say, can be resolved through wisdom and tolerance.

The two works also differ aesthetically. "The Scroll of Fire" is loosely constructed. Bialik admitted that it was a mosaic held together by the story frame and by a unifying rhythm. *The Legend of the Three and Four* (Second Version) is a straight and tightly knit narrative—its many subtexts are skillfully integrated and yet demand the active participation of the reader in fathoming its many implications.

❖   ❖   ❖

*There are three things that are beyond my ken and four which I
do not know. The way of the eagle in the sky, the way of the
serpent on the rock, the way of a ship in the heart of the sea,
and the way of a man with a maid.*
    —*Proverbs 30:18–20*

One day King Solomon prepared a grand banquet in his palace.
All the kings of the East and the West came to the banquet: the
King of Aram, the King of Tyre, the Kings of Amon and Moab, and
all the rest of the kings, great and small and smaller still. Foremost
among them was the mighty King of Egypt. All the kings arrived
with their ministers, their greatest sages, and their magicians. Each
brought with him his hidden thoughts. Some came to the banquet
sincerely and with an honest wish to see the wisest of kings in all
his glory and to honor themselves by honoring him, others as dis-
semblers, flatterers, and scoffers, and still others with masked envy
and with many evil schemes.

Now Solomon's table was laden with all the delicacies of the
world. Nothing that the human heart desired or the human eye
sought was lacking. The guests ate, drank, and made merry—yet
their eyes were watchful, as if they were waiting in ambush.

After they ate their fill, the king, as was his custom, took them
into the palace garden so that they might stroll under the shelter of
its shade and entertain one another with witty talk, parables, poetry, and ancient riddles, in accordance with God's gift of grace to
Solomon.

The king's garden was indeed very large. Numberless were its delights and splendors. All God's primeval trees were assembled there,
and beds of magnificent flowers and the choicest of herbs crowned
it with beauty. All day long, the garden resounded with the sweet
and cheerful singing of birds of all colors. Gushing fountains sprin-
kled their limpid waters without, ceaselessly splattering them like

crystal against basins of pure marble, and seemed to revive and loosen the tongues of all the garden's secret corners with this sweet tumult. Glass and crystal pendants and bells of gold and agate with pearl-like tongues hung like jewels on the foliage of the trees. The quiet breeze had only to touch them gently to set them tinkling, softly delighting the ear. The tinklings blended with the rustling of leaves, the murmurings of fountains, and the chirping of birds into a single glorious, divine chorus that was sweet to the listening ear.

The guests, seeing all this magnificence, were as if dream-struck. When Solomon broke the silence with words of wisdom, everyone put aside his petty connivings and his devious plottings. All eyes were suddenly fastened upon Solomon's lips. Everyone became totally entranced. Such was the magic of Solomon's tongue that it won the ears and minds of the listeners.

Solomon led his guests to a thick and leafy fig tree, which was entirely intertwined with sumptuous vines. He had them seated upon carpets of many colors around a limpid pool. The king's servants, handsome youths from Ethiopia, Saba, and Kedar, beautifully shaped and clear-eyed, were adept and fleet. They hastened to respond swiftly to every flicker of the guests' eyes, serving all sorts of refreshing wines and fruit juices in gold or crystal goblets, and they circulated silver baskets laden with every delectable fruit, to the delight of the guests.

Solomon sat at the head of the table. His face glowed with divine wisdom; his mouth was a fountain of understanding. On that day, he told parables about birds, beasts, and flowers and spoke with profound wisdom about God's ways, His providence, and all His wondrous deeds. As the spirit descended upon him, he expounded on the stars, the constellations, and all the heavenly host, whose goings and comings were by God's command. He set their paths and fixed their routes. Finally he also touched upon the nature of women, who, he averred, were God's gift bestowed upon every man in accordance with his deeds, be they good or evil.

When the King of Tyre (Solomon's boyhood friend) heard Solomon's words, his eyes reflected a subtle smile. It was a barely perceptible smile, sharp and thin as a needle's head. But nothing ever escaped Solomon's eye, and he promptly remarked, "Will the King of Tyre not tell us what he has in mind?"

The King of Tyre responded with a tiny imp dancing in his eyes: "Does a wife, indeed, come from the hand of God? I happen to

know a king who has a thousand women in his harem. Did God
bring them all to his bosom?"

The eyes of all the guests turned toward the speaker, some in angry rebuke, some in fear, and others with suppressed glee: "Bravo,
King of Tyre, your needle is thin, but its sting is fierce!"

Now the King of Amon, who was forced to become Solomon's
father-in-law, recalled what his son-in-law had done to him. How he
had entered his home stealthily as a waiter and abducted his daughter Naama. With this in mind, he said: "I, too, by the life of
Milkom, cannot believe that it is the function of God Almighty to
intervene in matters of love and courtship. Are there no other masters of this calling that we are compelled to assign it to God? I do indeed know competent people, skilled in their craft, who have cunningly stolen the hearts of foolish girls, as a thieving waiter purloins
a slice of meat from his master's pot, and who artfully enticed them
to leave their father's house. Did they not carry out this artifice
without God's help?"

The ears of the guests sharpened, their eyes shone sevenfold at
these explicit remarks. "That Amonite really cut him to the quick,
wonderful. This time Solomon's flesh was struck, not by a thin needle, but by a red hot spear." They all sat, taut as bowstrings, awaiting the battle's end.

Now the King of Aram, a scrawny, short man, consumed by enmity and jealousy, who for a long time had borne a grudge against
David's son, sensed that this was an opportunity to exact revenge.
Two tiny evil scorpions peered from his eyes as he said: "I know
more amazing things. I know a king who robbed a woman from the
bosom of his faithful servant. His son, the fruit of his sin, has succeeded him upon the throne. And I would very much like to learn to
whom did God intend to give this woman—the robbed or the robber? Or perhaps to both at the same time?"

The arrow that was shot this time was a burnished arrow, coated
with venom. It pierced the very innards.

The King of Moab, a fleshy, heavy-tongued man whose oily face
lit up with joy upon seeing that the sluices had been opened wide,
decided that he no longer need delay nor contain his emotions.
However, before so doing, he released his heavy tongue, so like the
tongue of a buffalo, and licking his greasy lips, he disgorged ponder-
ous, rolling words one by one, as though rolling stones, and said:
"Your ancestor, Ruth the Moabite, was scion of our family's stock,

a daughter of Moab's ancient chiefs—was it not she who built the house of the Kings of Judah when she married Boaz, the Bethlehemite, after the death of Mahlon, son of Elimelech, the husband of her youth, also a man of Judah! Now, would that I knew which God had twice placed the Moabites into the bosom of a man of Judah: Kemosh, the God of Moab, or was it the God of Judah, or did they both collaborate?"

Indeed, the King of Moab was a stout man, a fat bull of a man, yet the thrust of his horn was well aimed, right to the belly. His question suited him well: thick and heavy like the pole of an olive press, which could not be budged by seven Moabite strongmen.

All the royal guests, great, small, and smaller still, sensed the impending tempest and rejoiced greatly. This was going to be fun. In anticipation, their eyes glowed like small, gleeful torches. However, faint of heart, they hastened to hide their glee under their eyelids and lowered their eyes toward the carpets on which they sat.

Only the King of Egypt, the mightiest of kings, an old, angry-looking, haughty lion, full of majesty and pride, who had come to the banquet to bask in his son-in-law's glory alone among all the guests, boiled like a seething cauldron upon hearing these calumnies. All the layers of his flesh shook with rage. His eyes flashed and his nostrils smoked. His trembling right hand reached for the hilt of his sword, and only with great effort did he curb his passion and withdraw his hand: "Shall those dogs' heads insult Pharaoh's son-in-law, the ally of the King of Egypt and the husband of his daughter, and escape unpunished?"

A great silence suddenly fell upon the gathering, the silence of an expectation too heavy to be borne. All the guests held their breath, casting their eyes wherever they could. Their hearts felt an indefinable terror, as though an invisible sword was flashing over all their heads, about to rend them at any moment.

Then suddenly the King of Egypt darkened his brow sevenfold and cast a fearsome eye upon Solomon, as if commanding him, "Smite them, O King, crush their skulls!"

Many of the noble guests, too, kings great and smaller and smaller still, who had not dared to speak up against Solomon, now suddenly awoke from their silence and each raised his eyes toward the king, eyes of every kind: dogs' eyes and rabbits' eyes, foxes' eyes and hyenas' eyes, snakes' eyes and monkeys' eyes, owls' eyes and falcons' eyes. Snarling flattery, goading and craving scandal, they said in unison, "Smite them, smite them, O King, crush their skulls!"

But Solomon ignored them all. He simply waited in silence until they ceased talking. When their words were exhausted, he lifted his head like a young, self-confident lion and said with calm majesty, "Therefore, when my words shall be proven true, all of you—each from his country—shall make a pilgrimage to the house that I have built to God at Mount Zion, and there you shall bow and lick its dust." The guests then asked, "How shall we know that your words have proven true?" Solomon replied: "This is what we shall do: Everyone, myself included, shall write down the name of one of his daughters who is a virgin of marriageable age and we shall cast lots. The girl who shall be drawn by lot shall be placed by me on an isolated island, never seen or visited by anyone. I shall command my eagle, the white eagle of my chariot, to guard her and provide her with food from my royal house as long as she dwells on this isolated island. Then we shall see whether or not what I have predicted shall happen to her in the end."

All the kings said in unison, "Your good council shall prevail."

The lot was cast and it fell upon the daughter of the King of Aram. The King of Aram was furious at the decision, for she was his only daughter, a lovely maiden, the joy of his house, and the apple of his eye. He was exceedingly angry and gnashed his sharp mouse-like teeth; in his heart, he silently cursed both Solomon and his God, but he had given his word in the presence of the other kings. He could not retract it.

The King of Aram kept his word. After he returned home, he sent Ketziyah, his only daughter, whom he loved, to Solomon, the King of Judah, so that he might put his words to the test. And the King of Aram grieved greatly for his daughter after he had sent her away from him. He regretted his action and longed for her with concern and compassion, for who knows what God had in store for her.

2

Solomon knew of a hidden island, a secret place that he had kept to himself for many years. It was a small, isolated, and desolate island, planted in the heart of the sea, far beyond the sailing routes plied by ships. It was very mountainous, full of frightening, craggy hills and primeval forests. No human foot had ever trod upon its soil; no warship or trading vessel had ever entered its waters, because it was surrounded for four hundred leagues by dangerous rocks. No captain or crew could penetrate these perils, or if they did, none would return. No one ever knew the location of the island except Solomon, who had studied its topography. He had come across the island one day as he was gliding through the skies on his magic cloak drawn by his white eagle and had landed to explore it. He had kept this secret to himself, to be used by him when the occasion arose. Now that the matter of the maiden had come to hand, the hidden island seemed to him to be the proper place in which to conceal the maiden within a tower built for that purpose by his architects. There she might reside until her hour of redemption should come.

The king did not delay. He chose trustworthy master architects, the best masons, builders, carpenters, and craftsmen who worked in wood, stone, and iron and sent them to the island with their tools, supplying them with many provisions. There they built, in accordance with his wishes, a tower at the summit of a craggy peak, following the design he had drawn. The king did not send his craftsmen by boat, lest they might run aground in the perilous sea or lest they discover a safe passage to the island. He, therefore, brought them there by air on his flying cloak—his wondrous flying cloak. He landed them and all their equipment on the island.

When they stood on its ground, they lifted their eyes and saw that they had landed on a forest clearing atop a steep and precipitous hill on the highest part of the island, a hill that was unscalable from any side. In whatever direction they looked, mighty, thick-trunked trees covered by heavy foliage loomed. Here Solomon had decided to erect the tower.

After many days, the work was completed as ordered. The tower stood prepared and designed from top to bottom in accordance with the king's wishes. It rose on the mountaintop higher than all its environs, above the trees of the forest, like a proud neck stretching toward heaven. Within the tower, at its very apex, were ample living quarters, and there was a luxurious and spacious balcony on which the princess might walk about or recline in comfort. For the king had commanded the builders that the girl's refuge be generously built so that she not feel cramped for space and grow depressed. The upper part of the tower had windows and lattices, which could be opened for fresh air and sunlight, and through which the princess might look out like a dove from its cote and not be bored. But the lower part of the tower was windowless in every direction, with not a single aperture. The outside walls were also very steep and their surfacing was smooth. They had no projection or border, no hole, recess, or foothold larger than an inch. Only one exit was provided for the maiden; a small door that led from her boudoir on top of the tower to the roof, where she could walk about freely in the cool of the day. The tower had only a single gateway, whose door bolts and locks were all made of cast iron.

On the appointed day when the princess was to be taken to the tower, as agreed, all the kings, Solomon and his opponents, assembled. They took Ketziyah, the daughter of the King of Aram, and together flew upon the wondrous cloak to the island and landed on the hill upon which the tower stood.

The travelers explored the tower from within and without, checking its surroundings carefully from top to bottom. When they saw that it was constructed exactly according to plan, without any flaw or ruse, they escorted the princess up the ladder to the boudoir, where she was to be housed. Afterwards they descended and removed the ladder.

The princess wept bitterly when she was imprisoned. She stretched her arms toward her father, imploring him not to abandon her, for she was greatly afraid. The father's heart, too, was almost rent to shreds at her piteous appeal. However, he repressed his feelings, held his tongue, and hardened his heart. He was after all a king and had given his word. Solomon saw the princess's anguish and, consoling her, said with compassion: "Do not weep, my daughter, and fear not. No evil shall befall you in this tower. You will want for nothing. My white eagle shall visit you daily and bring you abundant and dainty delicacies from the best and tastiest dishes prepared for my table. Birds will frequent your windows and cheer you with song at dawn and at dusk. I have also appointed a wondrous bird, a talking bird, who shall come to converse with you from time to time and refresh your spirit. Night after night God's very eyelids, the stars on high, will flash their signs to you; often sweet breezes shall bear joyous tidings to you from afar, and the sea's billows will transport your soul to the outside world. Your youthful blood will seethe within you like new wine in a wineskin, like a cup overflowing. When you shall ripen and bend under the burden of your yearnings, your lover and redeemer shall come to you suddenly, although you do not as yet know by which way. Then he shall untie your bonds in a moment and free you from this tower."

Thus the king in his wisdom comforted the princess, and the more he continued to console her, the more her anxieties waned, until she was once again completely serene. She dried her tears and said: "This is my fate and I shall bear it. O my King. Do with me whatever you please."

The kings left the tower; the gate was shut behind them, locked and bolted, sevenfold. For the gate had seven bolts, each with seven heavy locks, and was sealed with the seals of all the kings and certified by witnesses according to the law. Thus there would be no opportunity for fraud or deceit.

Before they embarked, at the very last moment, the King of Tyre noticed that a very tall and sturdy oak tree, more than fifty cubits high, was standing close to the tower, only narrowly away from its wall. Its trunk, from root to treetop, was smooth and straight, and it had no branches except at the top. These reached out toward the upper windows of the tower. He called Solomon's attention to the tree and said: "Would it not be best if you would order this oak to be felled? Why should it be a snare for the princess or an excuse for those who might wish to find one?"

The king studied the oak tree for a moment and replied: "Why are you making such a fuss? Let the oak stay where it is, so that its branches might delight the maiden's heart whenever she grows morose. Shall we even deny her this pleasure? Moreover, my eagle has to land on this oak when it comes day after day to feed the maiden. From this position he will pass the food to her through the window."

When the King of Tyre heard these words, he cast a quizzical look at Solomon. He said nothing but stored the matter in his heart.

Following these events, Solomon, all the kings who had accompanied him, and all their men mounted the magic cloak and embarked, soaring above the island. The princess was left alone in the heart of the forest and in the tower surrounded by the broad expanse of the sea and the murmuring of its waves. She was committed to the hands of God.

3

The maiden sat imprisoned in the garret of the tower day after day with neither change nor news except that the white eagle would visit her daily, bringing her rations of the king's delicacies to her window or to the tower's roof, as the king commanded, ever since she was confined to the tower. Whenever the eagle was expected, she would ascend to the roof and cast her eyes to the edge of the sea, searching impatiently until she would sight what appeared to be a small speck flying in the sunlight along the horizon. Slowly the speck would grow until it had wings and a beak and looked like an eagle. It was the white eagle. It would arrive and descend on the roof beside the maiden or land on the treetop and pass the food to her. Then it would retrace its route. This the eagle did day after day.

Periodically, the magic bird, as Solomon had said, would come to the oak tree. It was a domesticated parrot with speckled feathers, a bald crown, and a crooked beak. Sitting on one of the branches facing the window, it would announce its arrival with a bitter screech, which sounded like a saw cutting through a dry beam, "It's me, it's me, O princess, I've just come." The princess would open the window for it, greet it cheerfully, and would converse with it, as one does with a friend about anything that occurred to her—straight talk or humorous banter. She would pose questions and the parrot would reply loudly. If it spoke sense, she would applaud and dance for joy. She would also try to guess what it was saying, and when she did, she thought of herself as recovering a treasure. But if it simply chattered nonsense or was contrary, the maiden became cross with it and from the distance would make a fist like a ripe fig or show it her sweet tongue and mock it with her ruby red lips. Insulted, the parrot would also rouse itself, angrily pouring out all its screeching imprecations one after another, and when exhausted, it would spread its wings and fly off.

The princess saw that all the signs and wonders that Solomon had promised did indeed occur. She now believed him and trusted his consoling words and was no longer angry. She dwelt alone on the island in her silent abode, hidden from human eyes, like a pearl in its shell. She filled her soul with all the sights and sounds that flowed to her from near and far through the caravans of light clouds, the roar of the sea's billows, and the murmuring of the forest's foliage. They entered her very being effortlessly, as the light enters the heart of a pomegranate or the flesh of an apple. The maiden matured silently; she was filled with juice, her skin became so taut that it was about to burst. One morning, as the sun shone upon her, she felt that she was like a ripe cluster of grapes hanging on the vine. Suddenly she asked herself: "When shall the grape gatherer come to me? Why does the wine presser tarry?"

4

In Sidon, a tumultuous city buzzing with commerce, there lived at that time a Jew by the name of Malkishuah, a leader of his community and a wealthy and enterprising merchant who descended from the tribe of Zebulun. He had settled in Sidon many years ago when he was still young and David, King of Israel, was yet alive. He entered its gates as an exile but because of his industry rose to high estate in his adopted city and married the woman of his desires, a pure, gentle, and delicate dove, who was the daughter of a nobleman from the tribe of Naphtali and also a resident of Sidon. In that city Malkishuah built his home, struck roots, and became very much a citizen of the country. As he became established, he branched out and prospered quietly. His property and his wealth increased, and all his endeavors were blessed. He dispatched camel caravans to distant lands and ships to remote islands, to Greece, Elisha, Tarshish, and Kittim. He gained renown among the merchants of the land as a mighty entrepreneur. He was admired and respected by kings and princes for his broadness of spirit and integrity. They would entrust him with their affairs and treated him kindly. Consequently, many important personages sought his company, and people from far and near were eager to do business with him. He, too, because of his generous spirit, never refused any overture and lent a helping hand to all who stumbled. He established a separate house in his courtyard in which every exiled or broken person who fled to him from Judah would find a haven, including men who had angered kings and princes. For he had experienced on his own flesh the anguish and pain of the persecuted.

Few knew the story of his early years, from the time he left Judah fleeing for his life until he arrived in Sidon. Malkishuah had drawn a veil over them. But those days were much marked by their many and varied agonies. While yet a young man, at the very peak of his vigor, he had left his father's home, the home of a nobleman, and gone forth bravely in quest of adventure, taking to the road in the pursuit of distant places. When he heard that Joab had rallied his forces to attack Aram, he rushed to the fray, showing his valor in battle and performing gallant deeds. His heart, like that of a leopard, knew no fear. Wherever the battle raged most fiercely, Malkishuah would race with his sword and bow. In one of these battles, his arrow pierced the heart of one of Aram's royal princes, and he earned a hero's accolade. His cunning was as great as his courage. His mind teemed with schemes. Several times a day he faced dangers but always extricated himself from them. He was taken captive frequently but always escaped by his wits. One day he was captured and brought before the King of Aram. A single step stood between him and death. But even then, his cunning succeeded in fooling his captors, and he escaped. Then suddenly he reversed himself and joined those who plotted against David. He had come to despise the King of Judah and called the people to revolt against him. There was no plot against David in which he was not involved. From then on, he made his home in the craggy hills of Judah or in its caves. Whenever he furtively came among the people to incite them to revolt, he would mask his face for fear of his enemies. When Sheba ben Bikhri[7] raised his hand against David, Malkishuah was among the first to join him. After that last revolt failed, he fled, wandering for many days in the desert and foreign cities. When, in those years of wandering, he sought to eke out a living, he never disdained the meanest task, changing his occupation many times. He worked for cruel and harsh masters and had his fill of bitterness and gall. There was no suffering that he did not experience, no shame he did not endure. Yet he was never broken by any misfortune or affliction. On the contrary, he was refined in the furnace of dire poverty. His burning ardor had indeed somewhat cooled, but his will remained strong as flint and his wit as sharp and burnished as a razor. Thus one day, he came through the gates of Sidon after having his fill of suffering and painful episodes, but he had also become much broadened and even wiser by his experience, and more adroit with his hands than he had been before. The sinews of the back of his neck were made of iron, his hands were skilled, his eyes were like

---

[7]II Samuel:1–23.

arrows touched with the poison of contempt, his mind a treasury of wisdom. When he saw the great international trade center, its masses, its trade, and its commerce, he decided to build his home within its walls and to demonstrate his prowess and his initiative in business and commerce. He did, indeed, accomplish what he set out to do. He became exceedingly wealthy.

Malkishuah's fame reached King David in Jerusalem. Evil advisers and secret detractors, who pretended to be zealous supporters of David and the throne, incited the king against him, saying: "See Malkishuah, who from his youth has been hostile to your throne, has now entrenched himself in Sidon. His home is a hotbed for every rebel and conspirator and a haven for disturbers of the peace of this land. Now therefore, ask the King of Sidon (is he not your friend and ally?) to extradite him into your hands." However, David was by then an old man and was likewise weary of tribulations. He therefore did not heed the whispering plotters and even rebuked them, saying: "One should not remember the sins of youth. I would rather recall Malkishuah's youthful loyalty when he risked his life for the glory of his nation in war and made a name for himself. He was a heroic soldier of absolute integrity. And if, as most men, he sinned in his salad days, he has long ago atoned for his transgressions with his years of exile and wandering. I have also heard that he serves as a bastion and protector of his people in Sidon. They are honored and find strength in the honor given him. Leave off. Let him rest peacefully in his abode and prosper in that foreign city. By so doing, he will increase the honor of God beyond the borders of Israel."

Nevertheless, Malkishuah denied himself the pleasure of making a pilgrimage to Jerusalem and Judah all the days of David's kingship. He also refrained from doing business there or engaging in large financial ventures, to prevent his enemies from criticizing him, lest the old king hear the slander and become displeased with him. However, because he was devoted to God and His festivals, he would send, through his agents and his few business colleagues in Judah, sacrifices and gift offerings to the great high place that was at Gibeon.

Malkishuah's gifts were a token of homage to God's altar, its priests, and the nation's poor. These were considered as acts of righteousness on his part. Moreover, on many occasions, be they a drought, a plague, or any other calamity, Malkishuah was the first to rush aid to the victims from afar and to afford relief to those in trouble. Hence Malkishuah's name was viewed as a blessing by many people.

After Solomon had built God's house and proclaimed peace and truth throughout the land, Malkishuah, fully repentant, once again supported the House of David. He made an annual pilgrimage to Jerusalem and contributed many vow and gift offerings. But he avoided the palace and never called on King Solomon, so that the king might never be reminded of the past and be distressed. He also desisted from doing business in the land of Aram and was careful not to step within its borders, for he feared the wrath of its people. For Aram had not yet forgotten the sin of his arrows. Malkishuah knew that were he to fall into the hands of those who sought to kill him, they would show him no mercy. He, then, remained safe in Sidon, running his affairs efficiently, enjoying much wealth, honor, and renown.

Yet with all this fame and serenity, he was not free of Satan's hostility even now. Suddenly, the bright light of his peaceful life was dimmed by the untimely and accidental death of the gentle bride of his youth, the pride of his home, and the mother of his only son. One day, as she was traveling by ship in the heart of the sea, she accidentally fell overboard, without anyone witnessing the accident. She found her grave in the deep waters. From then on, Malkishuah was overwhelmed by grief. He lost all pleasure. The joy of his Sabbaths and holidays ceased. He even discontinued his customary annual pilgrimages to Jerusalem. Malkishuah was able to assuage his heavy grief by lavishing his fierce love upon his son, her little orphan, the first fruit of her womb. He was the solace upon whom he showered compassion, coddling and guarding him like the apple of his eye.

The child grew into a boy, the boy into a valiant young man, handsome, intelligent, and able. None of his contemporaries could compare to him in bravery, intelligence, skillfulness, or good looks. Netanyah ably assisted his father in every endeavor, serving as his right hand. When the father realized the young man's sterling qualities, he put him in charge of his household and his possessions. Indeed, Netanyah so conducted all his affairs with great acumen, liberality, and courage that his father was delighted with him, adding even more love to the love he had for him and never denying him anything. However, he did not permit him to sail on his ships, for fear that Netanyah might experience the tragic fate of his mother on the treacherous seas. He, therefore, held him close to him because of his love and his concern for his safety.

All the Sidonean maidens who were acquainted with Netanyah, Jewish or gentile, admired him and sought his company. He filled their thoughts whether they were awake or asleep. Netanyah, however, was not attracted to them; none of them met his expectations. Moreover, his father did not urge him to marry. So although Netanyah had reached marriageable age, he was still a bachelor. One day, late in autumn, a ship chartered by his father was about to sail from Sidon to Tarshish, heavily laden with wheat, oil, and wine, and accompanied by one of Malkishuah's trusted employees. Malkishuah and his son went to the port in order to visit the ship and instruct its crew before it embarked, as was their custom. As they went to the port, a band of frolicking young men also descended to the shore, led by the playing of drums, cymbals, and fifes.

They were all young Jews who had gathered together from Sidon and its environs and were on their way to embark upon a ship sailing for the bay of Acco. From there they planned to go up to Jerusalem to celebrate the festival of Sukkot and to rejoice before the Lord. Netanyah saw the joy of the young men, and their spirit filled his heart, kindling a burning desire to see the City of God this time, come what may. He pleaded with his father over and over again to permit him to go to Jerusalem, as he deeply desired. Malkishuah was gravely concerned and said weakly: "Your request, my son, is granted but do not go by ship. Do not test the Lord. Go instead by land. In a few days a camel caravan is scheduled to depart. You may join it." But Netanyah insisted: "No, no father. I will go by ship and now. Is the God of the dry land also not the God of the sea?"

Malkishuah, this time, could not withstand the entreaties of his only son, seeing that he was consumed by the fire of his passion. His resistance broken, he granted Netanyah's request. However, because of his great concern for his son's welfare, he placed Netanyah under the care of the steward of his household, who was journeying on the ship, and ordered him to guard Netanyah and never let him out of his sight until he arrived at Acco, where the boat would stop en route for a short while. He was ordered to take Netanyah ashore and place him under the charge of Mr. X, an associate of Malkishuah, who faithfully represented him. This associate would concern himself with the young man and would scrupulously watch over him. And Malkishuah sent a letter by his son's hand to his associate who lived in Acco, imploring him to serve as his son's eyes and hands during his stay in the Holy Land, guard him constantly, and bring him personally to the City of God. He instructed him to oversee Netanyah's comings and goings and, once the festival had ended, not to delay him but return him quickly and safely to his father's home on whichever of Malkishuah's ships would first arrive at Acco.

All this was not sufficient in Malkishuah's eyes. He ran home and brought a heavy bag of silver weighing seven *manna* and a large and very precious emerald, the most carefully guarded jewel in his treasury and his most cherished amulet, which weighed twenty drachmas. These he placed in Netanyah's hand and said: "Shall Malkishuah's son undertake a pilgrimage to the House of God for the first time and come into His presence empty-handed? Never! Therefore, take what I have given you and bring it as a gift from my hand to the House of God. Present the silver for burnt offerings and sacrifices on the festival and this precious stone to adorn the curtain of the Holy of Holies."

But before Malkishuah put the precious stone in his son's hand, he paused for a moment and, overcoming his turbulent emotions, said in a shaking and at times hesitant voice as he regarded the emerald, which also trembled in his hands: "Do you see this stone, my son? It is for me the rarest of the world's amulets, a sacred relic. Like the morning star, it first shone on your mother's head on her wedding day. Like the planet Venus, it shone on her breast on the festivals. It is a wondrous gem, a rare stone in which a mysterious and mighty power lies hidden. It is more precious than royal treasures. For many days, it was hidden in the treasure house of an Indian prince, guarded by a great python. Through a miracle it finally fell into my treasure house. Let it now cast its light on the curtain of the House of God, and let its radiant brilliance tremble in His Holy Temple. Let it be an eternal light in memory of the soul of your mother, the purest of all the women on earth, like an immortal, everlasting tear, and let it commemorate the luster of her life, which ended before its time."

The emerald was passed from the father's hand to that of the son. It was still trembling and shimmering in Netanyah's hand. It appeared like a great tear of God, a tear of eternal sorrow.

Netanyah took the holy silver and the gem silently and hid them in the leather belt that he had fastened on his hips. Following these events, Malkishuah's anxiety for his son almost abated. Now, would not God surely command his good angels to guard the comings and goings of his son. For was not the young man sent by his father to the House of God on a sacred mission. He was going by the word of God and would fulfill his father's command.

Malkishuah embraced his son, showered him with many kisses, and sent him off in peace. Soon the ship set sail from the shore, bearing Netanyah the son of Malkishuah in its bosom to the far reaches of the sea. Netanyah, in his youthful innocence, did not know that while his heart and flesh were singing for joy at the sight of the sea and its broad expanse, his aged father still stood rooted to the shore, his eyes following the fading ship with fear and deep sorrow, eyes streaming with tears as his lips formed a whispered prayer.

5

A father's heart never lies. The ship had barely entered the sea when God cast a tempest into its waters, turning the depths into a seething cauldron. The heavily laden ship was tossed from billow to billow like a straw basket, and its officers and sailors were unable to keep it on its course. Every heart grew faint, every hand turned weak. The seafarers cried out loudly, each to his god, but the storm did not subside but grew stronger sevenfold. Sail after sail was ripped to shreds, ropes snapped, and masts broke one after another, crushing more than one skull as they fell. The eyes of the sailors turned despondent. They began lightening the ship, jettisoning half its cargo into the waters; sacks of wheat, barrels of wine, and jugs of oil were all heaved into the boiling depths and broke into a devil's dance around the ship's sides, rising, falling, and bursting as they smashed against each other. Soon the sailors realized that their action was foolhardy. As the ship became lighter, the billows raged even more and made it dance, playing their cruel game. Even worse was the realization that the cargo that they had cast into the sea now joined the waves goring the ship's sides and setting it atremble. After a few moments, the sides were penetrated with deadly holes, which could not be repaired. The waters rushed into its hold, swift and fierce. A deathly fear overcame the passengers, and they ran about wildly in all directions in panic. They were all disheveled and bleary-eyed, helpless and without recourse. Confusion, perplexity, and panic now reigned. Each man attacked his neighbor. The captain in command, realizing that nothing could be saved, remembered that his master's son had been placed in his charge and he devised a plan to rescue him. He lashed him with a thick rope to two inflated wineskins, tied a bottle of wine round his neck, thinking that if the ship were to sink, the wineskins would keep the lad afloat for some time and perhaps he might escape death. The rest of the voyagers also devised plans to survive, every man for himself. Some stripped themselves naked and lashed wineskins to their hips; some tied themselves to wooden beams or boards, or to sealed jars or barrels, or to anything that might float that could be found in the confusion. The treacherous waters continued to penetrate the ship, filling it to the brim. Suddenly the storm let loose a bitter and piercing shriek—a shriek boding catastrophe and death. The ship and all its contents plunged into the sea's depths. Only a small number of passengers were saved, among them, young Netanyah. They were now carried shrieking on the wrathful waves of the sea. But even among those in the water were many whom the storm carried away in all directions until they disappeared. Thus the boat was destroyed on a day of wrath, leaving no trace behind it.

6

What happened to the rest of the voyagers who had entrusted their lives to the sea, no one knows. But Netanyah son of Malkishuah was borne on the shoulders of the waves for two whole days, still nestling between the two wineskins like a baby between his mother's breasts, secured to them by a rope, and tossed from one wave to another. All the while, he neither ate nor drank, for the sea's billows confounded him and he was dazed. On the third day, the storm abated. Suddenly the healing and generous sun shone down upon the sea. Exultant, the sea burst into laughter, as if seized by an overwhelming joy. The young man opened his eyes and discovered that he was strapped between the two wineskins in the heart of the sea while boundless golden waters were merrily rippling all about him. Now he recalled the storm and what it had done to the ship and its passengers. His heart grew faint and he wept. He was especially upset at the fate of his father's steward, the ship's agent who, even when confronted by the terror of death, had remained faithful to his master and had first and foremost concerned himself with providing Netanyah with a safe refuge between the wineskins. His heart went out to the old man, and he suddenly imagined that he still heard his cry reaching him from the far and wide expanse of the sea and echoing in the moaning of its waves, "Na-tan-yah!"

And he vowed: "If God should rescue me from these mighty waves and return me to my father's house, I shall gather to me all the widows and orphans of the passengers and with God's help support them with great compassion all the days of my life, as God is my witness."

In the meantime, Netanyah's body regained its warmth. He grew stronger, opened the bottle tied to his neck, and swallowed a gulp of wine. His eyes lit up and his strength was restored. Groping about further, he found the belt still on his hips; the package he had tucked into it was undamaged. This he viewed as a good omen, indicating that he would still make his pilgrimage to the House of God and fulfill his father's vows as instructed. He was indeed, as his father had said, charged to fulfill God's commandments.

Netanyah lay in the lap of the two wineskins, floating and rocking upon the wide golden waters like a child in its cradle. His face was turned toward the brilliant sky, and his heart was full of prayer, hope, and consolation. As he floated with his eyes peering heavenward, suddenly a large, winged creature appeared in the sky, an all-white hawk of gigantic size, flying and hovering over him in the azure heavens, its plumage glistening in the sunshine like white silk. For a moment, the hawk ceased flying, as if suspended by a hidden thread between the sea and the sun. But a moment later, the thread seemed to snap and the hawk fell suddenly and descended from the heights like an arrow shot directly toward him. Before Netanyah could regain his composure, the fierce, heavy-bodied hawk cast a shadow over him as it fluttered its mighty pinions. Suddenly Netanyah's eyes perceived a pair of grasping, devouring claws as sharp as emery and a beak as hard as burnished flint curving in front of him.

Seized by a deathly terror, he lifted his hand as if to fend off the monster. At that moment, the hawk struck the rope tied to the young man's waist with its beak. One hard blow followed another and a third. The rope snapped and Netanyah was released. A mo-

ment later the white hawk soared to the heights, mighty and powerful, holding its prey in his talons—the unconscious Netanyah.

No one will fail to comprehend that the hawk that had descended
upon him was that very great white eagle, King Solomon's eagle,
which in its flight to the magic island to bring food to the daughter
of the King of Aram, imprisoned in the tower, had seen from the
heights a young man afloat on the sea, nestling between two wineskins. It had swooped down upon him and carried him away.

Thus Netanyah was drawn from the sea and held in the eagle's
talons. He was removed from the two wineskins, which continued
bobbing on their own as the waves shook them, moaning quietly,
abandoned on the wide expanse of the sea. The wineskins appeared
abashed and bereft like the twin breasts of a mother whose suckling
child had been snatched from her bosom.

7

The eagle carried Netanyah to the secret island and descended,
placed him under a tree in the woods, and flew away. When he regained consciousness and opened his eyes, he found himself under a
sycamore tree, surrounded by dry wild figs and leaves, which had
fallen from the tree. With his weak hands, he gathered a handful of
the figs and ate them and then washed them down with wine from
his bottle. His spirit was revived, his strength restored. Then he suddenly recalled the shipwreck, his floating in the sea in the wineskins,
and the fierce white eagle that had descended upon him. All these
events seemed like a nightmare dreamed while one is awake. He
could not be sure whether to believe they had really happened. After
his clothes had dried, he got up and walked about the woods to sur-
vey the area. Perhaps he would come upon some shelter or resting
place in a cleft of the rock or some cave or earthen tunnel or some
other hiding place in which he might rest for the night. Netanyah
wandered through the woods to and fro, walking, not keeping to
the path, and scanning everything he saw about him. As the day declined, he reached a high hill entirely covered with huge rocks and
bushes. Various wild plants were scattered over the hillside, whose
top was crowned by a thick forest. He heard the gurgle of bubbling
water, and he searched and found a limpid spring running along the
hillside, hidden by the rocks and the grass. Netanyah ate some mul-

berries, stuffed his clothes with them, quenched his thirst from the spring, and refilled his bottle. After he had refreshed himself, he continued to climb up the hill, striding over the rocks, cutting his way through the brush, intent upon reaching the forest at the peak of the hill.

The sun rested on the treetops. Netanyah stood on a plateau at the top of the hill, deep in the mighty and primeval forest. The cold forest air and its dark shadows encompassed him. He enjoyed the scene immensely. He was tempted to stretch out on the grass under a green fir tree and rest, for he was very tired from his exhausting journey and the heat of the day. However, while he was looking about, he suddenly heard what appeared to be a cracking of some twigs on which somebody had trod. Raising his eyes, he spied a tender doe leaping deep in the forest, now appearing and now disappearing among its trees. Netanyah dashed after the doe, following on its heels in a winding zigzag. Racing, he suddenly emerged into a wide clearing, entirely bathed in the light of the sinking sun. He was astonished to discover a tall tower in the heart of the forest. It loomed before him, high and prominent, casting its shadow like a dark carpet upon the grass. Its pinnacle stretched like a haughty neck toward the heavens. For a moment, he imagined that his legs had brought him to some human habitation, and he rejoiced. However, as he drew nearer and examined the tower, he saw that it was isolated; there was no other house beside it. He also saw its windowless walls, its bolts, and its locks. The tower made him wonder. This was an insoluble and somewhat frightening riddle. Was there something evil lurking within that tower? His mind told him to be very cautious and not to do anything before he first examined the tower and the surrounding country carefully. Who knows what snares were hidden in or around it? Perhaps it was a secret hideaway for bandits or murderers, a den or meeting place for witches and wizards.

Meanwhile the sun had set and night descended. A thick darkness enveloped the earth and all that was in it. In the forest the darkness was sevenfold heavier still. Pile upon pile it lay under every tree and bush, silent, brooding, and pregnant with mystery, covering every valley and depression, every rise and hillock.

All sorts of different sounds emerged from the depths of the forest, each more strange and more mysterious than the other: whisperings and murmurings, loud voices and howls, growls and roars, passionate mating calls and the lovesick groans of night birds, owls sick with desire, and the wailing of wild beasts writhing, crying, and aching with passion. The forest was steeped in terror. Netanyah's flesh began to creep; he abandoned the doe and the tower and retired to a cleft in the rock, which he had seen when it was still day, to hide there from the terror and the cold night air. He blocked the entrance to the cleft with stones, lay on the ground, and fell asleep.

Night fogs descended, groping their way like the blind, spreading their white sheets over the forest. Two lovely souls lay asleep in its bosom: the young woman in the tower's garret and the young man in the cleft of the rock.

8

Morning dawned. Choirs of myriads of birds filled the entire forest with joyous song, which gladdened the branches of every tree and bush. Their music rose to the heavens and poured down on the dew-soaked grass like golden rain and a hail of pearls. The forest stood wet, verdant, and robust; its trees tall and surging with sap, bathing their heads in the sunshine, and dipping their feet in the dew-filled grass. Bodies and faces glistened and were alive with joy. The singing of the birds woke Netanyah. He rose and went into the forest, full of his usual youthful vigor, for sleep had refreshed him, lifting his spirits and revitalizing his strength. Then he recalled the wondrous tower that he had seen in the clearing yesterday. He, therefore, returned to the site, choosing a hidden spot sheltered by the tangled brush growing behind a rock. As he sat there, he vowed: "I shall neither budge from here nor rest even at the peril of my life until the mystery of this tower is revealed to me."

He lay in ambush, his eyes peering at the tower through the branches. Suddenly, he heard a wild inhuman voice screeching: "It is me, it is me. How are you, my princess?" The youth was astonished, since he saw nothing. Suddenly he gaped in amazement, and his eyes focused upon one of the tower's windows that faced the oak tree. There, near the window but inside the garret, a gentle, sad-eyed maiden appeared, simple, youthful, and beautiful as an angel. Her face was pure and limpid as the moon. For a moment, she stood silent and doleful, looking toward the top of the oak tree. Then she thrust her head through the window and, as she glanced at its topmost branches, said sweetly: "I am very well, very well, my cute parrot, thank God, thank God, my darling bird! And you, you little devil. How are you?" Then the screeching voice pierced the branches again and shrieked, "I am well, I am well, my princess, thank God, thank God."

A slight smile covered the maiden's lips, although her eyes had a sad cast. She continued speaking in a tender but languishing tone: "Is this all you have to say today, parrot? Have you no news to bring me? Perhaps you might tell me how much longer I must remain imprisoned on this desolate island? Will my redeemer come to rescue me? Answer me, parrot, will he come?" And the strange voice shrieked, "He will come, princess, he will come."

The girl sighed deeply and cried out: "O my consoling bird. Why does he tarry? See, my eyes are wasted waiting for him day after day. My heart cries out for him as I lie on my couch night after night. Why has my redeemer not come, not come?"

"He shall come, shall come, princess, blessed be he who shall come." The maiden probed deeper and said bitterly: "If indeed he shall come, as you say, why does he not give me a sign? Why does he hide his face from me, keeping the light of his eyes and the majesty of his voice out of my sight? Why have I not seen or heard him?"

The voice in the treetop shrieked, "I have seen him, heard him." The princess's face was flooded with joy and she cried out: "Have you indeed seen him face to face; have you heard his voice? Where is he, then, far or near?"

The voice in the tree shrieked, "Far and near, peace to him that is far and to him that is near."

And the girl continued, faint with sorrow: "Will God make him wings so that he may fly up to me? Does he have arms powerful enough to break the iron bolts and locks? How can he enter my rooms and reach me while I am imprisoned behind double locks at the top of this high tower? Tell me, O magic bird!"

This time the only reply to her questions was a furtive rustling in the treetop. From his hiding place, Netanyah noticed that the wondrous bird rose from the treetop, flew hither and thither, then suddenly veered straight toward the bush where he was hiding, perched upon it, and shrieked fiercely, as if emptying his entire repertoire of shrieks all at once on the youth's head, "It is me, it is me, come, come, blessed is his coming, peace, peace, so be it, so be it."

After the bird had exhausted its breath, it spread its wings and vanished into the thicket of the forest. Astonished, Netanyah reentered the brush, trembling like a leaf. For these events came over him like an incredible dream. He could believe neither what he had seen nor what he had heard. "Who erected this tower at this fearsome site? Who is the princess hidden within it?" He was even more astounded by the talking bird. He had often heard about talking birds, but this was the first time in his life that God had brought him face to face with such a wondrous bird and enabled him to hear it speak with his own ears. He was not a cowardly man, nor did he believe in magic; nevertheless, his very bones trembled when the bird perched above his head on a bush under which he lay and when it shrieked at him. He held his breath, almost dying of fright at each word it uttered.

Netanyah did not know that even more mysterious wonders were in store for him.

9

When his shock had somewhat abated, Netanyah returned to his hiding place. His eye first sought out the maiden at the window, but she had disappeared. His heart was sad, as if the sun had darkened at noon. It was then that he recalled the words that were spoken by the maiden and the bird. He asked himself who was the lovely wan-faced, sad-eyed maiden who had appeared to him in the window, and who was the cruel heartless man who had imprisoned her in the tower. But he was not able to solve the riddle.

His heart and inner being were still yearning for the maiden, when suddenly he saw her again, this time not at the window but at the pinnacle of the tower. Gently and silently she walked in the glowing sunlight, pure and glistening like a small white cloud afloat in the blue sky. Her face shone like the face of an angel, reflecting the spotless robes in which she was dressed.

Soon she reappeared and, shading her eyes with the palm of her right hand, she scanned the sea's horizon. On the edge of the sky, a speck hovered between the earth and sky, coming closer and closer, increasing in size until one could discern that it had wings and a beak, and then took the form of a gigantic and fierce hawk plumed in white. The white hawk descended and landed on the tower's roof and stood before the maiden.

Netanyah saw the winged creature from his hiding place and his heart grew numb. He almost cried out aloud in terror and amazement. Was not this the fearsome monstrous hawk that had lifted him out of the sea and brought him to the island? He recognized it because of its white plume and fearsome appearance. Nevertheless, Netanyah restrained himself and sat silently in his hiding place, waiting to see how it all would end.

The great hawk was the white eagle that was ordered by King Solomon to feed the maiden. After loitering a little, it spread its wings and flew back along the same route it had taken, as was its custom day after day. The maiden likewise, after dallying for a little again, disappeared from Netanyah's sight. It was as if the sun's brightness had become tarnished for him. He waited till he grew tired, but she was gone, gone. A great sorrow filled his heart, and he sat in his hiding place despondent.

His very innermost chambers seethed with anguish like a turbulent sea. Ever since this wondrous maiden had appeared before him at the top of the tower and he had heard her sweet voice, his heart was shaken and he was restless. When she spoke, he was overwhelmed and felt great compassion for her. In vain did he seek to solve the mystery of the tower; it would remain a riddle.

When Netanyah grew too impatient with sitting idly by and waiting, he emerged stealthily from his hiding place and ventured toward the tower so that he might explore it at close range. Slowly, he cut through the brush growing near the tower, careful not to be seen or heard. He circled the tower, investigating its surroundings several times, always furtively, for he still feared the tower and its mysteries. He searched the reaches of the tower over and over again. Perhaps some entrance, gateway, hole, or underground passage might be found. His hopes, however, were dashed. The sides of the structure were impenetrable from ground to windows. He could never reach the windows, because they were much too high for him. The walls were smooth, without any projection, edge, or foothold. The single gate to the tower, with its bolts and locks of cast iron, was locked and sealed sevenfold and was invulnerable to the might of either a Samson or a Goliath.

Despite this, Netanyah did not despair and continued his search. He hatched numerous schemes to penetrate the secret of the tower. For a moment, the thought occurred to him that perhaps the oak tree might be his salvation, since it was close to the tower's wall and its branches reached out toward the window in which the maiden had appeared. But when he examined the height of the oak and the smoothness of its trunk, he faltered and abandoned the idea. Who would dare scale such a tall tree without breaking his neck? The height of the giant oak, with its dark foliage, almost frightened him. Sturdy and wrathful it stood guard, a faithful and solitary sentinel, as if warning, "No foot shall venture here; whoever dares approach will not escape unpunished." But with all that, the youth did not rule out the possibility of the oak tree, keeping it in mind for a more opportune occasion.

10

After Netanyah grew weary of his quest to devise a proper plan, he remained concealed in the forest. Meanwhile he grew very unhappy and was exhausted and overwhelmed as a consequence of all the mysterious events he had experienced. He went down to the berry patch and ate some fruit, slaking his thirst from the spring. Then he lay under a bush for a short rest and in order to think things over.

He lay under the bush, but all his thoughts were directed toward the tower and the maiden secreted within its walls. He could not erase the image of the wondrous girl from his eyes even when they were shut. Her pleading voice still rang in his ears: "Why has my redeemer not come? Why have his footsteps tarried?"

All of a sudden, Netanyah's heart was stirred. It was as if a bright ray of light had flashed upon him, and he asked himself: "Am I not the redeemer? Has not God chosen me to rescue the maiden? Was it in vain that He had showed me His many miracles and events, guiding me to this place? Did He not cast a storm on the sea, wreck the ship, for the maiden's sake? Was it not because of her that God's hand brought me here on the wings of the eagle?"

Netanyah held on to his imaginings and did not relent, as he continued to ask: "If this indeed was the finger of God, why did the process begin but not be realized? What point was there in bringing me here, when the tower is so tightly locked and I still do not know how to penetrate it, and how can I reach the wondrous maiden held within it? How can I redeem her when she is shut fast in a room at the top of the tower with seven bolts and seven locks and seven seals?"

Netanyah's heart sank again in bitter but soundless lamentation: "Alas, O God, why did You not command the eagle to cast me on the tower's roof instead of on the ground? Or formed me like the parrot, which can soar to the oak tree and speak to the maiden face to face at will, or even like one of the tiny birds that nest above her window and are able to alight and chirp on its sill, or on her prison roof, or wherever they please, unhindered?"

But even when he thought sad thoughts, Netanyah did not cease devising plans how to penetrate the tower at night like a thief by means of a tunnel. At other times, he contemplated approaching the tower unafraid and calling out to the maiden as he stood under her window.

Perhaps he might wrest the key to this entire mystery from her lips. Who knows, perhaps she might lower a rope through the window so that he could climb up to her.

He conjured up various schemes of this sort, but none satisfied him. He was not deterred by cowardice but by the fear that he might unintentionally endanger the maiden's life.

Netanyah lay beneath the bush for a long time, his heart rent and his head swarming with many plans. To the degree that these multiplied, so did the false and tiresome delusions they evoked. There was no scheme that he did not seize upon and abandon a moment later in despair. Finally, he became very dispirited; head and body weighed down heavily upon him and he sought relief. But the strength of the tower and its mighty mystery held him tightly in its grip, carrying him far off from where he lay. Once again, he saw himself cast afloat, lashed to the two wineskins, rocking like a baby in a cradle on the spacious sea, with his eyes fixed on the golden reflection of the sun upon the waters. As his eyes focused on the reflection, he discerned a figure rising out of the deep, a woman whose head was crowned with a sparkling diadem and whose forehead was adorned with a huge, glowing emerald. The figure looked like his mother, and the stone had the same color as the emerald that he had in his belt. A wave of emotion overcame him, and he tried to shout, "Mother, look, your son." But the cry cleaved to his palate. His tongue did not respond. He wanted to stretch his arms toward her, but they were bound to the wineskins, and the skins, instead of floating forward nearer to the figure, receded from it. Soon she would totally disappear. "Mother, Mother," he cried from the depths of his soul, "do not forsake me." In his great anguish, he de-

cided to try to free his hands from the ropes with what remained of
his strength. And wonder of wonders, before he even tried to do so,
the bonds melted away, and the ropes fell from his body. But, alas,
this too was to no avail; his outspread hands no longer found the
figure he so desired standing before him, for she had in the meantime disappeared and had sunk completely into the golden deep.
Netanyah's embarrassed arms turned limp and fell back into the lap
of the wineskins. At that moment, Netanyah hastily reached for the
emerald in his belt with trembling hands. "Was it still there?" When
he felt it, he grasped it with his fingers and rejoiced. He intended to
raise it to his eyes, so that they might enjoy its brilliant splendor, but
his hand did not respond. It remained immobile, glued to his side.
"Why is my arm stuck to my side?" he wondered. "Who has bound
me with ropes again?" he continued. He turned his head to see what
had come toward him and was struck with terror at the sight. No
ropes had weighed down upon him. It was a serpent. A spotted,
writhing serpent. It had wrapped itself around him and its coils embraced him. The serpent's neck and head stretched toward him; its
eyes stared at his. Its ugly mouth was agape, and between its teeth,
alas, was the sacred emerald.

And yet wonder of wonders, the more Netanyah stared at the serpent's eyes, the more his fear of it diminished and he could compose
himself. The expression on the serpent's face and its laughing eyes
proved that it had come with no evil intent. Had Netanyah's hands
not been bound, he would have now reached out to take hold of the
serpent's neck without fear. He also noticed that the serpent had
slowly relaxed its coils bit by bit, so that it was really only hugging
and caressing him. Undoubtedly its intentions were peaceful. It had
come to bring good tidings. But how was the emerald transferred
from his belt to the snake's mouth? Before he solved this dilemma,
the serpent turned its head away from him, as one turns the top of a
cane. Netanyah's eyes, entranced, followed the emerald as a needle
is drawn to a magnet. He was very much concerned that the precious stone might fall into the sea. When he turned his eyes away,
the figure of his mother reappeared to him, rising from the golden
deep as pure and luminous as she had been before. However, now
she was not alone but accompanied by another figure, completely
cloaked in splendor and younger than she. Her head was adorned
with a garland of white lilies, and she strode gracefully toward his
mother over the deep. The emerald no longer glowed on his

mother's forehead but on the forehead of the young woman who was walking toward her. The young woman resembled the wondrous maiden of the tower. Like two daughters of heaven who had descended to earth, both women strode toward each other gracefully, their lips radiating a splendid tranquillity and quiet joy. Then his mother turned to him, holding the hand of her younger companion in her left hand and waving her right hand toward him, as if calling and signaling to him from afar, her face flooded with joy. His eyes almost made out that her lips were moving, and his ears almost heard her whisper, "My son!"

The young man's heart was about to burst, flooded as it was with emotion, and he cried out in a superhuman voice, "Mother!"

As he cried, he broke his bonds with a surge of strength. He awoke; it was all a dream!

11

Astounded and overwhelmed, Netanyah remained seated for a long time while his mind wandered in another world. Dream fragments still roamed in the hidden corners of his soul, their broken cobwebs still clung to his eyelids. But slowly these faded away, and he realized where he was and awoke. Now he knew that indeed a day of miracles awaited him on this island, although he did not as yet understand what their exact nature might be or when he would experience them. One thing his heart told him: the emerald would guide him to them and would protect him. His father's words about this extraordinary gem and its mysterious powers were undoubtedly true. Did it not watch over him and save him from drowning in the deep sea, and did not its magical powers determine the miraculous events which brought him to this place? If this were so, what was the meaning of the vision of the emerald and the various incidents that he had seen just now?

Unconsciously, Netanyah's hands reached for his belt, and he felt for it nervously. Was the emerald safe? When he held the gem in his trembling fingers, he was relieved, as though a heavy stone had rolled off his body. Hastily he gazed at it, holding it very carefully in his fingertips, amazed at its size and the beauty of its splendor, which flamed and shimmered in his hands. It was indeed a magic jewel. He had never seen any gem in his father's treasure house that was its equivalent in size, splendor, coloration, or refraction. It was cut like a suspended teardrop—a large, full teardrop just about to fall—cut by a wondrous artist and polished to perfection. The more he looked at the emerald, the more he perceived every imaginable variation of brightness and coloration. It was as if God himself had stored the very essence of all His luminous splendors within it. Was this a tear of divine joy, the chief stone of his crown of redemption?

While he was still examining every facet of the stone and feasting his eyes upon it, his fingers trembled and the emerald fell and sank in the grass. As he stooped down to lift it, suddenly, the head of a speckled python, the size of a fist, darted out from a pile of dry leaves, seized the emerald—and fled.

A loud, bitter cry of distress startled the forest. Netanyah jumped to his feet in hot pursuit of the python.

12

The python glided along the smooth carpet of fallen leaves and grass, its winding spotted body like a thick rope, swiftly crawling and twisting through trees and bushes, with Netanyah in hot pursuit. Had he had a rock in his hand or any other deadly weapon, he would have crushed the skull of this ugly reptile at once and wrested its prey from its fangs. But he was empty-handed, and he could not pause to pick up a rock lest the python escape. He was confident that his swift legs would catch up with the python and prevent its escaping. Never for a moment did he take his eyes off the scaly, writhing, living staff—which glided along the ground ahead of him. He cunningly followed all its wrigglings and every turn of its head, always keeping his eyes upon it because he feared that it might elude him and the emerald be lost forever. Whenever the python passed a pit or a trench, or if part or all of its body sank for a moment out of sight in a pile of dry leaves or grass, the young man's heart would grow faint with fear. And when the whole python reemerged, he would take hope and his spirits would revive at the thought that with one further little effort he could reach his quarry. Then Netanyah would increase his pace and his legs would quicken once again. The python, too, did not slacken its pace but accelerated its speed whenever Netanyah increased his. So while one pursued the other, the gap between them never narrowed or widened. Netanyah began to believe that both pursuer and pursued were as if in a sieve, shunting back and forth, but never moving ahead. And as his eyes wearied of following the python and endlessly stalking its quivering body, he would sometimes have the illusion that it was not a python that he was pursuing but a curling, floating billow of smoke or, a moment later, a meandering stream of water cut off from its source, running and twisting through the grass, driven by pointless terror. At other times, he imagined that it was a black bolt of lightning shaped like a flying demon from the netherworld, the fruit of its dark womb or hatched from its cold bosom, one of those rods of black fire that the earth belches from its dark belly periodically to wander forth and scourge its surface, just as the sky sends out its bolts of lightning and its fiery white serpents to scourge the heights. But soon the fire dragon reverted and once again turned into a serpent made of flesh. To Netanyah, all these metamorphoses appeared to be weird fantasies and black magic. From time to time the python raised its whole neck and held its head rigid while still moving and turned to face its pursuer. It was then that Netanyah saw the emerald shining in the gaping mouth of the reptile and illuminating its whole throat. He was seized with terror. What was this all about? Was it a repetition of the dream? Or was some evil spirit terrifying him with weird hallucinations? But he knew that this time, whatever he saw, he was awake; this was real and he was quite sane.

Most wondrous was the fact that the more the python repeated this gesture of turning back his head, the more the terror that Netanyah first felt diminished and he regained his composure—just as in the dream. The python now appeared to him, not as someone who was trying to flee, but as someone in a hurry—a swift messenger, loyal to its dispatcher, diligently rushing to perform an important mission. Now when the python turned its neck and head toward him, it seemed to display feelings of kindness and goodwill toward its pursuer. Its face showed no signs of enmity or evil intent. Everything was as he had been shown in his dream. Nothing was omitted. The texture of the serpent's wonderfully speckled skin was beautiful. The python now seemed to Netanyah to be like a royal scepter, a long staff signifying power and courage and great dignity, and looked as if it had fled the world's most powerful and awe-inspiring monarch, who had rebuked it, or like the staff of God, a magical staff engraved all over with mysterious markings, which some great magician had cast from his hand and dispatched to the ends of the earth to perform great miracles. Slowly, Netanyah's anxiety completely disappeared, as did his concern for the emerald. Now he no longer pursued the python, but calmly and swiftly followed it. His heart was serene; his movements fleet. The python also slackened its pace, slithering along in front of Netanyah calmly, showing him what direction to follow. It was the guide and Netanyah, the follower. However, the gap between the two remained as it had been, neither greater nor smaller. Finally, they emerged in the forest clearing, and the python quickly went straight to the oak tree standing near the tower. Netanyah was drawn after it, as if moonstruck. Even if his eyes had been shut, he would not have strayed from the path to the right or to the left. A covenant of fate bound the two in an unbreakable bond. Both raced into the clearing, the python first and Netanyah after it. They reached the oak tree, and before Netanyah understood what would occur, the python stretched itself tautly and with one mighty leap, wrapped itself around the tree trunk and with great alacrity spiraled up the tree, reaching its top in a minute. There it halted. The tall, sturdy trunk that only a moment ago was totally bare now had its upper third entirely gripped by the python's many coils and looked like a gigantic screw threatening to rivet the earth to the sky.

Astounded and overwhelmed with wonder, Netanyah stood before the awesome snake pole, his eyes staring at the serpent wrapped at its top. Should he climb after the python? Could he reach it? Could he salvage the emerald from its mouth?

The python climbed even higher and stretched its neck and head toward Netanyah as if forming a rod. As it flashed the emerald in Netanyah's face, it cast from afar a gracious glance in his direction, eyes begging, entreating, waiting—all the coils of its body from head to tail trembled silently in anticipation.

Netanyah still remained rooted like a palm tree to his place, his eyes glued to the emerald, which trembled in the mouth of the python, as if it were alive, shimmering in its brilliance, signaling and beckoning him. But it was so high, so beyond his reach. Netanyah's eyes perceived it, but he was helpless. Should he try to climb toward the top? Would he have the courage? Could he make it?

While he was still hesitating between several options, the figure of the wondrous maiden suddenly showed itself to him. She did not stay long; she shone and withdrew. Was she watching for him, or did she retreat because of him?

Netanyah plunged forward, propelled by a mysterious force. His two hands grasped the trunk of the oak tree like two iron bands, clinging to it as a belt does to a man's hips.

13

At first, Netanyah's ascent was quick and easy. Foot by foot he grasped the trunk of the tree with his hands and sturdy legs. His arms were charged with iron and the calves of his legs with bronze. Two invisible ropes pulled him upward: the emerald and the image of the maiden, lifting him higher and higher above the ground. The higher he climbed, the more the python trembled with pleasure and joy at his approach. It conveyed its delight by the ceaseless and vigorous quivering of its tail. If it could talk, it would have cheered him on. From afar, it encouraged the climber with the glint of its eyes urging him on in every way: by the waving of its tail, the twisting of its body, and the moving of its head to and fro. When the climber reached the halfway point, he was exhausted. His arms and legs were weary, and his body became heavier and heavier. He held on to the trunk with what remained of his strength and inched himself forward. But he still had a long way to go before reaching the serpent. Could he do it? Would he find the strength?

He redoubled his efforts to climb higher, more and more, come what may. Netanyah dug his fingernails into the bark of the tree, tearing and scratching them until his fingers bled, and continued climbing. The emerald held in the python's mouth seemed to be signaling and commanding, "Climb on, don't falter, you'll make it!" Netanyah flexed his arms and climbed on. Two feet still separated him from the python, then just one foot, only one, and then only two more spans.

Just before he was one span away, his strength gave out. Hands and feet became rigid like wood and were unable to move even another inch. His body had grown much heavier; he was gasping for breath; his temples throbbed; he was bathed in sweat. In a minute his hands were going to slip.

Netanyah looked down at the earth from his perch and despaired. The ground below was very far away. Had his great effort and his climbing to this point all been in vain? Had he been able to conquer almost the entire height of the tree, yet would fail to cover the very last span?

With the last ounce of his strength, while he was still conscious, he hugged the tree trunk, and they became as one. Again, for the last time, he tried to move his hands, if only by a hairbreadth, but his hands did not respond, just as he had experienced in his dream. However, this time, every bone in his body knew that if his hand were to let go, if only for an instant, he would tumble down below. Would that his hand might not let go on its own.

As his heart sank and turned dead with fear, Netanyah shut his eyes and a cry burst from the depths of his soul, "Mother, come, hold me!"

With hope and strength gone, Netanyah's hands were about to lose their grip. However, at that very moment, a miracle occurred. The python, which had witnessed the struggle, had frozen in its tracks and fixed its full attention on Netanyah; now upon sensing the imminent catastrophe, it bestirred itself. Quickly it lowered its bottom coil toward him like a rope thrown to a despairing victim to clutch at. Unconsciously, Netanyah's hands clung to the lifeline. With his feet using the tree trunk as a springboard, Netanyah was drawn upward until he reached other coils and gripped them with both his hands. Now he could breathe freely.

Easily, like climbing the rungs of a ladder, Netanyah climbed from coil to coil while the python remained immobile, for it had flexed its entire body, making it rigid as an iron bar so that Netanyah would not slip until he had reached the lowest bough of the treetop and set himself upon it. Now Netanyah had regained his confidence and was no longer afraid. He was firmly seated on a branch. All he had to do was to seize the python by the scruff of its neck and wrest the emerald from its mouth. He was determined to get it, come what may!

Netanyah stretched his entire body along the branch and reached toward the python again and again trying to grab hold of its neck. But the python's neck kept turning away, eluding his grasp. And while Netanyah's hand kept reaching after it, the python's neck suddenly stretched out, emerging from its body as from a hidden scabbard, and slowly moved away from its pursuer toward the window in the tower's wall. The longer its body became as it hung between heaven and earth, the fewer became the coils that were gripping the tree trunk. Netanyah, drawn after the python's head, had also unwarily detached himself from his seat on the branch, slowly moving toward the edge of the branch that reached toward the window. But the branch fell short of its target by about a foot. It also grew thinner toward its end and bent under the weight of Netanyah's body. If he were to move forward another hairbreadth—it would snap.

Terrified and anxious, Netanyah followed the python's head with his eyes. Careful not to throw too much weight on the branch's tip, he rested most of his body on its thickest part and reached for the back of the python's neck. But his hand had missed its opportunity. Just as it almost touched the neck, the python quickly thrust its head through the tower window. Still gripping the tree trunk with its coils, it stretched its thick, round body between the oak and the windowsill like a slanting beam, a sloping bridge.

Netanyah almost fell off the branch because he feared that an evil fate might befall the emerald and that the python might now drop it onto the tower.

But as if impelled by a hidden hand, before he was even able to consider what action he might take, Netanyah suddenly slid off the branch that he had grasped with both hands and found himself hanging between heaven and earth. Finding a foothold, for an instant, for one of his feet on the python's body stretched like a bridge beneath him, Netanyah sprang like a leopard through the window into the tower.

On the floor, the emerald glistened in front of him, and from the wall opposite him, a pair of startled eyes stared at him in amazement. Pale as the plaster on the wall and the whiteness of her garments, the wondrous maiden stood, rendered seven times more beautiful by her fear.

When Netanyah turned his head to look for the python, he did not find it. The python had fulfilled its task and had disappeared, as if it had never been there.

14

Once their amazement and their fear had left them, Netanyah and Ketziyah sat together on the carpeted floor of the garret, like two long-parted lovers who had met each other again after a lengthy separation and who could not satisfy their desire to look at each other or relate to each other all that had happened before meeting again.

As night fell, Ketziyah took Netanyah up to the roof, set before him all the delicacies that she had kept for her evening meal, fed him, and gave him drink. Afterwards she laid out a bed for him on the roof, while she happily hastened to her garret, leaving behind her the sweet scent of her soft body and white garments—an aroma as gentle and as delicate as the finest of perfumes.

Netanyah remained on the roof alone, his feelings stirred and his blood seething. He could not contain the wonders he had experienced that day, wonders whose number was even greater than its terrors. But was he not fully rewarded? Indeed he had now received full recompense for all his tribulations. Here, in the garret just below him, a passionate loving doe will climb into her lonely couch, her heart trembling and her flesh aglow. As she turns and tosses alone in the grip of her desires, she will bear his name on her lips and silently whisper, "My love, my redeemer." This morning she was so distant, and now she is so close. Couch below couch. Only the thickness of the ceiling separates them. Had not God hidden this pearl, this most enchanting treasure in all the world, just for him? And he, had he not gained her at the risk of his life?

From the very first moment she had appeared to him at the top of the tower from afar, before he was able to reach her, his heart was drawn to her; how much the more so now, after he had climbed to her at the risk of his life and she so near to him. Is she not the bride for whom he had been willing to die?

Netanyah threw himself on his bed, laden with indescribably wondrous feelings. His heart overflowed with new thoughts that had never before entered his mind. What is this deep silent melody so sweet and full of yearning that comes to his ears? Is it the singing of the evening stars or the sound of the ebb and flow of his own flesh and blood?

He fell deeply asleep, lying on the tower of the roof under the canopy of the sky. His sleep and his dreams were more delightful than any he had enjoyed in so many nights.

Early next morning, before the warmth of Ketziyah's flesh had cooled and while the dew still rested on Netanyah's hair, the two stood upon the rooftop like two loving young gazelles. Facing the east, they gazed at the majestic sun as it rose in holy splendor from behind the mountains and shed its light upon them. Embracing one another, the two leaned against the parapet, a man and a woman. The sweet scent of their bodies mingled with the chilled morning air and the touch of their secret and loving caresses. A single hidden passion overwhelmed both of their bodies, and a great spontaneous joy illuminated their faces. Indeed, on that morning the sun appeared doubly glorious and powerful. The gleeful singing of the birds also rang out with special vigor that morning. Had God declared a holiday on earth? As they embraced, soul pouring into soul, even before the sun had risen above the horizon of the earth, their lips suddenly met in a long kiss. It was as if each had completely imbibed the other's soul. Then the intoxicated Netanyah murmured, "My soul thirsts for you, my morning star." And Ketziyah, clinging to him, whispered, as she cradled her head in his bosom, "My body yearns for you, my savior."

Soon, when they caught sight of the eagle approaching in the distance, soaring nearer and nearer to the tower, bearing his pleasant burden on his pinions, the lovers shook their ecstasy away as birds do the morning dew and, waving their hands, greeted the eagle warmly, over and over again, until it landed in the garden. They hailed its arrival as children hail the coming of an uncle or brother who has returned from holiday in a distant country carrying a delightful present under his arm.

Deftly and joyfully Ketziyah unloaded the package carried by the bird. However, seeing that the size of the portion had not been increased, she scowled at the eagle, pretending, like a spoiled child, to be angry. In her flightiness, she had forgotten before whom she was standing, and she pointed her sweet little finger at this most powerful of eagles and reprimanded him in a charming mischievous tone: "What a small portion have you brought today master eagle! Indeed you are niggardly, O chariot of the King of Judah! Do you not yet know that there are two of us in the tower today. Two today and two we shall be from now on. Did you not yourself bring the guest to my home. It is your duty, then, to fill all his needs. See, he stands before you. Isn't he a valiant young man? Return to your master and tell him that I am no longer alone in the tower. There are two of us! Did you hear, two! Ask all the morning birds and they shall confirm that we are two. Even the waves of the sea will roar from afar: we are two. And the mountains around us will repeat again and again: we are two; we are two!"

And as this surge of glee seized Ketziyah, she burst into a dance, taking quick mincing steps, which she strung together like a string of small pearls. With her toes touching her ankles, she tripped lightly around Netanyah, circling gracefully and silently gliding, as if afloat. At times, she withdrew like a frightened doe. As she backed away, she stretched out her two tiny and delicate palms, and her eyes prayed. It seemed to him that she was offering him her body and soul as a morning gift of love. At other times, she would come forward and approach him very closely, standing erect before him, brow to brow, and as her entire body swayed before him, taut as a violin string or straight as a beam of light, she scorched him with her eyes and set him aflame with her breath. A moment later, she again withdrew. Hands on her slender hips, she swayed and pranced gracefully, looking like a fine double-eared silver punch bowl just about to fall from its perch. Netanyah's hand almost rushed to catch her. The more she danced, the more she changed her mood and became bolder. The doe was converted into a fiery lioness, and her dance transformed itself into a flaming storm. Her golden curls caught fire and, loose to the wind, ran wildly along the back of her neck like raging and consuming flames. She was a live, burning torch. Netanyah, swept by her storming and singed by her fire, stood immobile. His soul drank in her flame and he was intoxicated. His heart was pierced by her deadly arrows. His trembling hands quickly reached out toward the fire, but he did not know for what purpose—were they to save her or grab hold of her?

However, the flame of the great fire had already gripped Netanyah, and he was no longer able to retract his scorched hands. A moment later, when Ketziyah, all afire, fell into his arms, he lifted her on his shoulders and carried her to her garret as a reaper bears his full stack to the threshing house. The strange, white eagle viewed all that was happening with stranger's eyes, as if it saw nothing. But no sooner had Netanyah disappeared into the castle with his prize than the eagle suddenly bestirred itself and soared to the sky frantically, as if scalded by boiling water. As it flew about to and fro above the roof for several moments, flapping its wings, it seemed to be beating against a hidden net in vain or like a night bird groping at the moon. Suddenly it veered powerfully, as if freeing itself from a trap, and hurled itself all at once, without thought, into the void, cutting with both its mighty pinions through the wide spaces of heaven, tearing through the distance and sending its mad screeching to the ends of the earth.

When the parrot arrived after the eagle had departed to call upon the maiden and greet her, as was its custom every morning, no one responded. The window did not open that day, and the head of golden curls did not show itself. It was most perplexed. Why does no one hear its screeching or respond to its call?

15

On that day, Netanyah took Ketziyah under his wing and married her. The next morning when Netanyah and his wife went up to the roof, the eagle had doubled the portion of food that he had previously brought. This act they considered as a sign that God approved and blessed their love, and they greatly rejoiced. Ketziyah almost hugged the eagle's neck in her delight, but the angry glint of its eye, the flinty shine of its beak, deterred her, and her eyes greeted it from afar. The eagle acted as though it did not know her and paid no attention to either Ketziyah or her greeting but stood alone, silent and estranged. This morning its eyes and neck were haughty, and it looked more dignified and more majestic than ever before: king of the kingliest of eagles.

Henceforth this routine became law: each morning the eagle would bring two portions of the best delicacies from the king's table, one portion for each of the two. Netanyah and his wife lived in the tower like a pair of doves in their cote, contented as they drank, ate, and rejoiced in their love. Only one matter disheartened Netanyah, despite the fact that he was now imprisoned in a tower on an isolated island with his beloved: it was now even more impossible to fulfill his obligations in this hopeless state. He was despondent that he could not realize his plan to appear before God and fulfill his father's vows.

With the passing of many days, he became saddened and depressed. But Ketziyah consoled and encouraged him by referring to Solomon's words. "Has not everything that Solomon said happened thus far? So too will the rest of his words prove true. Our redemption is indeed about to come. The King of Judah, the wisest and handsomest of all kings, will remember the silly little maid of Aram who had surrendered her insignificant self into his white and long-fingered hands and believed what his tender and honeyed mouth had uttered. Shall the ruler of Judah and Israel lie and act traitorously?"

Ketziyah's prophecy was indeed fulfilled. The redemption of the tower's prisoners was not late in coming, as we shall soon discover.

16

One day, King Solomon's chefs noticed that an additional portion, beside the one allotted to the maiden and borne each day by the eagle to
a designated address by order of the king, was missing. This absence
puzzled them, but they ignored it, assuming that it was a mere accident. Perhaps their figures were wrong, or perhaps it was stolen by
some rat. But when the shortage was discovered again and again, they
became very concerned and set an ambush for the thief. Indeed he
was soon apprehended. And who was he? The great white eagle, the
master eagle, the king's haughty mount. He and none other. The matter was brought before the king. When Solomon heard about it, he
smiled and his face lit up, but he acted as if ignorant and said: "I did
not know that the master eagle has the habits of a magpie. He has
embarrassed me very much, and I shall have to teach him a lesson in
honesty." And, then, as if undecided, he said: "In any case, let him
steal as much as he wishes until I decide what to do. Whoever makes
snap judgments prevents justice. Who understands the psychology of
a bird? Sometimes the tiniest fly is wiser and more righteous than
even the giant Og, King of Bashan. Moreover, does it not sometimes
happen that their evil instincts are wiser than our good sense? Perhaps
their deeds, which might appear to us to be sinful and stupid, will be
considered by God to be wise and very just."

On that very day, Solomon dispatched his couriers to all the kings
who had disagreed with him at the banquet and requested them to
stand ready on a date that he specified to go down to the island with
him, they and their retinues, in order to visit the tower to determine
what had happened to the daughter of the King of Aram.

And Solomon and all the kings who were at his banquet, including the maiden's father, they, their highest ministers, their greatest
sages, and their chief magicians, all gathered again as one at the
court of King Solomon. All were clad in majestic robes; the kings
wore their crowns and their royal gowns of purple and scarlet, the
ministers donned their majestic miters and their coats of fine linen
and crimson, the wise men came with their striped shirts, white
staves, their turbans with long trains, and their wide and tasseled
girdles with scribes' ink pots on their side, the magicians with their
towering hats shaped like fortresses and embroidered in white, vio-
let, and green. When this entire multicolored company mounted the
magic cloak, it rose above the earth and embarked for the island.

All the wild life on the island, ranging from wild fowl to the beasts of the forest and the crawling insects of the earth, again witnessed in great fear how the wondrous eagle, so terrible, mighty, and broad, descended suddenly from the sky. It looked like a flying tract of land, unequaled in size by any flying creature since the creation. When the eagle landed before the tower, a company of wondrous creatures swarmed out of its hold, very strange and weird beings, bipeds who stood erect and gathered as one body at the tower's gates.

The passengers walked round the tower, carefully examining its structure, feeling and smelling every stone in its walls, every splinter on the trees, every beam or brick, to ascertain whether it had any breach or hole or had been touched by human hands. Then they turned back to the gateway, checking it as well, its bolts, its locks, and its seals. Had anything been lacking?

When they found that everything was as it should be, they ordered that the seals be removed, the locks opened, and the bolts drawn. The doors of the gate, which had rusted because of the years, squeaked as they swung open. The entire company entered the tower.

The ladder that had been removed was replaced, and the voyagers climbed into the tower, each according to his rank, first the greater, followed by the lesser members. All except the bitter and tense King of Aram, who was short and scrawny, who jumped the line and entered first. His superiors, anxious as they were to know what had at last happened to the maiden, forgave him this time and did not reprimand him, since they recognized the advantage he enjoyed over them. He was the maiden's father, and he was most anxious to discover his daughter's fate. He was short-tempered and impatient (some say he suffered from piles). He never knew a moment's peace.

As they all ascended to the garret, they lined up in rows, each according to his rank, position, and the honor due him. In the first row was the mighty King of Egypt on one side and the irascible King of Aram on the other, with the even-tempered and smiling Solomon between them. Behind them, in the second row, were the minor and even lesser kings. And behind them were the wise men, knowledgeable and literate. Bringing up the rear was the band of magicians and astrologers, who knew the art of interpreting dreams and foretelling the future. Thus the company of those who had gathered on the island stood in the ample garret, and their eyes searched out every one of its corners to find the imprisoned maiden.

They were all impatient to learn what had happened to her during her days of imprisonment. Would Solomon's words be confirmed?

But the girl was not to be found in the garret. Was she hiding in the bed chamber? All raised their eyes to the door leading to the bed chamber. At that moment, the door was opened. The company turned to stone. They could hardly believe their eyes. Instead of the single individual who had been imprisoned in the tower, instead of the dainty and gentle maiden, the daughter of the King of Aram, there now emerged before them, standing tall at the threshold with heads raised high, two people, a man and a woman.

Everything that occurred on this day as well as all the other events that followed it—all the excitement and tumult, their effect upon those who viewed and heard them, and, moreover, the look on the face of the King of Aram and his anguish upon learning who was the father of the man whom God had chosen for his daughter—all these would exhaust the pen of even a skilled writer. Let each one, therefore, imagine them in his own way.

17

On that very day, Solomon and all the kings who had accompanied him, their retinues, and the new lovers, who had been dwelling in the tower, returned to Jerusalem to the royal palace, in order to partake of a banquet, which the king had ordered to be prepared before he had departed, anticipating the result of his visit.

A swift courier came to Malkishuah in Sidon with the king's command, saying: "Hurry to Jerusalem to attend your son's wedding, do not tarry. The king is summoning you."

Old Malkishuah was taken to the palace. When he found his son, he fell upon his neck, embraced and kissed him over and over again on his forehead, his cheeks, his curls, his shoulders—wherever he could place his lips. He wept so profusely that he almost fainted, calling out in a broken heart and in a shaking voice, as his tears streamed like a gushing river, "Ah, my son, my son, you have sorely distressed your old father; I had almost followed you to the grave in my anguish!"

All those assembled were moved to tears at the sight of the poor old gentleman. They retired, leaving father and son alone in the room, as each poured out his soul to the other in the absence of strangers.

18

The great banquet that Solomon had arranged at his palace had never been equaled by any held in any palace. This was, after all, the wedding banquet in honor of Netanyah and Ketziyah.

The guests were seated, each in his proper place. At the head of the table sat Solomon, Queen Bathyah, Pharaoh's daughter, and Netanyah and Ketziyah. He was crowned with myrtle and she wore a wreath of white lilies on her head. Beside them sat their two fathers: the King of Aram, still angry, at the bride's side, and Malkishuah, still aggrieved, next to the groom. On each of their sides sat the Kings of Egypt and of Tyre, they and their queens, as well as the friends of the bride and groom. And then, the rest of the guests: the foreign kings and their retainers and the chiefs of the people of Israel—all of whom were men of renown, princes, lords, nobles, generals—and the wise counselors of the king: judges, poets, and men of letters, as well as many scholars and elders of the people. Never had so much greatness, wisdom, glory, honor, justice, and bravery come together at one single table.

Everyone of the king's musicians and singers who made sweet music gathered at the palace on that day, forming a single large and numerous choir. Their voices sang and their instruments played before the king and his guests some of the psalms composed by David and the sons of Korah. Then came the dancers, who performed both as a group and as soloists—all this enhanced the merriment.

The king's servants and butlers served every delicacy of the highest quality in gold and silver vessels. There were all sorts of choice preserves, products of the rivers and the seas, succulent meats of the field, and hunt from the forests, rare, cooked, roasted, and well spiced—the work of master chefs. Chief bakers lavished upon them delicious breads of finely sifted white flour ground from the richest wheat of Miletus, Zanoah, and Minit. The head butlers brought wine from the king's wine cellar, new, old, and even older. Pure and blended wines as well as distilled liqueurs. Those who abstained from strong drink refreshed themselves with the juices of pomegranates and other sweet fruits. Each in accord with his taste and the preference of his palate. No servant faltered or dallied.

The more the guests ate and drank, the more their appetite grew, and they ordered dish after dish. For such was the quality of Solomon's delicacies that those who ate them seemed never to be sated. They simply slipped down the gullet into the belly without anyone being aware that they did. Not in vain was it said that the fish of the sea, the fowl of the air, the beasts of the field, cattle and sheep, all flowed en masse, rushing happily to Solomon's kitchens, since they considered it a fitting honor to be served at his table and fill the bellies of his guests.

Yet the King of Aram was the only guest who still sat angry and irascible, his green, wrinkled face growing greener and even more wrinkled. His hand did not touch any dish that was placed before him. He neither ate nor drank. Ever since he had learned whose son was the young man who took his daughter, he was filled with the venom of pythons and vipers. Twitching and evil scorpions peered from his eyes, dancing wildly as if running amok. Malkishuah, too, still sat like a mourner at a wedding, his face dark. The joy at finding his lost son did not assuage his sorrow. He sat quietly but mournfully, although his eyes looked with loving affection at the face of his only son. The king perceived that the two were sad. He silenced the band of musicians and singers and suddenly remarked to Netanyah: "Please tell us, O Malkishuah's son, before all our guests, how you came to the island and its tower, and how you managed to reach your loving dove in her cote. Tell us everything in detail, speak up and do not be embarrassed."

Netanyah rose and clearly and honestly recounted all the adventures he had experienced from the day he sailed by boat bound for the bay of Acco, bearing his father's vow offerings, in order to go up to Jerusalem to celebrate the Sukkot festival before God, until he entered the tower, joined Ketziyah, and cleaved to her. He also told them about the episode involving the emerald and the python and all the dreams he had, not hiding anything. When he concluded, he took out the emerald and placed it on the table before the eyes of all, as faithful evidence confirming his account.

All the guests, the people from Judah and Israel and the foreigners, upon hearing these wondrous events, were very astonished. The eyes of the beautiful ladies, including lovely Queen Bathyah, filled with tears, although they were fixed upon the large emerald that glistened at them with its seventy-seven eyes and its thousand rays.

Solomon waited until the astonishment and excitement of his guests abated and then said: "My dear guests and friends, today your ears have heard the miraculous episode and all the wonders that Netanyah has described, as well as all the events that contrived to bring him, a Jewish lad, dwelling in the Canaanite city of Sidon, to a hidden desolate island unknown to man and to a doubly locked tower, which even the most valiant of heroes could not breach. There he found a loving dove who was imprisoned alone, a maid of Aram, and took her as his wife. Now tell me all of you, could this have occurred without God?"

The guests, their eyes still chained to the marvelous, magic emerald, responded as one: "Indeed it was the hand of God that did this. It was He who caused this to occur."

And the king continued: "You have spoken the truth. This has come from God. However, if you said what you did honestly and wholeheartedly and if your heart and your mouth are in concord, then: magnify the Lord with me and let us exalt his name together." And lifting a full glass of wine, he rose to his feet and said: "I raise this glass of blessing and redemption in the name of God; please respond together with me: 'Praised be God of the spirits of all flesh who gives a woman to a man.'"

All the guests rose and, with one eye still fastened upon the emerald, repeated after Solomon the blessing word by word and said, "Amen and Amen."

And all the band of musicians and singers, upon hearing the blessing, broke into a loud and powerful song in praise of God, as their voices and instruments proclaimed, "Fortune is cast in the bosom and all its ways come from God."

And the sound of the singers and musicians engulfed the entire hall like a roar of mighty waters. However, the guests ignored the music because, as the king's blessing was concluded, they once again scrutinized the emerald with both their eyes and were not able to remove them. All their attention was centered upon it. In order to distract their eyes from the emerald to the bride, the king said, smiling with good-natured mockery, "O kings of many lands and princes of the earth, have you so lost your good taste that you turn your eyes away from this charming beauty and stare at the jewel?"

The eyes of the guests suddenly shifted to the bride. Then the king also turned to her and said: "And you my lovely dove, princess of Aram, because you heeded the call of your fate and of your heart and bestowed your love upon a Hebrew lad who came from afar whom you did not know, may God bless you. Fear not, nor be ashamed. Rejoice with the prince of your youth, follow him to his father's home and family, and cling to their God and their ways. I know you will not regret your decision. This event is wrought by the arm of God, who brings the distant near in wondrous ways and joins those apart by means of the mysterious pathways of wisdom in order to mix blood with blood, living springs with living springs, rendering the many and mighty fields of God fertile, and raising rich produce on the earth anew everyday and every moment. This great hand spun the wheel of fortune for you and brought you from afar, imprisoning you in the tower, in order to have you taken by him who sought your soul and your love and to have you planted by his hand in foreign soil, in a place that was appointed for you from days of yore.

"And know this—the king, your father, should also know this, but he forgot and is angry—you are indeed not a foreign twig nor a mixed seed in the land of Judah. Although Aram separated itself from Judah in ancient days, both peoples are hewn from the same quarry. Our earliest fathers are hewn from the same rock, which originated in Aram. They took their wives from the family of Aram. Therefore let your source be blessed, and on this day, your wedding day, receive a sevenfold blessing, as you come before the eyes of this community and in the presence of the elders of Israel to seek shelter under the wings of Israel's God and dwell in his shade forever. Our sister, may your descendants be counted in myriads."

And all the assembly responded to the king's remarks in joyful tumult, and the choir of musicians and singers echoed the blessing with a fanfare of song, "Our sister, may your descendants be counted in myriads."

The king and queen kissed Ketziyah on her pure white forehead to the cheering of the assembly and the choir. When the roar subsided, the king, his hand still resting on the bride's shoulder, declared: "I haven't finished my remarks. It is indeed true and clear as the sun that you were shown that only the hand of God can perform all these miracles and render the circumstances that brought these two distant souls together, but bear in mind that it was I who was chosen by God, unbeknownst to me, to be one of his instruments in this matter, and I in no small way caused the anguish that this dear girl, the apple of her father's eye, had to endure. This silent dove, completely innocent, was forcibly ejected from her cote and forced to suffer isolation on a desolate, uninhabitable island, where she was confined to an impenetrable tower. I empathized with you, my daughter, felt your agony from afar; my heart trembled for you. But now your joyous wedding day has arrived, and you will be married in my home. I, therefore, decided to atone for the wrong that I did you by presenting you with a gift, which I have prepared for you. May it serve as a small compensation for your great and incomparable pain, for your immeasurable courage, and for the strong trust that you had in King Solomon and his word."

The king had barely finished his speech when one of his servants, a prince of the court, brought him a silver platter covered with a small, but remarkably embroidered, silk kerchief. The king removed the kerchief before the eyes of the curious company. Beneath it was a small, sealed golden box, which was entirely covered with pearls and precious stones; it was a wondrous box whose fine design had no equal. When the king opened its lid, the assembled were blinded. Inside the box, on a soft backing of green silk, there shone with a thousand powerful rays scintillating splendidly like a living thing a large emerald, the identical twin of the emerald that was lying on the table.

The entire assemblage was at first astounded at the sight—struck dumb. Then an indescribable sound rose from the depths of all their souls and receded after a while. It was like a lengthy sigh of astonishment, as if a thousand empty water skins, pierced by swords, had all at once exhaled their air in unison and collapsed. The eyes of the assembled, struck blind, darted alternately from one emerald to the other, never seeing their fill. Then all at once all eyes were fixed upon Solomon, as if asking, "What is this?"

The king removed the emerald from the box, raised it to the view of the assemblage, and said: "Indeed, this, too, is one of God's miracles and mysterious ways. This most precious emerald, the queen of gems, was given to me as a gift by one of the trusted servants under my command, the king of reptiles, the greatest of snakes, on the day I ascended the throne. I secreted it in my treasure house in a secret place for a propitious occasion, appointing the king of the serpents to guard over it and assure its security. And now its time has come. It is the twin sister of the emerald on the table. Birds of a feather do flock together. Undoubtedly God's hand united these two living souls. It was His hand that brought together these two distant gems. Who knows, perhaps these still stones also possess a living soul, perhaps this stone's soul also yearned for its distant sister or brother and it was God who arranged the circumstances to satisfy its desire. For God did not create man alone but in pairs, man and woman, and all flora and fauna as well. Why should nonorganic substances be inferior to them? Perhaps all the mighty forces of the universe, its very foundations, hidden or revealed, near or far, great or small, ranging from the host of heaven to the very dust of scales, from the tiniest atom of matter to the spirit and power of all things, were fashioned in pairs—male and female. And God implanted within them the urge and desire to cleave to each other as one, and when they longed for each other from afar, circled each other, constantly pursued or were pursued, wandered to and fro, they knew no rest. Is this not that great and eternal love, that mighty love of God, love everlasting, the soul and spirit of every living being, which is stored like fire in the bowels of the universe and of which no place is free? It suffers neither end nor destruction, and when it bursts forth and reveals itself, it blazes mysterious roads and paths never foreseen or hoped for by man."

And as he fixed the emerald as a headpiece on the wreath of white lilies crowning the bride's forehead, he continued: "The emerald that Malkishuah's son carried to the House of God by his father's command is a holy emerald, the holiest of the holies, because within it are stored the grief of a father deep as the abyss and the mourning for a mother, which is inconsolable, the true anguish of the heart, and a pure hidden tear. This emerald, which I place as a beautiful decoration on your curls, is likewise a sacred gem because it rises to shine upon your pure brow on your wedding day like the dawn of a new life. As it casts its many splendid rays upon you, may it be filled with the splendor of the great love, the very torch and flame of God, which at this very moment illuminates your inner soul, overflowing with its radiance. Therefore please take this gem as a blessing from the king's hand, and it shall be yours, for I give it to you."

As he spoke, the king turned to Malkishuah and said: "Your amulet, Malkishuah the Zebulite from Sidon, shall be brought to the House of God and shall be set in the curtain of the Holy of Holies, as you have requested. When it casts its light upon it, as a candle of grief and a pure tear of mourning, in memory of the wife of your youth who died so suddenly, before her time, its twin sister will gleam as a light of love and consolation on the head of your new daughter, like God's joyous dewdrop, as she now enters your home to illumine the darkness of its sheltering beams and gladden its mournful corners like a bird. Enough, then, old man, of this draining of the cup of sorrow to its dregs. Arise and smash it to the ground in smithereens. See, God has now given you the cup of great consolation. Seize it, drink, and bless God doubly. For he has granted you a double consolation; he has returned your lost son and has added a lovely daughter to your household. This is not a time for mourning but a time to dance!"

The king signaled the musicians and the palace resounded with the sound of music, the resonance of lyres, the blasting of trumpets, and the crashing of drums and cymbals. The dancers joined in dancing, prancing, and stomping vigorously. The very ceiling trembled at their reeling. Joy flooded the palace.

When the table was served meats, they were selected from various animals: venison and antelope meat and all edible fowl, both domesticated and wild. The diligent waiters continued to serve one delicacy after the other, many sweets, and every type of wine and drink, never tiring. Who has not heard the fame of Solomon's banquets! The king commanded that a platter containing a whole tender doe be placed before the groom. Silencing the musicians, he said: "I have spoken words in honor of the bride. I cannot send off the bridegroom empty-handed, for he is my brother today, my equal. A crown shines on his head. You know, 'A bridegroom is like a king!' How much the more so, one who is of the choicest of men, an exemplary and valiant young man who has experienced wonders and is blessed with good fortune, upon whom God has showered great favor and many omens, too many to bear, while he is still tender in years. By my soul, I shall not send him off before I, too, shall, bless him."

The king continued at first in a slightly mocking but good-natured vein and then more earnestly: "See, I have commanded that you be served a young doe, for I find that you are a brave hunter and a skilled marksman who has no equal. On the day to which you referred, you tracked a wild doe, but you captured a loving, tame doe, a dainty and sweet doe who is a delight to the eye and one's heart's desire. Indeed you are a swift hunter and deft. Let your quarry then be doubly blessed. May your bow always be taut and may your quiver never lack sharp arrows throughout your life. Delight your wife in your youth; she is a loving and enchanting doe; may her love always be fulfilling and constant. A woman of charm honors her husband, and he shall gain glory from her beauty. Let the woman who is entering your home be a blessing and a joy to you and a great solace to your aging father. May you establish a new and faithful home in Israel, as did Ruth the Moabite, who established my father's royal house in Judah, and as did our first three patriarchs, each of whom married daughters of Aram and founded the house of Israel."

Raising a cup of blessing before all the guests, the king continued: "Let it not be said that King Solomon dismissed the bridegroom with mere words. I have prepared an additional blessing for him: I have today appointed you overseer over all the foreign trade of the realm. You shall be in charge of the ships and caravans that enter and depart from its borders. You shall oversee the commerce of our land, its imports, and its exports and shall conduct its affairs faithfully and justly. As you served your father, you shall now serve me. Although it is true that you are still young and have had not yet been in the king's service, nevertheless, since I know your diligence and your good sense and am not ignorant of your honesty and your youthful courage, I do not fear placing this heavy and honorable office upon your shoulders. 'If you see a man who is quick and diligent, let him stand before kings.' I have also appointed your father as your mentor to assist and guide you. With his broad experience and his great wisdom, he will be your eyes, and you, with your competence and practical talents, will be his arms. The two of you shall serve your king and nation with intelligence, with integrity, and with vim and vigor. Your activities will bring a blessing to the land and provide a livelihood for many people. Long live the valiant Netanyah, and long live Malkishuah, the king's chief agent for external trade. Be strong, and be courageous!"

All the guests as one cheered the two loudly to the sound of drums and cymbals, echoing the king: "Long live Netanyah son of Malkishuah. Be strong and be courageous."

Netanyah rose to the applause, made a modest bow to the king, and said: "I bow before you for having found favor in your eyes, my lord the king, and for the recognition you have given me. I am unworthy to have received all your kindnesses."

Then the king turned toward the King of Aram and continued: "To you, too, King of Aram, I have only one more word to say and then I shall desist. I have watched you sitting here all the time angry and dispirited, as if upon a pile of scorpions. Who is pouring hot coals on your head or roasting your flesh? What evil spirit has possessed you ceaselessly? Who is it; tell me its name. I know that you have a grievance against me and my father's house. For a long time,

you have been consumed by your hatred for David's seed and all the
seed of Israel. I have not overlooked the fact that you are displeased,
very much displeased at the joke that God has played upon you by
giving you as a son-in-law the son of Malkishuah, the enemy whom
you hate so intensely and against whom you have plotted for many
years; and even worse for you, that you must sit at the same table
and be unable to do him harm. Your heart is heavy, but you yourself
are a lightweight, O King of Aram! Have all the many peaceful days
that separate us from our fathers not diminished the fierce hatred
you bear against us, a hatred that you had inherited from your forefathers? Even if we grant that this man had committed a bloody
crime against them, must you forever nurture your enmity? Is there
no reprieve from sin? Must a man carry hostility in his breast with
him to the grave, as a leper bears the rot in his bones and the
spreading cancer in his flesh? Lift the corners of your cloak and bare
your hips; are you not carrying an avenging sword hidden under
your clothes? Our ancestors hated one another but are long since
gone; their hatred and their jealousy have died with them. Shall we,
their sons, maintain that enmity forever? See now, the joviality of
friends and the happiness of love bursting all about you. The fountain of glee flows freely and tumultuously as a powerful river. Can
your heart withstand this flood? Do you wish to stem it with your
disdain? Hate is indeed deeper than the pit, but love is more powerful and stronger than hate and can overcome it! When love pours its
spirit upon man, it returns him to his primordial state, as God created him. He no longer keeps petty accounts.

"Sons can tear down the walls of enmity, which the fathers have
erected row upon row and, in their great anger, have heightened
over the years to divide nation from nation and people from people—this wall can be destroyed by the sons, together with its time-
worn stones and crumbling plaster down to the very foundations,
when in a single moment the spirit of love gathers them under its
wings. The eyes of vicious and arrogant hatred are like those of a
standing frog. When it stands erect, its eyes look backward, but
love's eyes look straight ahead. Why have you fastened your eyes on
the ground? Lift them up and see what stands before you. Are not
these two young souls, the chief cause of this banquet, your own
daughter, O King of Aram, and the son of your enemy Malkishuah
the Zebulite? Are they not living and true testimony that not the
breadth of the seas, not the desolation of distant isles, not prison

walls locked and sealed sevenfold, not even all of these together can serve as barriers or withstand the power of love and its mighty roar when it storms, terrible, beautiful, and full of godly valor, toward its joyous destination and when it cuts its mysterious path, despite all barriers, toward the goal it desires to attain? Shall the high walls of the tower withstand the assault of the Israelite lad as he strives to climb up to the Aramean girl? How do you dare stand as a dividing wall between them with your petty hatred? Are your eyes displeased with the union? Is the doe of Aram not a fitting partner for this handsome fawn of Israel? Or do you really think you will be able to sunder what God had joined together? Enough, O King of Aram, forsake enmity and desist from vengeful wrath. Uproot them, as one uproots a poisonous thorn. When love shouts its joyous song, hatred turns dumb. No more vengeance, no more begrudging from now on, no more quarreling or conflict. Let the former resentments no longer be remembered."

Suddenly the king held the bridegroom with his right hand and the bride with his left and raised his voice: "Today we shall discover how superior is the way of God to the ways of man, with his petty and evil plots and deceits. Like a snake behind a fence, like a leopard in his lair, the avenger lies in ambush waiting for his hated enemy in order to kill him furtively and extinguish the fire of his passion with his spilt blood. Year after year, he lies in ambush, never resting until he carries out his abominable design. Afterwards, he considers it a laudable act of great courage. But God has paths to redemption yet unknown to man. God does not place the task of revenge in Satan's hand but in the hands of the best of his angels, in the hands of love. Blood for blood, a soul for a soul. Not by bloodletting or killing does God redeem, but by giving seed and by increasing life upon the earth—seed and new life, which are superior to that which previously existed. Look here, these are the true avengers of your brother's blood, O King of Aram. They stand before you today: your daughter and the son of Malkishuah. Today your brother's blood has been redeemed by them. This is a redemption of peace; Malkishuah and his house are now cleansed of guilt. You have arrived too late, O King of Aram. God has preceded you and avenged you. Rise and praise His name for redeeming both your soul and your brother's blood by preventing you from taking innocent blood. For indeed, Malkishuah was always innocent of the charge of murder, and you have persecuted him unjustly. You hated

him in the past for a crime he did not commit. Did Malkishuah
shoot his arrow at your brother from some back alley, or did he
come upon him in an open field? He encountered him as a valiant
warrior, and your brother died in battle like a brave soldier.
Malkishuah is free of bloodguilt. He is a man of honor who de-
serves the reward of heroes, for he faithfully served his king, nation,
and God, as did your brother, who shall be remembered forever because he risked his life in his people's honor. Who then is he who
makes false demands upon his neighbor to pay a debt that he never
owed him, and how much the more so when it is an obsolete debt
incurred many years ago? Can a throne be stable without mercy, can
it stand without justice? Come then, forbear, and view Malkishuah
as a man of peace. Accept the precious atonement that he has prof-
fered you, his only son, in whom he takes pride. Is this atonement
too little in your eyes? And if you reject it, by the life of God and all
his good angels, I shall not leave this place until you bless this marriage and make your peace with Malkishuah. Let us see whether
you will have the courage, after all that has been said, to reject with
hatred the hand that is offered to you in peace."

The king rose as he spoke and rent the sheep that stood before
him into two equal parts. As he presented one part to the King of
Aram and the other to Malkishuah, he raised his voice and declared: "I have split this sheep in two today. Let it be a sign of a
covenant of peace between the two of you. As your children cleave
to each other and become one flesh, so shall you two become
united heart and soul forever. May true peace abide in your hearts
all the days of your life, and may your covenant never be violated
from this time until all eternity. Let it be said of your families that
love and peace have met—Amen, may God so do. Peace, peace to
them who are distant and them who are near. Peace, love, and
mercy."

The eyes of all the guests turned toward the King of Aram and
Malkishuah to see whether Solomon's words had succeeded in
changing the hearts of both for good. Indeed Malkishuah rose and
went toward the King of Aram to greet him in peace. But the King
of Aram still hesitated, as if struggling with his soul at the very risk
of his life. When he raised his hitherto lowered eyes slightly from
the ground, the little scorpions had almost disappeared, as if retreat-
ing to their holes, and only the ends of their tails still fluttered there
and writhed. Then Solomon lifted his glass and shouted an imperi-

ous command, "Scold Satan, O King of Aram, the angel of peace awaits you."

The call broke the resistance of the King of Aram. He crouched even lower and, as if forced by a devil, quickly buried his scrawny hand in the broad, strong hand that Malkishuah had extended to him. He hid his face, as if to conceal his embarrassment. Solomon saw his anguish and spoke words of encouragement to him: "Lift your head and stand straight, O King of Aram, and dare to take a risk. Today you have demonstrated that you are a true sovereign and yours is the kingdom and the might. You have struggled with yourself and have prevailed. This act of courage is greater in my eyes than all the great deeds that you and your fathers have performed until today. There is no greater ruler than he who rules over his own spirit. No greater hero than he who conquers his own soul. Long live the King of Aram and long live valiant Malkishuah as well. May this double covenant, which you have made between you, be a covenant of life and peace for you and your children after you forever. Choirmaster, a song of praise!"

Who can recount what followed at that time in the banquet hall? All the court rules were forgotten, and even the emeralds were ignored. From all ends of the table, the guests rushed to the king and crowded around him. All stood high, their necks outstretched, their hands extended. Everyone wanted to see the pact of peace that the King of Aram and Malkishuah had concluded. And when the king's "Long live" toast was offered, a thundering response rolled through the hall and everyone shouted: "Long live King Solomon, prince of peace, forever. Long live Jedidyah,[8] the elect of both God and mankind! May his throne be established forever and may his kingdom endure from generation to generation."

A mighty storm of joy swept the hall and engulfed all who were in its precincts. Throats roared, mouths resounded, musical instruments thundered, feet stamped—the very hall seemed to quake at the sound of dancing. Soon the joy spread, flooding the courtyard and its surroundings. The merrymaking of the banquet merged with the celebration of the holiday. Masses of reveling holiday crowds flowed from every street and alley. Pilgrims to the House of God streamed to the king's palace, singing joyous songs. Like the waters

---

[8]One of King Solomon's sobriquets, meaning friend of God.

of a river, they poured into the king's outer and inner courtyards and joined the banquet guests to form a single turbulent human sea of limitless revelry. Joy filled the palace road.

19

The banquet lasted for all the seven days of the festival. On each of these days Solomon and his guests would go up to worship in the House of God, rendering many vows and gift offerings. Each day of the festival, Solomon would sacrifice seventy oxen on the altar, a number equal to the number of the nations of the world. The foreign kings each sacrificed twelve sheep a day, the number of the tribes of Israel. And God's name was honored by the gentiles during the holiday. Never had the House of God witnessed so much joy, honor, and glory during all the days it existed in Jerusalem.

On the eighth day, which marked the close of the festival, Malkishuah, Netanyah, and Ketziyah, his bride, went up to the House of God to fulfill the vows that Malkishuah had given through Netanyah when he had sent him away.

Now when Netanyah gave his father's emerald to the officer in charge of the treasury of God's house, Ketziyah removed the emerald from her diadem, that is, the emerald with which Solomon had decorated her, placed it on Netanyah's emerald, and said: "Let this gem, the gift of King Solomon, be sacred to God and let it be placed on the curtain of the Holy of Holies beside its twin sister so that they might both shine forever before God. These are twin sisters whom God has joined, why should I separate them? I know that the king will not be angry at this act, for there is no one wiser than he who comprehends the heart. Am I not right, Netanyah?"

As she spoke, a very strange and mysterious smile crossed her lips, but Netanyah's eyes failed to discern it. His heart flourished like grass as he recognized his wife's piety and her holy innocence, all of which added to the beauty of her youth and her charm.

The two gems were fixed in the curtain, each alongside its sister, as Ketziyah had desired and declared. They were a pure pair in the presence of God. Whoever came to the House of God saw the two emeralds high on the curtain and would say: "These are the two tears of God, which have fallen from his overflowing cup. It is God's double gift to humankind in order to relieve and redeem them: a tear of sorrow and a tear of joy."

That day the kings who had been Solomon's guests and their retinues hurried to return to their countries and their thrones. Even now we do not know what they thought. Were they pleased by Solomon's greatness, were they happy, or were they sad? They were all silent when they departed, closed-mouthed like silent dogs.

Unique among them was the King of Tyre, who remained unchanged. His eyes smiled the thinnest of smiles, as before. But his heart was like a child's, generous and guileless. He was Solomon's closest friend and was proud of him and his greatness. But he considered himself to be wily and enjoyed playing the wise man, scoffing and posing as unconventional and skeptical. He had faith in only one thing, his true love for Solomon, a strong and fierce love, which showed no favor but which, nevertheless, would forgive any offense. This is why Solomon returned his love in equal measure and chose him alone as his confidant. He would bring to him his innermost thoughts and permit him to look behind their mask. Solomon's conversations with him in the privacy of a room where no stranger was present greatly delighted him. Now, too, when the King of Tyre came to bid him farewell with the rest of the kings, Solomon kept him in his palace for an additional day. In the evening, at the close of the banquet and the festival, when melancholy overtook Solomon and his soul was troubled, the two closeted themselves, room within room, while the shadows of evening gathered them under a single wing. But whatever occurred between the two within the walls of the room no ear has ever heard—that is why the words of this scroll must now conclude.

Glossary

Aḥad Ha-amist a supporter of the cultural Zionism articulated by Aḥad Ha-am, the pen name of Asher Ginsburg (1856–1927).

Aleinu prayer recited near the end of Jewish worship services.

Aleph the first letter of the Hebrew alphabet.

Baal Shem Tov "Master of the Good Name." The title of Rabbi Israel Baal Shem Tov—the alleged founder of Hasidism.

Bar Mitzvah the age of responsibility, according to Jewish law, when a boy is thirteen.

Beit Midrash communal house of study.

Cholent a Sabbath stew prepared before the Sabbath and kept warm overnight, usually eaten at midday.

Golem creature made in an artificial way by an act of magic, hence something untamed and dumb.

Goy (female: *goyah;* plural: goyim) gentile.

Ḥallah a loaf of white bread eaten on the Sabbath.

Hamantaschen a traditional sweet roll eaten on the festival of Purim to commemorate the hanging of Haman.

Ḥametz foods containing leavened material and therefore forbidden to eat or touch during Passover.

Hanukah a minor Jewish holiday celebrating the rededication of the Temple in the second century B.C.E. Traditionally, children were given gifts of small coins as part of the festivities.

Ha-Pardes a Hebrew journal advocating Aḥad Ha-amist ideals.

Ḥaroset a mixture of grated or chopped fruits (apples, walnuts, and wine) eaten during the Passover Seder (meal) to symbolize the clay mixture that the Children of Israel had to prepare to form building bricks during their enslavement in Egypt.

Ha-Shiloaḥ an intellectual Aḥad Ha-amist Hebrew periodical.

Haskalah the Jewish enlightenment movement, which strove to modernize East European Jewish culture in the nineteenth century.

Havdalah   a special home service that marks the end of the Sabbath.

Ḥeder   one-room classroom for religious education.

Ḥovevei Tsion   "Lovers of Zion," a pre-Herzlian Zionist movement, formed in the 1880s.

Ḥumash (plural *Ḥumashim*)   the Pentateuch, the first five books of the Bible.

Ḥupah   wedding canopy.

Iluy   "genius"—a name given to a bright Talmud student.

Kaddish   a doxology often recited as a memorial prayer.

Kapote   a long coat or caftan, worn by ultraorthodox Jews.

Kashrut   the observation of the laws pertaining to the selection and preparation of kosher food.

*Katsap*s   Russian farmers settled in Volhynia by the czarist regime.

Kiddush   a short service held at home before partaking of meals celebrating the Sabbath or holidays. Also used for a buffet to celebrate special occasions.

Kreplach   plural of *krepel*, a traditional ravioli-type pasta eaten on festive occasions.

Le-ḥayim   "To life." The customary toast said over wine or liquor.

Little Talit *[Tzitzit]*   a four-cornered ritual undergarment worn by male Jews.

Lokshen   noodles.

Loshen truvki   a derisive term for the Hebrew language.

Lulav   a palm branch, one of the "four components" used at the Sukkot (Tabernacles) service.

Maamadot   originally, a term designating the twenty-four "watches" of priests, Levites, and representatives of the people who served as officiators at the Temple rituals in Jerusalem. After the destruction of the Temple in 70 C.E., special prayers, including readings of the order of the sacrifices, instituted to commemorate the sacrifices overseen by the *maamadot*.

Matzah   unleavened crackers used instead of bread during Passover.

Mazel Tov   congratulatory expression, literally "good luck" or "good fortune."

Meḥokek   an engraver.

Melamed (plural *melamdim*)   the traditional Hebrew teacher of the ḥeder; hence "melamdism" is a disparaging term denoting an incompetent, unworldly view of life or culture.

Melaveh Malka literally, "accompanying the Queen" (i.e., the Sabbath). The late-afternoon Sabbath meal marking the approaching end of the Sabbath.

Mezuzah amulet placed on Jewish doorposts containing biblical verses.

Minyan (plural minyanim) quorum of at least ten adult males required for the holding of a public act of worship.

Mishnah code of Jewish law compiled circa 200 C.E.

Mitzvah a religious law or commandment. The term is also used to designate a kind of righteous act.

Phylacteries see Tefillin.

Purim a minor festival commemorating the saving of the Jews from the wicked Haman, as recorded in the Book of Esther.

Rabbi title of an ordained religious leader of a Jewish congregation.

Reb designates a respectable Jewish personage.

Rebbe teacher.

Rebbitzin Rabbi's wife.

Rosh Hashanah the Jewish New Year holiday, usually occurring in September.

Seder Passover service and meal.

Shalom Aleichem Hello—literally: peace be upon you.

Shavuot Pentecost.

Shiksah a gentile woman.

Shkola Slavic word for school.

Shofar ram's horn, blown at the service for the New Year and the Day of Atonement.

Shohet an authorized slaughterer of fowl or other kosher animals, who had to be well versed in all the regulations regarding the proper procedure.

Short Friday the Friday closest to the winter solstice. Orthodox Jews must cease all work on Friday prior to sundown.

Shulhan Arukh codification of Jewish law by Rabbi Joseph Karo in the sixteenth century.

Sukkah a festive booth used traditionally during the Sukkot (Tabernacles) holiday.

Talit a prayer shawl worn by adult male worshippers.

Talmud code of Jewish law compiled circa 500 C.E.

Tefillin phylacteries, worn by men on the head and arm during the weekday morning service.

Tikkun   a private midnight service held by the pious at home consisting of psalms, supplications, and lamentations at the destruction of Jerusalem.

Tikkun Leah   specific *tikkun* recited on ordinary weekdays (excluding Mondays and Thursdays) and on the Sabbath and festivals.

Tikkun Rachel   the *tikkun* ritual reserved for Mondays and Thursdays.

Tikkun Shavuot   a compilation of readings after midnight on the first night of Pentecost.

Tsaddik (plural *Tsaddikim*)   holy man, especially among Hasidim.

Tsimes   a dish of various cooked vegetables, usually including carrots, slightly sweet.

Yarmulke   skullcap.

Yeshivah   an academy for Talmudic learning and the training of Rabbis.

Zhid   a derogatory Slavic term for a Jew.

Further Reading

English Translations of Bialik's Works

POETRY

Carmi, T., trans. *Penguin Book of Hebrew Verse* (bilingual). New York: Viking Press, 1981. Pp. 18–33.

Efros, Israel, trans. *Selected Works of Ḥayyim Naḥman Bialik* (bilingual). New York: Bloch Publishing Co. and Histadrut Ivrit, 1965.

Nevo, Ruth, trans. *Chaim Naḥman Bialik: Poems from the Hebrew* (bilingual). Jerusalem: Dvir and Jerusalem Post, 1981.

Rivner, Tuvyah, trans. *The Modern Hebrew Poem Itself* (bilingual). Edited by Stanley Burnshaw, T. Carmi, and Ezra Spicehandler. Cambridge, Mass.: Harvard University Press, 1989. Pp. 18–33.

FICTION

Danby, Herbert. *And It Came to Pass.* New York: Hebrew Publishing Co., 1938.

Danby, Herbert. *Knight of Onions and Knight of Garlic.* New York: Jordan Publishing Co., 1939.

Lask, I. M. *Aftergrowth and Other Stories.* New York: Jewish Publication Society, 1939.

Lask, I. M. "Aryeh the Brawny." *Israel Argosy* 7 (1960).

Patterson, David. "Aftergrowth, Chapter 1." *The Jewish Quarterly* 20, no. 4 (winter 1973). Pp. 17–18.

Works on Bialik

Aberbach, David. *Bialik.* London: Weidenfeld and Nicholson, 1988.

Bateson, M. C. "The Riddle of Two Worlds." *Daedalus* 95 (1966). Pp. 740–762.

Patterson, David. *The Foundations of Modern Hebrew Literature.* London: Liberal Jewish Synagogue, 1961.

Spicehandler, Ezra. *The Modern Hebrew Poem Itself.* Cambridge: Harvard University Press, 1989. Pp. 199–200.

Spicehandler, Ezra, and Samuel Leiter. "Ḥayyim Naḥman Bialik." In *Encyclopaedia Judaica,* Vol. 4. Pp. 795–803.

Yudkin, Leon. "The Quintessence of Bialik's Poetry." In *Escape into Siege.* London: Routledge and Kegan Paul and The Littman Library of Jewish Civilisation, 1974. Pp. 19–38.

Index